AUSTRALIAN AUTOPSY

Australian Autopsy

The gory details of how England
dissected Australia in the 2010/11 Ashes

Jarrod Kimber

Published by Pitch Publishing

Pitch Publishing
A2 Yeoman Gate
Yeoman Way
Durrington
BN13 3QZ

Email: info@pitchpublishing.co.uk
Web: www.pitchpublishing.co.uk

First published 2011

A CIP catalogue record for this book is available from the British Library.

13-digit ISBN: 978-1908051028

Printed and bound in Great Britain by CPI Group

This book is based on true events.

ACKNOWLEDGEMENTS

Special thank you to mum and PK, Sarge, Mimi, Joel and Nicki (Issy and Lucy as well), Astrid and the Lees, Blair and Gazz and Mazz for letting me crash and mess up your places. Thanks to Pitch, Cricket Victoria, The Wisden Cricketer and Cricinfo for giving me cash to make the trip. And thanks to Sampson, Soph, Hendo, Paul, Sally and most of all Miriam (for letting me disappear for a couple of months).

SYDNEY

Sydney was like the end of a made-for-TV-based-on-a-true-crime story starring someone off *Melrose Place* and a child actor from a sitcom that didn't last its first season. The *Melrose Place* guy is playing the older brother – big, strong, the main guy in town and with one of those creepy smiles that tells you he's gonna enjoy hurting you. The sitcom kid is small, wiry, emotional and has the eyes of a friendly puppy. The premise is simple: younger brother accepts 20 years of torture, really sadistic stuff like the gluing of cocks to stomachs, public nudity and cigarettes on the nipples, plus mental torture about adoption, not having enough money for an abortion and everything else an older brother can do to break his younger brother.

Then the younger kid goes to join the Marines, gets that stupid haircut, beefs up, becomes real tough and learns to kill a man with a beer coaster. He comes home and his older brother acts like he is still the swinging dick in town. It's clear to everyone else that he is a fading force; he's still big, but now it's turned to flab, and he's still trying the same piss-weak jokes he did for years. Everyone has stopped laughing and he's taken the odd beating.

One day, the older brother is pissing off everyone at the local bar and some of the locals are getting angry. Then the younger brother walks in. The background noise fades out and all you can hear is the older brother being an asshole and the footsteps of his younger brother. The older brother turns around when he realises that no one is listening to his shit, sees his younger brother and can't help question his sexuality. The younger brother uses all his training and preparation to force his brother to the ground.

The locals all gather, cheering for the little brother; this is a raucous, entertaining ass-whipping. The older brother's head is smacked against the floor. The older brother still has one last play left in him and he squirrel grips the younger brother hard and then gives him some lip. In the past this might have been enough to put the younger brother off, but this time he grabs his sock knife that he had for just such a need and digs it deep into his brother's chest.

It's not an angry stab, but a precise thrust. The anger is why he is there; the training is why he is winning the fight.

The younger brother could stop there, his brother has now given up, but he doesn't want to. So he continues to stab with all his force over and over again, thrust after thrust. Powering the blade into the chest until he is covered in blood. Bits of flesh and organ are scattered all over the place. The brother hasn't moved in an hour. The bar has shut; no one wants to watch anymore.

The younger brother doesn't stop. He's trained so hard for this moment, so every time he stabs he remembers a time when his brother ruined his life. Once the flesh is gone, the knife hits bone a while, but soon that is gone and the younger brother hits the concrete floor until the noise of the knife striking it snaps him out of it. He drops the knife, stands up, wipes off some blood.

And does the sprinkler.

BRISBANE

"Good luck, mate" said the complete idiot. Me. In retrospect it was a dick move. I mean, he had a frown on his face, was looking down, and most importantly was dragging his cricket kit into the airport two days before the Ashes series was about to begin in that very city. To his credit, he said thanks. He could have stopped me and said, "Seriously, mate, how stupid are you? I'm walking into the airport with my kit, clearly I have been let go from the squad. Try and pay more attention."

It was Steve Smith, the young batsman who people were trying to pretend is a leg spinner. Since Michael Clarke, no player had arrived on the scene with as much boundless enthusiasm and energy. It did him no good; the selectors had gone for Xavier Doherty instead. I didn't need to spend an hour questioning him to know he was pissed off at the decision. I liked that though. Too many players seem to say things like, "I understand the decision and I'll go back to state cricket and try hard." Deep down you know they want to grab the nearest sharp implement and start cutting up people in Cricket Australia uniforms.

Like any micro-blogging, social-networking wannabe journalist I tweeted the information. It was perhaps the best way to start the tour as I accidentally broke the story. Since my journalistic instincts are so poor, I often end up breaking things by accident rather than on purpose. On the trip to Sarge's house,

11

my accommodation for the trip, I thought about whether I'd see Smith in the Ashes. And whether I should apologise for my stupid remark. I'd like to think that a real journalist would have seen Smith, worked out why he was there, tried to interview him, and then tried to file before the announcement was public.

This was my first time back in Australia for three and a half years; I'd left Australia as a bit of a fuck-up and, until the Smith moment, I thought I'd moved on. Not that Queensland was like home to me; I'd never spent much time here and, as a Melbournian, I'd spent most of my life mocking the place.

Sarge's car radio was playing talk radio, and the reason I nickname Queensland 'New Texas' was painfully aware to me straight away. The DJ had one of those voices that implied everything he said was nothing but the truth, and he then said, "Of course in the great state of Queensland…" The great state of Queensland? It was like riding through the Deep South of America. I've never got Queensland. I'm one of those left-wing pinko commie assholes that DJs in New Texas like to take the piss out of. I don't blame them; I take them piss out of their right-wing, pseudo-Christian, sponsor-paid, ill-thought-out-hate-of-the-week crap as well.

Part of the reason I don't get New Texas is the heat. I don't do hot. I may have spent 28 years in Australia, but in all that time heat and I never got on. I once got sunburnt in Wales in September. I'm whiter than white, my wife laughs at my skin colour on a daily basis, and even redheads mock me. It wasn't just the sun in New Texas, it was, "the humidity, mate, that's what kills ya". And it fucken does. It makes me irrationally mad at the place I am in. It could even explain my hatred of New Texas. That or conservative nut bags.

Sarge took us to his main house. He has a few. He is a white-haired short man who is painfully working class – and a millionaire. On some people being a working-class millionaire looks rather odd. For Sarge it fits about right. He is my dad's best friend.

My dad was also in the car. I don't know how I'd explain him: a grumpier, older, fatter version of me, without the need to write about things. He was the one who got me into cricket. By that

I don't mean he bought me a bat and a ball (we couldn't afford bats, we were too poor, one was cut down from a big bat for me), I mean he taught me how to be a cricket fundamentalist. I knew about field settings before I learnt fractions. My dad is a very thoughtful person who comes up with opinions and who sticks with them even in the face of great evidence. As a cricket teacher he was perfect. He coached me in cricket from the age of eight till 16, and without cricket I don't think I'd ever have really got to know him.

During much of his working life he was a stony son of a bitch. Spending day after day working for people who he was – or thought he was – smarter than, and not being able to jump them due to a lack of subtlety and college education. When he came home he was silent or thunder for much of the time. And that was when he was working; there were also the three times when he was made redundant. So he had a well-earned chip on his shoulders. This meant that when he came back very late from work, he wasn't in the mood to know what went on in anyone's day, but he had a view about the world in sport.

In those days, sport meant cricket or football (Aussie rules). Getting pissed off at the sports news was his vent during the week; playing golf was for the weekend. We bonded through this sort of grumpy joint hatred of every stupid thing happening in sport. When he talked about the actual sport, and not the bullshit administration, he was much different. He went from Darth Vader to Yoda. At his best he could pick out the important moments in a sporting contest and explain them to me in such a way that I always understood what he meant. It was just him chatting to me. Now it's clear all that anger and information was setting me up for a life doing the same thing for money.

Sarge and Dad were also the perfect representation of Australian cricket fans. Sarge was the sort who only really watched the cricket when it was the height of summer. He cared little for his state team, and didn't really realise what had happened in the months prior, but he was interested now it was Ashes time. Dad was the other Australian fan, who followed them on their tours, and watched as much as he could on TV if it was in a good time zone. He always had an opinion; some of them were right.

I was the third kind of Australian cricket fan, by far the rarest kind. A real cricket sadist. I'll stay up late to watch West Indian domestic cricket just because … well, just because. I don't drink much during play of a Test match, in case I miss something. I know the names and statistics of key Sheffield Shield players who will never play for their country. I even know who captains Glamorgan, and why a left-arm wrist spinner is called a Chinaman. You might say, well that is your job, but I knew all this before, hence why I was really only trained for one thing.

As such, we all had our opinions on who would win the Ashes. Sarge was sure the Poms would revert to type, and we'd crush them, even though he thought Peter Siddle was useless. Dad thought Australia would win, but as a keen punter he wouldn't have put any of his money on them. And I was unsure. Call it professional fatigue. The more you know, the less you're sure.

When paid for my professional opinion I came up with 2-1 Australia. That was weeks out from the Tests and since then some things had changed. Australia had picked the entire country in a Test squad for a start. In such situations, there is little you can do bar take the piss.

> Greg Chappell said, "It's a holistic cricket squad; we could have limited ourselves to just the 13 or so players that are most likely to play for Australia, but what about Mavis Brown from Epping – the Poms know nothing about her. How will her plastic hip help her get turn? Also, it is important to not give the Poms what they are expecting. This squad might look like we have just put the entire voting registry on it, but it is way more than that. Way more."
>
> Simon Spehr of Camperdown was over the moon to be selected, "I'll be honest, I've been waiting for this call all my life. It wasn't a call, obviously, they couldn't call everyone, but to know that my name was in the squad was more than enough. My mother was so excited for me, but even more excited for herself."

Former legend Dean Jones was also ecstatic about the squad, "I knew the selectors hadn't forgotten about me. Commentating may not seem like the ideal preparation for playing in a Test. However, since my time out of the game I think I've learnt a few things, especially from Hashim Amla."

While almost every Australian selected in the squad was happy, there has been some negative feedback. The English press believe this is a desperate move from an insane cricket selection panel who have completely lost the plot. Russell Crowe and Sam Neill were both visibly upset at not getting selected. And Germaine Greer complained bitterly about Steve Irwin's inclusion.

The squad is expected to be trimmed down to 10,000 by the 20th of November.

The announcement of 17 players while it rained by Sydney Harbour was one of those occasions when it was obvious that Cricket Australia had put marketing gimmicks ahead of winning the Ashes. According to the born-to-wear-a-suit James Sutherland, the 06/07 Ashes squad was announced just as early, it's just that he forgot to add that it had a lot fewer than 17 people in it. It was classic Cricket Australia. "We haven't done anything wrong – you're just blowing it out of proportion." It was blown out of proportion, but only because it looked like Australia was a fish on the deck of a ship. The best part was that the marketing department also failed to attract more than the 40 people. Most cricket writers saw it as all kinds of pathetic.

England were Cool Hand Luke in comparison. Strolling around the country getting runs into batsmen without them, having their back-up bowlers chew up and spit out Australia A with helpful conditions, and giving their main bowlers a week off in New Texas before the Test. England were looking so smooth it hurt.

Sarge, Dad and I sat around a pool drinking beer trying to predict what would happen next. Then we had a barbecue and tried to predict what would happen next. Later that night we tried to predict what would happen next.

The more I talked Australia up, the more I felt as sick as I had when I'd eaten the world's most expensive hamburger in Heathrow airport. Luckily the beer took all the doubt away, and I think I was back to us winning 2-1.

2-1 to Australia is about as clever as saying good luck to Steve Smith.

THE GABBATOIR

I'd never been to the Gabba before; I'd never even seen Australia play in Australia outside of the G (Melbourne Cricket Ground). So the first time I took the stroll down from Sarge's Kangaroo Point river-view apartment I had no idea what to expect. When hitting Vulture Street, I could see down to the ground, and also see a huge cowboy billboard overlooking the ground. It probably wasn't a homage to me calling Queensland New Texas, but you never know.

The ground was wedged into a suburban street with a dodgy-looking thing called the German Club over the road. Somehow I made my way to the nets, where I asked dozens of people wearing lanyards where I should go to pick up my accreditation. No one knew. So many lanyards, so little clue. Then I started looking through the small, sweaty-looking media pack, but I knew no one there either. I've worked a bit in the cricket business, but I'm still little more than an occasional pimple on its ass, and there is no better way to work this out than when 50 people are watching the teams train and you don't know one of them.

Eventually I was sent by a security guard to an office and I lined up in anticipation. Sure, it was only an ID, but it was my gateway to the Ashes. A free Cricket Australia accredited pass that meant I got to pretend to be a part of the establishment. It was all thanks to Cricket Victoria who saw my pro-Victorian dogma as a good fit for their branding. For the last Ashes I had to beg for only a few days' access, now with Cricket Victoria on my side I had the entire series. When the Cricket Australia guy handed it over with no fuss, I grabbed it and ran. I didn't want them having to think about it in case they changed their minds. I'm always waiting for metaphorical rugs to be pulled out from under me.

Once I had gotten far enough from the office I had a bit of a stare at my pass, and there was a problem. The ID stared at me, and just beyond my uncombed, unwashed, ratty mop of hair was writing that said, "Melbourne Only". The one place I didn't need accreditation was the only place I could go. I raced back into the office and stood behind others getting their accreditation while I nervously bounced from foot to foot like Mark Nicholas talking to camera. This could not be happening. In my head I was thinking of who I could contact at each ground to get in. I had no contacts at the Gabba, and after years of abusing the Queensland Bulls, the only reason they would know who I am was from what I had written about them. And what of the other grounds? I couldn't pull out of the tour now I was here. How would I get into the Adelaide Oval, where would I plug in my laptop, how would I afford my lunches? This was the worst news ever. My pass was the policeman knocking on your door at midnight when your kid still hasn't got home.

When I got to the front I explained my problem. The Cricket Australia man decided that I must have applied only for Melbourne. I assured him I only ever applied for all the Test matches. Why would I apply for Melbourne only when I work for Cricket Victoria? Surely the more obvious explanation was that some key puncher had assumed I only wanted Melbourne because I worked with them. This explanation didn't seem to sway him; instead he rang Cricket Victoria.

They, probably largely unaware of who the hell I was, pointed him to Lachy Patterson, whom some people call 'the Lachsmith', as he is a problem solver for Cricket Australia, as well as being their media guy. He's never solved their spin problem though. I'd never had much contact with him. I tried to listen in to the conversation and read what Lachy was saying by the face of the young Cricket Australia guy in front of me, looking for some message of salvation on his face. Then he hung up the phone and started assing about, and suddenly a new pass was given to me, just like that. Whatever Lachy said was enough to get me an all-access pass for the rest of the Ashes. So, if he ever wants any sexual favours from me…

Luckily I had not become another victim of the Gabbatoir. Visitors to this ground, whether in Aussie rules or cricket, often ended up slaughtered. It was clear why: it's a fucking labyrinth. Now I knew why the other lanyard people hadn't known in which direction to point me – they had no idea where anything was either. Nothing seems to lead to anything, just endless hallways and doors that all look the same. Like something in a Canadian sci-fi film. In these sorts of situations I'd usually just follow someone else to the press box, but you could tell by the other faces that everyone was waiting to follow someone.

The first thing you notice about the Gabba is the matching seats. Whether on TV or at the ground, they stand out, because most grounds don't have patterns of maroon and yellow in the stands. I heard someone say once the idea was to make the ground look full even when it wasn't. That is a sensible guess, but I prefer to think of it more as a New Texas form of hypnosis. This is the Maroon state, and we will bewitch you with our special chairs.

Other than that, it's just a modern sporting stadium. I don't mean that in a bad way, I'm sure people like coming here. It's just that it's simply a small modern coliseum with one whole stand that wraps around the place. It wasn't really the Gabba I expected, the one where countless touring countries have been sacrificed – it was clean and professional-looking. Of course, it did have the best pitch in world cricket, so who cares about the corporate stands?

I sat down on the field and watched Michael Clarke prove his back was fine with a bit of fielding practice. This almost completely useless act led to something worth watching, the photoshoot. I've now come to realise that the day before the Test is not as exciting and thrilling as I had dreamed as a kid.

Even the day before the Ashes – but a photoshoot between the two captains had a certain something.

Ponting came out for the photoshoot dressed in his Aussie creams and Steve Waugh-approved baggy green. Strauss was still dressed in his training gear – he wasn't really ready for a photoshoot – and Ponting took the time to chat to a kid who was at the ground. Then the whole world collapsed as Dean Wilson from the *Daily Mirror* whispered to me, "I don't think Strauss has his whites here."

He was right. Suddenly cricket officials sprung into overdrive. It always amazes me that cricket officials don't make better cricketers, because no one would ever beat them between the wickets. They are the quickest species known to man when a photoshoot or press conference is in the balance. Strauss then told Ponting that he didn't have his whites and Ponting tried to act nonchalant. But the great thing about Ponting is that his poker face is really shit. Everything you need to know about Ponting is written on his face. And when Strauss told him that there were no whites, you could tell he was pissed off. He must have felt like the guy that got to the party before they were finished setting up and realised he was overdressed.

Luckily Strauss was given someone else's whites and the photoshoot was saved. That is how professional NuEngland is, they always have a set of reserve photoshoot whites. Ponting was now playing cricket with the kid as a way to pass the time – an excellent photoshoot in itself. Then Strauss came back and Ponting handed him the replica urn and said, "You should hold this, it isn't mine." At this stage they had chatted three times without ever looking each other in the eye.

Then the main event started and all you could hear was shutters clicking and the occasional "move here, turn, come forward, go back" from the hungry photographers. They face the cameras, each other, the urn, and put on their serious, yet relaxed, Ashes faces. There was also a bit of out-relaxing each other. Each man wanted to portray that he was at once better prepared and more relaxed than the other, without trying to look like they were trying to do so.

I couldn't help but wonder how the players prepare for such

a situation. Strauss and NuEngland would probably have a coach for body language and modelling. I can imagine Strauss standing in a room as two coaches and Andy Flower walk around him, Flower saying to the others, "I want him to look confident, but not over-confident. He should have an air of 'I'm in control, but I am also flexible enough to change at a moment's notice'. He needs a swagger in his eyes, but relaxed lips. They need to see the photo and know he is here for business and yet relaxed enough to not tense up at the wrong time. OK, you guys have three days to get him right for this, the Ashes may depend on it."

Ponting wouldn't have any consultants; instead he'd rent a sleazy motel for the night, go into the bathroom and just work on his smile with a camera filming his every move. After an hour of smiling into the camera he'd take a look at the footage and then review it to see where he could improve. He may even have footage to compare it to from previous photoshoots when he was in good form.

Of course, all that practice means nothing if you can't pull it off in the heat of battle. Both men did. At times I assumed they were just cardboard cutouts, as they had their looks stapled to their faces.

After about an hour the photoshoot was over and the teams went about their preparations. England seemed more relaxed, but only by 12 laughs to ten. Shane Watson almost hit Brad Haddin when batting in the nets. Justin Langer stood on a wooden box to throw the ball down from a height from which a bowler would actually deliver. Graeme Swann seemed to produce more one-liners than deliveries.

Then there was the Ponting press conference. I'd love to tell you what he said, or what he was talking about. I just can't remember. I'm amazed that real journalists can remember what cricketers say at press conferences. It just sort of hits my forehead and then rebounds as I start to wonder whether taking a time machine trip back to Germany in the 30s to kill Hitler would make that much difference or if fast zombies or slow zombies are cooler. Other reporters hear what Ponting says, and then make things out of it.

For instance, if I was at the press conference where Ponting was asked, "Is it possible for you to win 5-0?", and he said, "It's absolutely possible, there's no reason why not," I probably wouldn't have walked away thinking that this wasn't an important piece of information that the world needed to know. The other journalists walked away thinking it was. They were right. As was Ponting. Even with the world's biggest home Test squad, bad form, and the ritual sacrifice of Nathan Hauritz, it was possible that Australia would win the Ashes 5-0.

England winning 5-0; Shane Watson outing himself as a lover of plush toys (plushophile); Jimmy Anderson scoring a run-a-ball hundred to beat Australia in the deciding Test; Dean Jones holding a press conference to announce he was a rubbish cricketer; Xavier Doherty taking off his shirt and doing the Warne dance when Australia win. Andrew Strauss getting caught with his dick in an exhaust pipe. If you asked me if these were possible, I'd say yes. I probably wouldn't say, "There's no reason why not. It's all in their hands." I'd probably say, "None of these events are likely to happen, but there is a slim possibility that if you fucked Tony Greig in the eyeball for an hour straight you'd get nothing more than a sore dick as he is clearly an indestructible motherfucker, but what is more likely is that you'd end up with eyeball under your foreskin."

Some might say it is also possible that a captain in the twilight stage of a long career could be asked such an obviously inflammatory question and fuck it up. If the conditions favoured it. At a press conference way back in August, Ponting also called Hauritz a lock-in for the first Ashes Test. Being that Hauritz was going to miss out on the first Test, someone probably asked him about Hauritz, but I can't recall it. It also had no talk of 5-0 or Tony Greig's indestructible eyeball. It just had some sort of endless droning on. I decide to leave my first trip to the Gabba without hearing what Strauss had to say.

Four hours later I managed to find a way out of the ground.

Back at the flat we let Issy, Sarge's very lovely girlfriend, make us dinner while he talked all sorts of beery nonsense. Actually, I was on the Woodford Reserve after Issy stupidly said, "Don't buy any bourbon, I have some." As the night went on I'd made a bet with Sarge that Ben Hilfenhaus would end up higher in the wicket-takers' list than Watson would in the run-makers' list. Comparing batsmen and bowlers in a bet is never that clever. So the rules didn't make that much sense, I just knew Sarge wanted to make a bet. He is a natural betting man. While I never really knew him before he had money, I'd think he even made bets back then. It's almost like his natural conversation ends with, "Lets put some money on it." I'm not sure he believes anyone's opinion unless it ends with them willing to put their money on the line.

It all started when Sarge suggested Watson was the first player picked for Australia these days. I argued that Ponting was still that man, more on past deeds than current form, and that Hilfenhaus was the man I'd pick next. This seemed to get him unnaturally fired up, as can happen late at night on the balcony. My thoughts were that while Watson was the in-form player in Australia, Hilfenhaus was the most dependable bowler in a group of flaky individuals. Therefore, I'd pick him before Watson. This sent Sarge into a rage.

It's such a beautiful bullshit conversation to have, as it really doesn't matter if your player is picked first, second, third or fourth – just so long as they pick them. With alcohol it just seemed more important. Then the rules of the bet were made by me. I tried to make it as fair as I could to both men while Sarge yelled various expletives at me. Eventually I'd receive AUS$100 if Hilfenhaus was Australia's second leading wicket taker, and Watson third leading batsman. If the opposite happened, Sarge would win the money.

It seemed that this Ashes would be me making half assed bets that I never really believed in. At least I knew that Hilfenhaus would play all five Tests, give me an honest try in each of them, and end up with at least 15 wickets…

DAY 1 – THE GABBA

There was an extraordinary amount of pressure put on the first ball of the Ashes thanks to Steve Harmison's career-defining cock-up of 06/07. Australia losing the toss meant that that pressure was on Ben Hilfenhaus. A very different character to Steve Harmison, he wasn't about to bowl to second slip. Hilfenhaus reminds me of every brickie I have ever met. Sure that is stereotyping him via his former profession, but every cricket writer is a snarky bastard, so I think it's OK. Hilfy had the sort of manly good looks that you can see in any suburban Aussie pub, just without the beer gut and smoke hanging out of his mouth. I like the fact he would look just as comfortable in a backyard eating a snag (sausage) as he would opening the bowling for his country. Solid shoulders, decent height, scruffy, short-enough-to-get-away-with-it hair and a solid jaw meant that he was not the man for second slip bowling.

That didn't mean it wasn't about to be just as momentous an occasion. Anything could happen on the first ball of the Ashes as we know from the one time it happened.

The umpires strolled out and Andrew Strauss prepared to face the first ball from a man wearing a comedy moustache (for charity). The crowd swelled, because that's what crowds do. Once you see the first ball of the series, watching the rest of the series is completely useless. When Hilfenhaus came in to Strauss, it wasn't just a normal delivery, it was a story, a fable –

epic and far-reaching. Steeped in history, mystery and folklore, you'd tell your kids where you were when Hilfenhaus bowled it. The ball was outside off stump and left alone by Strauss. But what a story it told.

The Ashes is well and truly on when reporters are racing to file after one delivery, and that is what the press did, taking the name of Steve Harmison in vain. If this had been in the day of typewriters the noise would have been deafening; everyone was tapping away at full speed trying to fill a couple of paragraphs on a ball that sailed through to the wicketkeeper. Phone calls were made, while others searched for the meaning of life in Hilfenhaus' wrist position.

People were still talking and writing about the dreadfully dull Strauss leave when, facing the third ball of the day, the England captain hit the ball straight to gully. Australia had jumped out of the gates. Unfortunately for Australia the third ball of an Ashes series doesn't usually predict what will happen in the whole summer.

This brought the Ashes' two most exciting men together at once: Alastair Cook and Jonathan Trott. Cook looks like he has just auditioned to play a posh public school kid. Dark brown curly hair always cut into a style far more conservative than suits his age. I know Cook's brother, and they both have strong faces in that sort of, "I was built for upper management" sort of way. Nothing on either of their faces says they are built for fun. It should also be pointed out that the two paragraphs of Cook's autobiography I read said that he wasn't brought up middle class, but that his family often went skiing.

Trott is shorter and plumper, not fat, just less athletic-looking. I like to describe him as someone who has spent his whole life trying to walk tall and look like Steve Waugh, but got it all slightly wrong. If Steve Waugh's baggy green ever goes on sale – over his dead body – Trott will be the one trying to buy it to cover up his slightly receding hairline. I can never tell if he looks old, or just looks older because of the hair. Perhaps it's the slightly old world charm about him. Making him perfect to appear next to Steve Waugh in an old photo from a trench in the First World War.

It's almost impossible to stay tuned in to the Ashes while Cook bats. The only person in the world who could watch every ball of his innings is Alastair Cook. He has a sick, desperate form of patience. While he and Trott slowly edged the game forward I went into some sort of coma. I respect both men, but there is a horror film called *Incident on and off a Mountain Road*, which has an almost unwatchable drilling-of-eyeballs scene that feels like a treat compared to when they're in together.

Maybe that's harsh, but I think boring run-accumulating batsmen should be moved as far away from each other as is cricketly possible. Australia did the viewing public a favour by moving Mike Hussey and Simon Katich further apart. But the NuEngland management are far too professional to think about the punters who trudge into the ground looking for entertainment. The bastards. Some think Strauss is boring as well but I like the way Strauss bats – that sort of self-assured command of back-foot shots, with punches down the ground. Strauss also has more than one gear, he doesn't just nudge and accumulate and can cut free like a real boy at times.

Strauss had had a stress-free entrance to the Ashes from the media. Australia were stumbling and bumbling around Pakistan and India, while England did Pakistan in with ease. Considering he came into the series without a hundred in 14 Tests at the sub-Marcus North average of 33, he'd done well to keep them off his back. The last hundred he'd made had been gifted to him by the Ashes-defining opening morning at Lord's in 2009 when Siddle got wayward, Johnson hid in a closet and Hauritz ended up in hospital.

In his three-ball innings at the Gabba it was hard to say whether he was in form or not.

Trott continued to knock the ball off his pads like he does, until he was done by a straight one from Shane Watson. Australian fans rejoiced. It's hard to know if later they became worried that it had been Watson who had made the breakthrough. Cook kept going, a prod at a time, and KP came out to increase the pace and sexiness at the wicket. With the appearance of KP – in recent months a walking wicket to the slow left-arm orthodox bowlers – Australia's Irish bullfighter, Xavier Doherty, started to warm up.

Doherty was the replacement for Hauritz, a like for like in many ways. A struggling first-class finger spinner plucked from nowhere, who could bat enough to be handy, and was a decent fielder, but was largely unremarkable and had a very poor first-class record. While I never truly understood why Hauritz had ever been picked it made even less sense to get rid of him for someone who was mostly the same kind of cricketer. Hauritz had some scars from international cricket – India had played with him like a cat with a mouse, KP thought so little of him he decided what shot to play before he bowled and Chris Gayle described facing him as like facing himself – but he had stuck around, fought, got more confident and ultimately did better than anyone thought.

His first five-wicket first-class haul had been in Test cricket; his second had come in the next Test. Sure, both of these came against a Pakistan who many thought had thrown the game, but he had worked hard to get himself a way better average in Test cricket than he had in the rest of the first-class game. That along with Ponting's lock-in quote had seemed enough to get him a gig in Brisbane. It wasn't. It seemed that the big problem was that Hauritz wouldn't learn to bowl the way Ponting wanted him to, wider of the crease and quicker like Murali and Harbhajan Singh. It was completely contrary to the way Hauritz had bowled and which had got him modest success. It seemed he couldn't do it, and Australia couldn't wait any longer.

The Australian carousel of spin took on another member. The first time I saw Doherty bowl I thought he would play for Australia. He was assured, clever, got decent spin, had what my mum would call a spunky disposition and looked like a bowler. Six years later I'd given up on him as a Test player, but thought he was a handy one-day container for Tasmania. The boy has some timing. He destroyed Victoria with a five-wicket haul that led to Victoria's rare loss of a first-class game, and, in combination with his four wickets against Sri Lanka at the MCG one-day international, it was enough for him to leapfrog Hauritz. With KP in, and at least 70 per cent of the reason for Doherty's inclusion being to bowl to him, Doherty delivered his first over in Test cricket. It wasn't a chapter in his autobiography, but it was tidy.

KP's career has stuttered since he was sacked as captain for daring to say that he couldn't get on with the coach. It was perhaps the best move for the team, because since that time England have played some of their best cricket in years. KP hasn't. His form problems seem to be partly to do with confidence, and partly because he has some sort of allergy to left-arm spin.

It's like watching a kid chase after a butterfly. He charges at it when he should stay still. He swats at it when a slow move would do better. And it ends up freaking him out when really he should never be scared of it. Yuvraj Singh's awful bowling started the rot, and since then every pie-chucking left-arm orthodox in the world seems to have gotten him out, as have a few good ones. Doherty's selection was 30% wickets at the right time and 70% KP's problems with butterflies. It was surely less to do with his bowling average for Tasmania, which stands at a Hauritz-like level of 48.

Doherty's first overs may not have made the selectors pencil him in as Warne's long-term replacement, yet he showed that he wasn't overawed by the occasion. He looked very focused, like a kid who had been told to be quiet at a funeral. His mind was whirring away thinking about what he should be doing when Watson let go a short ball, and Doherty, fielding at point, dropped Cook twice in one chance, and then almost broke his wrist.

This mistake did inspire a touching moment when the cranky old Tasmanian captain went over and gave young Xavier a low five, the most respectful of the five family. It showed why Ricky's team love him so. Though I could have misread the situation, and perhaps he slapped his hand so hard to remind him not to drop another simple chance. But it wasn't just Doherty who looked sloppy in the field.

While Xavier was tempting KP into the odd stupid shot, Siddle was heating up at the other end. A hot Siddle was an uncomfortable sight for anyone. Perhaps the best line from the 09 Ashes was something like, "Siddle looks like he would run through a brick wall for his country, and looks like he already has". I had no idea who wrote that, but I liked them. Siddle is mostly chest, with a little hair on his head and under his lip. He'd make a more convincing cartoon boxer than a fast bowler.

Siddle had been out of fashion due to some ordinary bowling at home during Australia's great unbeaten summer over the sixth-, seventh- and eighth-ranked Test nations. Then there were the injuries. And the fact he had to lower himself to training with the Carlton football club. But they kept him around – Ricky seemed to like him. He's like a charming pitbull: he won't always rip a team apart when you want him to, but he is loyal and will bite all day. There wasn't really much between him and Doug Bollinger, the left-arm paceman. But for some reason the selectors went with Siddle. Even when everyone else wondered why Bollinger wasn't playing.

That all seemed to make sense around the time that he got the ball full enough to nip out KP and Paul Collingwood within a couple of overs. Like male pornstars, length is often what people talk about when discussing fast bowlers. You've gotta find your length. That isn't your natural length, that isn't the length for this pitch, you're too short, too full, pull your length back, get it up there, aim at the base, and you know, short balls are dangerous to this man. Siddle found his length nicely, just full enough to make you want to drive, just dangerous enough for you to want to be very fucken careful when driving. KP isn't often careful, and he was soon out even though he looked like he'd found some form.

Collingwood came to the crease like a condemned man. A self-condemned man. He only feels truly at home if someone is about to torch him, and with England three down in the middle session it was the sort of time when Collingwood digs in for a spoony leg-side innings full of ugly nudges and crude defence. Instead he just played a wafty excuse for a drive. Siddle, the pitbull no one had wanted, had found a home. Ricky patted his head and gave him a snack. There was a sniff of an exciting Test in the air.

Bell came in, and he was no longer the ginger punchline that people had seen for years. Now he was a respectable batting machine. His batting was no longer a pretty little 30-something – well, it was still oh so pretty and I'd still happily oil him up naked in a birdcage at my swinging 60s party – but something just felt different. There had been talk that his tour to South Africa had made the difference. I didn't see it then. Others pointed to his innings at the Oval in the 2009 Ashes, which I think was described by me as largely crap (I'm paraphrasing). I noticed it in domestic cricket.

Bell just looked manly, and that was odd to me. For years he had looked mostly like a scared little boy. Suddenly in one-day games for Warwickshire he looked like someone who knew where the best pubs were, how to get late-night booze and how to walk up to a woman with confidence. He also looked bigger somehow. Sure, his hat was still pulled down amazingly low on his forehead and he hid his emotions behind his sunglasses, but it all sort of worked for him now. I had always assumed that when Bell went to McDonald's to get a plain sundae, he always ended up with a milkshake instead. While he was disappointed that the McDonald's staff had got his order wrong, he wouldn't dare correct them on it and would just drink the milkshake (not a Daniel Day Lewis reference). Now if he went in and asked for a plain sundae, though, one way or another he'd get the sundae, and probably the phone number of the part-time model who worked the cash till. There was a bit extra to him, 50 per cent more Bell for the same low price.

Of course, I still bet against him making many runs in the Ashes. It was instinctive to me. If you walked up behind me and said Ian Bell, I'd yell "shithouse" and walk away. So when Tom Clark, the producer on the cult internet cricket commentary service Test Match Sofa, wanted to bet me that Bell would average over 45 in the Ashes, I took the bet. Even I thought the bet was a bit stupid, so when a few weeks later Tom told me that Stuart Broad would average more with the bat than he would with the ball, I took that as insurance.

All this went through my mind as Bell almost chopped on first ball. I felt it still when Simon Katich, from short leg, was so positive that Bell had edged behind he convinced Ponting to unsuccessfully review the decision. Bell continued to bat, as

Cook picked up a noble, dour fifty. If you could take Cook's patience and determination and put it together with Bell's talent you'd have Sachin Tendulkar, but both men are working hard on becoming better cricketers, and it's hard to hate them for that.

After tea the cricket took a turn for the worse. Australia had been flirting with what Bill Lawry calls the Queensland line, only wider. Modern teams are getting keener on this theory that if you bowl three feet outside off stump you can bore out a wicket. It seems a weird tactic to try to bore out Alastair Cook. In the 35 minutes after tea, Bell faced only two balls that would have hit his stumps. When I start counting things like this, you know the cricket has jumped the shark. Australia bowled wides and slowed down the game. People didn't know who to blame. Some blamed the captain for this tactic, others thought the bowlers should have just ignored it and bowled near the stumps and still others blamed the batsmen – after all, if it's wide, just smash it.

I blame conservative politicians and people who like reality TV.

Siddle didn't bowl as wide as the others. I think by the time he came on Ponting had tired of his tactic, or he just thought Siddle could be his one attacking option. This led to Cook prodding at one and nicking off. Had I been at my desk, and not at the back of the press box planning a new cricket chat show – *Two Pricks at the Ashes*, more of which later – it would have woken me up. It was such a typical way for Cook to get out that I can barely finish this sentence. This brought Prior in, the man who had reinvented his 'keeping and started struggling with the bat at the same time. First ball he was gone, bowled by Siddle.

Stuart Broad had to try to survive the hat-trick – the hat-trick the Victorian demon had been promised when he was born in the right state. Victorians take a lot of t

Test hat-tricks. Before you get all pissy and start saying I have a bias for the People's Democratic Republic of Victoria, this is based on actual facts. Hugh Trumble took two, Jimmy Matthews popped in for a couple in one match, Lindsay Kline took one, Damien Fleming should have taken two, Shane Warne took one and cost Fleming the other, Merv Hughes got one in three separate overs and now Peter Siddle was about to fulfil his destiny.

There have only been 37 hat-tricks in Tests. Victorians have eight of them. More than South Africa, India, Sri Lanka, Zimbabwe, Bangladesh and New Zealand combined. Sorry, now it's nine from 38. Broad tried to pretend that he got his bat somewhere near the searing death yorker, but he wasn't dealing with one of his dad's mates in the referee's chair. The umpire saw through the Broad façade, and Siddle added to a fine history.

It was the third time I'd been at the ground when an Australian had taken a hat-trick. Not that I counted myself as a good luck charm. I'd seen Warne take one in 1994-95 and jumped around like a crazy Victorian kid who'd just seen Shane Warne take a hat-trick. At the 2003 World Cup I'd seen Brett Lee's hat-trick against the mighty Kenya and jumped around like a drunken idiot who'd just seen Lee take a hat-trick.

Those two hat-tricks felt very real; this one was more surreal. First there was the whole press box side of things. Then there was the whole first day of the Ashes side of things. And thirdly this was Siddle, the stray who shouldn't have been playing according to most people. You see, you can't really yell in the press box – not because it will get you in trouble, but just because one person yelling in the press box makes you like the old guy who dances with all the wives at the country wedding while he is still sober. I didn't know the press box well enough to pull off the yell.

The rest of the day was a bit of a blur. I'm not going to lie and say I remember every ball, or that I saw any of them, or that I wasn't tweeting about Victorians taking over the world. Siddle removed Swann, and then Brad Haddin dropped his chance of getting seven wickets. Bell moved past his fifty as Ponting put the fielders out on the boundary, just far enough to let a good batsman in top form score twos at will. Then Xavier took two charity wickets that I was glad he got. Bell was the first, having made 76, his best Ashes innings in my closed-minded book.

Then Anderson did what Anderson does: he played shots well beyond his talent level which ended when he played the reverse sweep leave.

England had reached 260. By recent standards at the Gabba it wasn't horrible, but it felt a bit icky, like the taste of your finger after putting it in your ear. While Tests against New Zealand and Shield matches had provided sporty wickets, this didn't look all that sporty. Apart from Siddle, no Australian bowler really looked dangerous, and all the English batsmen other than Strauss got in. You just had the feeling that there were runs in this here pitch.

Australia got through a few early overs without too much trouble. England let their best bowler have a go, and Swann's first two Test balls in Australia were hit to the rope by Katich. Rejected twice by the ugly girl – not how Swann dreamt of his start to his Australian Ashes adventure. Not that this would dent his confidence. Swann saw himself as a dashing man of the people, a cooler-than-ice kind. Even the fact that he had a chin that was as large as a newspaper caricaturist would have drawn it didn't seem to bother him. That he was really just a better than ordinary player who was really good at a boring skill that never really worked in Australia wouldn't bother him either. Swann lived in his own world, and it was working for him mostly. Some fours from Katich wouldn't change him.

That night I started something special: *Two Pricks at the Ashes*, an internet vodcast chatshow that I'd been working on earlier in the day. My co-prick was Sampson Collins, a posh, tall, pretty, former Etonian who worked for *The Wisden Cricketer* and wanted to make his name at this Ashes. People with bullshit hope in their hearts were my kind of people. Sampson had it, and I had this camera and no idea what to do with it, so why not? Sampson came up with the name. It suited me well as I'd once asked my mother what one word described me for some nonsense project and she'd said, "'Prick' comes to mind."

The first episode wasn't great, other than the fact we filmed it in front of the press conference banner. When you do shocking sound, hardly worry about lighting at all and film yourself in front of a well known background the whole thing has that strangely captivating feel to it. I'd say that's about all it had.

Sam and I weren't best friends or anything like that, but we'd hung out a few times before. In my experience he was a top guy, very intelligent, and, like Brad Pitt's character in *Ocean's Eleven*, constantly eating in situations when no one else was. We just thought that since we were given accreditation, enough money not to starve and the opportunity to follow a whole Ashes, we might as well try to do something with it.

After our first rather dismal effort, we went to find beer with Andrew Miller, the editor of the UK Cricinfo. Miller was a great guy, who at once seemed to live in his own bubble and still take in everything around him. Bumbling posh I'd call it. If others dressed like him, they'd look like bums, but it just made him look even posher. His stupid Akubra hat was with him, and while it was a terrible fashion mistake, it made perfect sense on his head. We made our way across to the German Club. It was the sort of place that looked like it should have smelled of piss and vomit. It was, as so many weird places like this in Australia are, a members' club. You had to be a member of a club to get in. Any club. Miller, ever the quick thinker when beer is involved (until he's had one), whipped out his cricket writers' membership book and we were allowed in.

It wasn't all plain sailing. Someone saw Sampson's press pass, then heard his soft English pomp, and decided he was going to give him some abuse. It is people like this that make Australia great. And a cunt of a place. This drunken assclown just wanted to yell at poor Sampson, and there was nothing he could do. If he told the guy to piss off, he'd be a posh twat. If he sat there and took it the guy would just continue yelling at him. If he pushed the guy away, he'd probably be punched by a whole group of yelly, drunken dickheads. I figured that Sampson could stand a bit of yelling, and that me getting involved would help no one, so I followed Miller to the bar. It could be misconstrued as a coward's move; I'd like to think of it as the decision of a thirsty man. Sampson was fine, and we went outside to drink and talk shit.

Eventually I went back to the flat and waited for Big Daddy, my cousin/best mate, to come in. As it was my first week back in Australia, he and Dad had made a special effort to fly in and use Sarge's flat to see me. Big Daddy and I caught up, like you do, but we had to pause when Sarge left his bedroom very late to get something from the fridge.

All Sarge was wearing was bikini-cut underwear. And even with very little in the way of cock-protecting material, he thought it was a great time to start up a chat with me about how wrong he had been about Siddle. While I respect a man admitting he is wrong, any conversation with a 60-year-old bloke in bikini-cut underwear who also is off his skull should be avoided.

DAY 2 – THE GABBA

Somehow I'd ended up with a regular radio gig with a regional radio station in Port Lincoln, South Australia. The reason I agreed to it was that he'd called me cricket's Stephen Colbert, and because, like most people in this industry, I was a massive media whore. The problem is that in the morning you may ring me for expert analysis and piss taking, but what you get is random noises and endless unfunny sentences. But the host seemed to be really into it, and for his sake I wanted to engage him.

I'm not expecting stellar book sales in Port Lincoln.

Big Daddy and I headed to the ground after Issy had made him a sandwich. How he convinced her to make him a sandwich I don't know. He just had that effect on people. Although not on me, I wouldn't make him anything, and even if I did, he'd assume I'd spat in it as a gag. Or worse if it had mayo on it. Big Daddy convincing a woman to make something for him was one of those things I missed about home.

Unlike me, who felt mothered by the whole world, Big Daddy could make anyone feel like his mother, even single women far younger than him. It wasn't like his mother was inadequate; it was the opposite. He just knew he liked women to do things for him, and that by complimenting them, being very polite, and, importantly, never ever asking for anything directly, he'd get whatever he wanted.

Even so, getting Issy to make him a sandwich before she started her shift as a nurse was very impressive.

Big Daddy went to find a seat and convince some woman near him to get him a beer I suppose. The Gabba felt less angry than the day before. While the first day had been a bit of a lad crowd, this was more of a family atmosphere. The Gabba has never really strived to be sophisticated in the way Sydney and Adelaide Oval are. It is really more like a smaller version of the MCG. Even the fact that it doesn't have an obvious members' section makes it feel harder than most grounds in the world: the yobbos and morons seem to be all around you and not focused in one section.

Australia's fear of losing the Ashes, which was largely unspoken even though you could feel it, had disappeared with Siddle a day earlier. Katich and Watson were a good partnership, the old and new of Australian cricket. Katich could have played in any of the previous four decades and not been out of place. His penchant for chest hair, getting dirty and playing as hard as he could were old school Australia. I've never seen a photo of him slumped drunkenly in the changing rooms with a cigarette and a beer, it's just how I picture him. He's hard, and while his technique is as ugly as you can be while still hitting the ball, he makes it work with sheer, working-class Australian ethic. He's the sheep-shearing, beer-drinking, hard-as-nails Aussie man. Tough, but fair.

Watson is nothing like that. At first glance he makes Katich look like a skinny little man, but it doesn't take long to see that while Watson is a solid unit, he is not the manly man that Australians are often mistaken for. Watson spends more time on his hair than Katich spends mowing his lawn – and Katich looks like a man who makes sure the edges are trimmed. Watson's physique was built up by years in the gym, and has now been refined through yoga or Pilates, or yogalates. His ex-girlfriend was a dancer on one of those dancing celebrity shows. His wife is a model/actor type that is sort of well known. He is the modern Australian metrosexual man. Perhaps not a bad person or even a prick, he just comes across as a solipsist and vain. It is this demeanour that makes so many people hate him.

He looks like the sort of person who loves the surfing look but the actual thought of surfing has never occurred to him.

Together, they made an unlikely team. Neither was an opener, neither was all that popular with fans for long periods – even though both were chosen as potential superstars early on – and they had now been thrown together more out of luck than planning. It shouldn't work as a pairing. They should be too different to get along: Katich should be mocking Watson's sexual preferences and Watson should be giving Katich his chest waxer's number. But somehow they make it work. They've made it work so well that when these two get out the collapse starts. Their partnerships seem to always range between 40 and 110, and once one of them goes, Australia wobble. An all-time great is at number three; a once in a generation teddy bear comes in at four, and the statistical anomaly of the mid-noughties bats at five. None of them seem to be able to stop the rot, once Katich or Watson go. It's quite weird.

It might be an illusion, but I thought I'd seen seen their partnership broken at 80 about ten times only for Australia never to pass 250. These outcasts had become the backbone and, without them, Australia ended up as spineless, over-rated idiots. The problem is that while Katich and Watson could make runs, they didn't make millions of them. Katich seemed to make 40 or 80, rarely 120 and as good as Watson looked putting his massive leg down the wicket, he didn't get much past 50 very often, and had made only two Test hundreds. It shouldn't have been a problem; the other higher-rated batsmen should use their solid base to put on a big total, but it didn't seem to happen that way.

The only other problem Katich and Watson had was their running between wickets. I don't think either man really trusted the other one. If you were going to steal quick singles, as both men liked to do, you had to have trust. I'm sure sometime in the past some coach has gotten batsmen to play the trust game and let Katich fall into Watson's arms. It must have gone wrong, perhaps like the time I did it and got it so wrong that I caught the person but also kneed them in their spine (I did that to a girl once – from the look on her face, it wasn't nice). That's why when Katich pushed one into the off-side and took off, Watson screamed no. Katich was left mid pitch while Trott wondered whether to shy at the stumps or wait for Prior to get to them. Prior didn't hurry and Trott's shot missed. With the time Trott had, it should have been out. Katich and Watson always seemed to have these moments. Maybe because Katich always seemed to be diving for the crease. They just don't communicate well.

When they were trying not to run themselves out, Anderson was working them over. Anderson had recently appeared semi naked (don't you hate it when they call something naked that doesn't have genitals in it?) on the cover of a gay magazine in the UK. Had he not been a cricketer, I think he'd have been one of those serious-faced jeans models you see topless all over billboards in America. Pretty enough to sort of be a girl, but manly enough to wear a pair of jeans. Anderson was better looking than Sampson Collins, and that was saying something.

His spell was every bit as professional as you'd expect from NuEngland. Line, length, pace, guile and plenty of testing deliveries. While Anderson was in charge of his game, his game was being rebutted by the review system. After Billy Doctrove gave Katich out lbw, the Virtual eye machine deemed it was too high. Then when he thought the onfield umpire was wrong he put his same faith in that machine, and this time the ball was just clipping leg to Watson, and not the 50 per cent or more that is needed to reverse the decision.

Channel 9 had changed from Hawkeye to Virtual eye, because Virtual eye was as good as Hawkeye and cheaper; there was also Eagle Eye, which was perhaps the same thing as Virtual eye, I think. Sometimes you write a sentence just because it's fun.

The crowd had started to get excited. England's low total, luck going against them, two set batsmen and some overthrows meant they were ready to get very animated. I couldn't get excited. Australia were near 80 with no wickets down and appeals happening every over. It seemed that any minute now England would get one. Then Anderson did just that. Watson in the slips. Bringing Ponting out to the crease in his last Test at the Gabba.

Maybe.

You never know, do you? He could get run over by a bus (why is it always a bus, why can't it be a tragically oversized four wheel drive driven by some stupid fuckwit who thinks they are safe) or could just retire at the end of the Ashes. Ponting still had the hard-to-like face, was still quick to anger, had the built-for-hard-labour disposition and the I-want-to-make-a-difference stare, but they were all fading. Where he had once been the man for any occasion, he was now rarely the man at all. It seemed the deeper the lines on his forehead got, the less likely he was to make a difference. Even in India when he was Australia's most consistent batsman, he made three scores in the 70s, not one hundred. The old Ponting would have killed an Indian politician for a hundred. The young Ponting would have just made one.

I'd spent my whole adult life with Ponting, and this was new. He looked unlikely for the first time I could remember. There was something missing; it could have been age, or the fear of a third Ashes defeat. It just wasn't Ponting. He had the whole series to prove me wrong, but it just didn't seem likely. I knew he'd never command the crease like he did at the Oval in 09. That day he would have needed a North Korean missile to take him down. Or a comedy run-out.

Right now, Ponting's innings made me think he'd been cryogenically frozen, found in the year 2243, brought back to current times by an Australian fan hoping he'd be the difference, but wasn't thawed correctly.

Ponting's recent record is bad enough that you can mock him, but not to his face – never to his face. According to Ponting all his recent statistical low points could be directed back to the term 'bad luck'. That was a good catch; never mind that I hit it in the air. That ball kept low, as it did to other batsmen. I got run out again, more than any batsman in history. That flying saucer that was behind the bowler's arm put me off, never mind that I played a pull shot 12 seconds after the ball was released.

I'd seen reporters try to push Ponting about the elephant in the room, but he was too scary-looking for anyone to nail him on it. While his form on the field had gotten progressively worse, his performances in press conferences had got fiercer.

I once said – more than once – that Ponting's form is now reserved for what I call the fuck-you-hundred. It's an innings he makes through sheer angriness. Usually it comes early in a series when he has been under the pump in the lead-up. It's a one-finger salute, sort of like an Eminem song from his first album.

Considering Ponting's team and form had been slated in the lead-up to the Ashes, I expected him to come out and show that he meant some kind of business. This innings was about as far from a fuck-you as possible. It was more "excuse me, am I in your way"? I can't think of too many times when Ponting wasn't facing Harbhajan Singh that Ponting ever looked like this. It hurts me to watch him. When, after a lovely lunch of rice and various unidentified meats, he was out caught down the leg-side, it wasn't a shame, but a mercy. Ponting can claim to be unlucky but he now looks rubbish off his hip. And his habit of jumping inside the line of the ball is going to mean more balls will go past his hip. Hopefully he would have had some more time to thaw out for the second innings.

Swann, meanwhile, was having the kind of shocker I thought he might on Australian pitches. Actually, he wasn't. I thought he might work for hours on end, day after day, without much luck. Instead, for two days running, he had started with filthy filth. The sort of deliveries that even most club off-spinners don't bowl. That said, if you gathered up all the club spinners from across England, and combined all their turn and put it up against Swann's, he'd still get more spin. While that might be a fun task, it didn't help Swann on this tour.

Off-spinners and Australia don't mix. That isn't a Nathan Hauritz joke; it's a cold, hard fact. Murali and Harbhajan have suffered; Richard Dawson, the former Yorkshire bowler who played four Ashes Tests in Australia in 02-03, is now only seen on Steve Waugh's highlights. England turning up with the world's best spinner didn't change the pitches over here. Swann also started the last Ashes badly. He was outbowled by the same Nathan Hauritz that no one wanted back then. Now he is showing that same nervous twitch that he had at Cardiff about 18 months ago.

Katich made it to yet another fifty and then went – it's as if he and Watson don't trust the other one when they're in the changing room alone. It was a soft push back to Finn. According to Big Daddy, Katich was limping. He could have been right, although Katich looks like he's limping on a good day; it's something to do with the way his shoulders move.

Swann was twitchy, Ponting stiffy, Katich limpy, yet all of them looked far better than Clarke. I'm not talking about his normal mobile phone salesman look, inoffensive small face, short hair, blinky eyes, designer tattoo, shirt tucked in just right, clothes nice and clean. I mean his back. His injury was one of the main concerns coming into the Test, which is why some of us cricket writer types had watched him doing fielding practice the day before looking for signs of pain or stiffness. We saw none. Two days later Clarke was out in the middle looking like his back had been replaced by an old Hills Hoist clothes-line. It was as horrible as I'd ever seen Clarke bat. Clarke is a pretty batsman. He doesn't hit the ball, he strokes it. His footwork is precise, his shots crisp, and his execution stunning. His batting is almost feminine. Actually, it is feminine. It's how a classy female lawyer from a cheap Hollywood film would move. All its hairs are in place, it plays straight, and never gives too much away.

When a batsman like Clarke has a bad day, you notice it more. This was the worst day I'd seen Clarke have. I'd seen him in bad form before, I'd seen him look out of sorts before, and I'd seen him doubt himself before. I just hadn't seen him combine the three. A bad back doesn't sound like an injury that would affect a cricketer that much. Batsmen don't move as much as most sportsmen and general fitness for a cricketer is not the same as other sports.

The back is really only important when you get fast short bowling. In Test cricket, unless you play India, you get fast, short bowling. Clarke hasn't been able to get out off a short ball in a long time. Ducking and twisting are hard when your spine is not kind. Stuart Broad bounced Clarke out in a T20 match a few months before in England, and the terrible way he played the ball was so obvious that even casual fans knew England were going to bounce him in Australia.

Three Tests earlier, while touring New Zealand, Clarke had achieved perhaps his greatest moment: making a hundred days after his biggest PR disaster. While on tour he was confronted with a huge problem, a naked photo of his glamour model fiancée, Lara Bingle, taken by her ex-boyfriend, the married-at-the-time Brendan Fevola. I met Brendan once. It's not relevant to the story, but I like to mention it.

In New Zealand, here was poor Clarke trying to score runs for his country, while dealing with sickening Twitter pleading from his fiancée. Not for the first time, he chose his fiancée over Australia. Or so it seemed. Instead of going back, comforting her, and missing a Test, he went back, dumped her, and then strode out on the field to make his top score in Test cricket, 168. It wasn't the most emotional fiancée crisis in Test cricket – Bob Blair once saved the follow-on for New Zealand after his fiancée died in a train crash. Clarke's version was the soft cock modern cricketers' PR crisis, but to fly back and make runs was still a huge effort.

My grandmother is 88 and in a wheelchair, and she would have moved as well as Clarke in this innings. She would have handled the short balls far better. She probably would have dumped Bingle earlier as well. The only good thing that could have happened to Clarke was if Ponting had come out on the field and retired him hurt. Clarke missed over a quarter of the balls he faced. He was hit on the body, hit pretty close in front, had a massive appeal for caught behind given not out (snicko disagreed with the verdict) and then eventually got out to perhaps the lamest pull shot in the history of cricket. Rodney Hogg once erased a tape of himself batting because it showed how cowardly he had batted. I could imagine Clarke doing the same, not because he batted like a coward, but just because he wouldn't want a child of his seeing him looking so unstylish.

That brought Marcus North to the wicket, gifting Swann his first wicket in Australia. That's all.

Then it was Mike Hussey and Brad Haddin, with Australia in enough trouble for me to give up my 2-1 prediction and never speak to anyone ever again. Australia found themselves at 143 for five. Yet again they'd managed to erase all the good work of Watson and Katich and dive mouth open into a bucket of shit.

Brad Haddin was once described by Alex from the blog King Cricket as exactly how you'd expect an Australian wicketkeeper to look. That bland round face, with sun-damaged eyes, he looked like he could have been an eager swimming instructor. If you were forced at gunpoint to draw an Australian cricketer you'd end up with Brad Haddin. In recent times Haddin's body had been breaking down with such amazing regularity that Tim Paine's assured batting and fewer mistakes had brought him mentions in replacement talks.

Hussey looks like he's a swell guy. He could be cast as an extra in *Gallipoli*, or coaching your kid's basketball team. His eyes are close together, giving him that eager old world look. He was a young man's old man and he should have been dropped years ago. Well, at least 18 months ago. Maybe longer, I'd forgotten since I'd been saying it for so long.

It had been ages since Hussey was in any sort of form that resembled Test form. Since January 2008, Hussey had made three Test hundreds, and if you looked at it closer, two of them didn't really count. The first one was at the Oval in the last Ashes Test of 09. That one didn't count because he knew that part of the reason he had to make a hundred was so that I and others who had called for his head couldn't lynch him and that Test was already over. The other hundred was in a Test match that a man who recently ran into undercover *News of the World* reporters claimed was fixed. Even if it wasn't, Pakistan's effort to get Hussey to a century in that match was spectacular.

In this period of his career he had managed to average 33, even including these fraudulent hundreds. Whilst his batting average was once a statistical anomaly of over 80 from 21 Tests, after 54 Tests he had brought it down to 49.75. Say it out loud, four-nine-dot-seven-five. When his average got to 49.75 I had a little party. It was a small affair, just me and some dodgy bourbon, but everyone enjoyed themselves. For years I had heard about how Hussey must still be good to keep his average above 50 which, other than being the sort of nonsense that people who like reality TV would say, is just plain wrong.

If your average was over 80 from your first 21 Tests, then your next 33 Tests must have been pretty damn ordinary to get it to 49.75. That sort of logic never really seemed to bother most people. They were still talking about Hussey like he was Neo from *The Matrix*, when he was more like Bernie from *Weekend at Bernie's*. My voice had gone, not literally, from all the times I had called for him to be dropped. Plus, I'd moved on to Marcus North; you can only work on one weak link at a time.

At the point when the magical number of 49.75 had come up, Hussey had come under some pressure before from the press, but never enough. They never even brought up the stats that made me spit when I talked of him. They also never mentioned that when a man over 35 hasn't made runs for three years, even if he comes back to form, he should still be discarded. The Australian batting line-up is perhaps the most stable workplace in Australia. While John Howard had done his bit to make sure there was little job security in the country, he must have left a clause in that protected Australian batsmen. It didn't seem to matter than more than a few of us had noticed problems. Those being: age, reliability, clubhouse and shit.

If you'd been casting for a movie about this top order you could use the *Space Cowboy* stars to fill the team up. James Garner could play Katich, and make him a bit more likeable. The two youngest men in the top seven were 29. Being that Australia were supposedly in a rebuilding phase, it seemed odd that they were using men who in some cases had less than 12 months of cricket in them. I suggested it was time for James Sutherland to purchase some gold watches.

Recently I built a mansion made of cards, rested a bowling ball on top of it, sat it outside in Chicago and put the Australian batting order next to it. Guess which collapsed first? In their previous 17 Tests, ten of them had produced massive collapses or pathetic totals. Nothing happens though. It was almost as if the Australian selectors don't watch the team bat at all. When Katich and Hussey bat together, that is not a bad policy for everyone.

It is often said getting into the Australian side is harder than leaving it. That isn't so true now; the bowling line-up changes often because of injuries, mostly because Ricky slowly puts his bowlers to death. But getting into this batting line-up was harder than being a lesbian trying to get into the panties of a born-again Christian member of the God Hates Fags group. Getting out was non-existent: it's the Hotel fucken California. North was being given an extended run, Hussey was given 18 months' sick pay – it was hard to know what you would need to do to get dropped from this line-up. Perhaps sodomising a goat live on TV and not running it past Cricket Australia first? Especially if the goat was branded with a non-sanctioned sponsor.

If your dog continues to fall over and pisses himself around the house, it is OK to take him to the vet to get him fixed or put down. I know you love the dog, but the falling down and pissing are quite obvious signs that something is wrong. Don't wait for him to shit in your bed.

Mike Hussey should be the poster child for Australia's saggy old batting line-up. He had probably only made this Test because he stole a hundred from a depleted Victorian line-up in the second innings of the Shield match for Western Australia. I feel sick that the Victorian people have had a hand in him being in this Test. I would have dropped him and not lost a wink of sleep.

While I was writing all that, Hussey reached his fifty.

He was batting in such a way that I couldn't mock him. I don't say that lightly. There was a spring in his step; his shots were crisp and on purpose. He even walked out like he expected to make runs, not his usual gallows walk. Hussey hadn't intimidated a player in Test cricket for a long time, but his furious feet, front and back, were all over Swann's neck. Full balls were played with ease, short balls pulled like a father trying to prove he is still better than his son in backyard cricket. There was a brief time when I felt like Swann was trying to bounce Hussey out, perhaps inspired by the English quick men who were trying to do the same. It was a doomed theory for Swann and the rest of the bowlers in the end. When the world's best spinner has five men out on the boundary you know he's got something very wrong.

This was the best batting I'd seen from Hussey since he'd averaged more than 80. Warne and McGrath played then. He was doing what they say on the telly, making batting look easy. He had his luck: his first ball dropped just short of second slip from Steve Finn. It was the only time he looked nervous in the innings, and even then he was only nervous because the ball was flying towards a slip fielder who could have ended his career. Now his 50 had guaranteed him another 10 Tests at least, maybe another hundred. For all my talk about his age, he looked as virile as he ever had.

Haddin was good too. Not in a classic Haddin way – he was barely scoring. He played the Tim Paine innings, perhaps so Tim Paine couldn't come in and do it for himself. Haddin put all his shots away and just let Hussey carry the bulk of the load to stumps. Australia got there just as the new ball was being brought out; stumps were taken early due to Queensland aversion of daylight saving and the rain.

This was also the night of my great breakthrough. Late at night, while looking for a suitably cool place to film the seminal *Two Pricks at the Ashes* series, we were in some corporate boxes. There we found the magic bounty, the uneaten food of the corporates. The cricket might finish at 5pm or 5.30 due to a slow over rate, but the cleaning crews don't come in for hours. I'm not saying the food is everything you've ever wanted, or hot. It's free food, and if it's good enough for the pompous assclowns in there, it's good enough for me. It's also true that free food tastes better. Especially the party pies and sausage rolls. Party pies are one of the great foods in the world's history. Like a normal family meat pie, but shrunk down to bite size. Genius.

That night I didn't stuff myself as there was steak to be had on Sarge's balcony cooked by him and Issy. Dad, Big Daddy and I watched as they both tried to drunkenly put together a meal in much the same way a *Three Stooges* sketch would go. At one stage my salad had been on three different plates before getting to me. Although I'd never complain about free steak and bourbon.

With Big Daddy there, Sarge decided to move into him for a

bet. Big Daddy was far more sober than Sarge due to his overall size and the fact he'd sat in a dry zone of the Gabba (something he was less than happy about). He took the bet with Sarge, which involved the newest AFL team, the Gold Coast Suns, finishing above Collingwood, my team, on the ladder. I can't remember the amount, but I remember thinking it was the worst bet of Sarge's life, and the safest of Big Daddy's.

This stupid bet also let us all ignore the precarious position of the cricket. Australia were 200 for five, but England could still grab a lead. The majority of the cricket chat was about how someone on TV had angered my father by saying that Haddin's innings was exciting. Watching my dad yell about someone on the telly getting it so wrong reminded me of thousands of our conversations in the past. As he got so angry that he spat and got all the details wrong, I also knew how I'd made a career: this angry, ranty shit was quite captivating.

That night I convinced Dad and Big Daddy to do a podcast. They both did quite well. They're natural born bullshitters, and never was there a better outlet for that than a podcast. I spent the rest of the night chatting to Big Daddy and editing the Two Pricks episode. I'm not sure that when he came up to visit me for these Tests he thought he'd gently fall asleep at one end of the sofa while I sat and edited at the other end.

Just before he did fall asleep, Sarge came back out of his room in his underwear again. You were never drunk enough for that. Mike Hussey would go to sleep tonight thinking of a possible hundred. Big Daddy and I would go to sleep thinking of Sarge's package.

DAY 3 – THE GABBA

Big Daddy and I were going to walk to the ground together, but instead he went off to dump some garbage for Issy. Now I understood why women did things for him – he does things for them. It seemed like hard work, so I just went down to the Gabba on my own.

Sam pointed out the walkers. Two men decked in Cricket Australia clothing doing laps of the ground in the morning. It was the sort of walk that two men could happily do in any middle-class suburb in any city in the world. The problem is their Cricket Australia pale blue (why pale blue, it's surely a colour invented to make bridesmaids look ugly) and orange costumes made them stick out, and the constant laps meant we could easily identify them. Eventually it became clear that one was my accreditation saviour, Lachlan Patterson, and the other was Australia's chairman of selectors Andrew Hilditch. There was something nice about this walk; two men who don't get much spare time during the season just waddling around the ground getting fit.

It was also quite odd. The crowd ignored them, but only because they didn't know it was Hilditch, luckily for him. Sam wasn't the only one to notice it, David 'Bumble' Lloyd had as well. I was sitting next to the *Daily Mails'* Paul Newman, and Paul was Bumble's ghost writer. Every day Bumble would come over and chat to Paul. It made one of Bumble's columns, and when they were chatting about it I couldn't help but be sucked into the conversation. Especially since he was taking the piss out of Hilditch. "Wouldn't get Ray Illingworth doing that, would you?" he said.

The other key story of the morning was Jimmy Anderson. It was the sort of spell we've all had in our dreams. I'm going to put the ball here and move it here, because I can. Then I shall make this man in good form look like an idiot, and make the other guy look second rate. The problem with a dream spell is that in it you take eight wickets for 12 runs, run someone out from the boundary with a direct hit and take a screaming one-handed catch, then go off the field and satisfy 12 women all on your own. Jimmy took no wickets, hit no stumps and never even took a one-handed catch. There were no women either.

At one stage Jimmy hit Hussey in front enough for the Poms to refer. It wasn't a terrible referral, but it was hopeful. Not out was the decision, meaning they had lost both of their referrals. So a few balls later when Hussey was hit dead in front, and there were no referrals left, Jimmy's dream turned into a less happy dream. Not a nightmare – I mean he's out there playing for his country sledging Brad Haddin, so it's not all bad.

There was a time when Anderson was perhaps the most embarrassing world bowler when the ball wasn't swinging. Those days were at their worst for him during the 06/07 Ashes when his action was being remodelled by Troy Cooley, now the Australian bowling coach. Now he was a pretty good bowler when the ball wasn't swinging. Not the vicious match-winner he could be when it was swinging, but a clever leader of the attack who gave little away. When the ball was swinging he was Natalie Portman in a bathtub of whiskey.

Jimmy's last tour was a nightmare. He was almost overcoached to extinction. Jimmy's head drops when he bowls and he has other technical issues that mean his action is not pure. Jimmy was remodelled; he was twisted, turned, and thought to be fixed. This led to him bowling a collection of the shittest deliveries he had ever bowled until he almost was lost forever.

The 06/07 Ashes was not good to him. When I say not good,

it was prison rape. Three Tests for five wickets at an average of over 80. That he still exists is a testament to his doggedness. He shook off the coaching, worked on doing things when the ball wasn't swinging and has now become the leader of this attack whilst nearing 200 Test wickets.

Cooley was supposed to be the reason behind England winning the 2005 Ashes, when he took a top bowling attack plus Ashley Giles and turned it into a swing-bowling machine. Jimmy was not required in that series. Then Cooley took off back home to Australia and he got Mitchell Johnson to bowl an inswinger. He bowled 17 of them, but they were the only 17 he ever bowled, and considering Australia beat South Africa away after losing to them at home, Cooley was a hero on two continents.

Not that Cooley is universally loved: other than his tinkering with Jimmy, there is also his tinkering with Kabir Ali. I once tried to find out what Cooley did with Kabir Ali, but the mere mention of Cooley's name in Worcestershire gets you chased out of the village by people with pitchforks.

David Saker, like Cooley an Australian (actually a Victorian), was now in charge of Jimmy Anderson and the other pace bowlers, and he is the best fast bowling coach in the world. I say this with as much bias as I can as Saker was one of my teenage heroes. My first memory of David Saker was in the early 90s. I heard a story about this really talented bowler who should be playing for Victoria, but wasn't because he was considered a behavioural risk. Among his many crimes was that he was suspended for bowling a bouncer off about 18 feet in a club match. I was only about 12 at the time, and it seemed insane for a bowler to bowl a bouncer off 18 feet in anger. I think he did it twice. This is only one of many stories from Saker's angry past.

Victoria knew he was talented, but it seemed to take them years to finally have the guts to play him. When he did play, he played very hard. He forced his way into an attack that at times had Damien Fleming, Paul Reiffel, Merv Hughes, Tony Dodemaide, Brad Williams and Ian Harvey to choose from. He was a bullocking outswing bowler who was always up for a fight. Saker never took a lot of wickets, but he was the sort of bowler you could wind up and let bowl into the wind all day. He was easily the loudest cricketer I have ever watched. It wasn't sledging, it was more like a series of vicious public service announcements.

Recently his former team-mate Darren Berry had written about a Sheffield Shield final incident, "David Saker was reported and lucky not to get life. He at one stage threw the ball from the boundary line, a little ill-directed and aimed at the umpire, such was his anger." This may have been retaliation for Saker's involvement in the attempted kidnap of Berry's Rajasthan Royals teddy bear mascot at the last IPL.

When Dean Headley was interviewed on a Test Match Sofa podcast, he was asked who was the most annoying cricketer he played against, and immediately named Saker. Saker was also once charged, and then cleared of, ball tampering. It should be noted that he was not playing but coaching in that game. He is the sort of man that newspapers would talk about having a chequered past. Even in a feel-good story from a few years ago, when Saker and his nephew took all ten wickets in a club game together, he was referred to as the crazy uncle.

But none of this, and I am just skimming the surface, is to say he is not an exceptional bowling coach. Since taking over from Rodney Hogg (another with a chequered past), Saker had helped the careers of Andrew McDonald, Dirk Nannes, Peter Siddle, Clint McKay, and Shane Harwood. Saker had made every one one of these players a better bowler. He just has the knack. He even produced an English Test bowler, Darren Pattinson, before becoming England's bowling coach.

His philosophy had always been pretty sensible: "The thing I stress [to Jimmy] is about making sure he keeps the game as simple as he can," he said. "There's a lot of coaches out there – and I'm a coach as well – trying to make the game of cricket very complicated. But you keep to the simple rules and you'll have success. As a bowler, if you bowl to the right areas for long enough, then you'll get some results."

With two hard working but not overly talented bowling line-ups in this series, the bowling coaches become an important factor. Saker could claim the upper hand with Anderson's spell today and Siddle's hat-trick. Although, Cooley might want to claim that as well. If they had to fight for it I think Cooley might get beaten up.

On the pitch, Anderson was even becoming more like Saker. He'd been getting mouthy before Saker was around, but with him on the scene, the whole bowling unit had become just that bit more sledgy. Jimmy now had trouble getting through an over without abusing someone. With Haddin at the other end he had a real friend, so the two were getting friendlier as the amazing wicketless spell went on. Geoff Miller, the England chairman of selectors, wandered through the press box carelessly whispering that it was the best spell he'd seen in years.

It really was, but Australia continued to survive. Haddin even lifted Anderson back over his head for four before unleashing a bit of Haddin magic on the game. With Anderson tiring from carrying England, Steven Finn came on and Haddin smashed him twice for four to bring up his fifty. It had come off 137 balls, yet he had made 26 from the last 23 balls.

Once Jimmy was off, Australia took over. To celebrate this fact Australia's former Prime Minister Kevin Rudd came into the press box with some random Chinese mayor and Geoffrey Boycott. I'd never really liked Rudd. I was glad he came along at the time to finally get rid of John Howard, but I don't like conservative left types, or people who pretend not go to tittie bars. Plus, why did he always have to be standing next to a Chinese person? I know he speaks Chinese, everyone knows he speaks Chinese. It's a cool skill. But so is the pull my finger fart gag, but a little goes a long way with both.

With Australia smashing his bowlers around, and Kevin Rudd speaking Chinese, Andrew Strauss lost the plot. I think the best thing ever to happen to Andrew Strauss as a captain was the fact that Ricky Ponting was his opposite number. It meant that if people were going to abuse a captain, it would be Ponting. Not that all that abuse is unwarranted. Most of it is very much warranted, but Strauss can be just as stupid as Ponting; he just looks calmer and sounds posher.

When Haddin started beating up England, I knew Strauss would shit himself. Hussey charged down the wicket to Swann, hitting a lovely lofted off drive, and Strauss put out a deep point the next ball. It was reactionary captaincy, and bad reactionary captaincy since lofted drives over mid-off don't often end up at deep point.

Just as I assumed most people were about to start pointing and laughing at Strauss, Hussey brought up his twelfth Test hundred – and a real one. There was no match fixing, and it wasn't a pointless one in a losing cause. This was a proper hundred, and he celebrated it that same way, with jumps, whoops and the sort of endless enthusiasm the man has. Even Haddin was genuinely excited. It was so exciting I almost didn't notice that when Swann continued to bowl to Hussey he did it with three men out on the boundary, but not one at deep mid-wicket, where Hussey had hit more fours off Swann than anywhere else.

I very nearly didn't see that.

England then got ropey. Cook missed a tough chance from Haddin off Collingwood. That Collingwood was bowling, and looked as though he had a chance of getting Haddin out, was a huge worry for England. Then the fielding started disintegrating. Haddin brought up his hundred by hitting Swann for a six. Jimmy watched it at long-on looking quite uninterested. Even a spell by Jimmy failed – Hussey and Haddin attacked him as well. It was brutal.

The calm and measured Lawrence Booth from the *Daily Mail* said, "This now feels like any other Ashes series." Lawrence takes times over his tweets. I don't think Lawrence would do anything in a hurry; even his hairstyle seems to have been carefully placed through hours of work.

There was now little to distinguish this from any other Australian Ashes series since I was old enough to masturbate. I even had these visions of some huge conspiracy and that Channel 9 had, in conjunction with Cricket Australia, just put on a tape of some game from the late 90s or early 2000s knowing that no one at the ground, especially the journalists, really watched the cricket. It was North Korean magic.

It couldn't be real. Australia were supposed to struggle, not plunder. Hussey was finished, a tragic waste of cricket carbon,

Haddin was held together by sticky tape and on-field rage. They weren't supposed to be having their way with England. Especially not the professional NuEngland. This was pretty far from professional. England's field placings looked random and made up. Their fielding went back to the good old days. Their bowlers were spent.

The one thing they kept doing, and you couldn't miss it, was the organised patting on the ass. If you did a good piece of fielding – let's say, a firm ball is hit to your right and you have to drop down and dive to your side, that's worth three players coming up to you and patting you. Stopping a hard ball belted straight at you is worth one. And a dive to save one you should have never got to can mean as many as five players patting you.

A fielder can be at fine leg and 50 metres from the nearest player, but if he does some really good fielding, at least one player will give him the pat. The actual ass patting is not enforced. They also do low fives, shoulder taps and occasionally just walk close to the player and give him a clap. The thing is they always do something.

It seemed so exact that it was part of a plan. They'd got an ass-patting manual somewhere that they came up with in a meeting. That was not even a one per center. It was further than crossing the T's and dotting the I's. This was hardcore planning. It's admirable if from no other perspective than from an OCD standpoint. For me it might have been a bit of a put-on. When I want an ass pat, I want it to be spontaneous and loving, not just because we've talked about encouraging each other.

Steven Finn was getting some proper punishment; there were few congratulations from his team-mates. Finn, taller than necessary, and skinnier than a bulemic, didn't look like a fast bowler. He looked like he should be knocking on doors for the Mormons. Finn had been brought over as a tall fast bowler capable of putting it up the Aussies. Well whatever he put up them they seemed to like. Why he thought the key to bowling in Australia was floating up half-volleys, I'll never know.

I, like most of you, judge a fast bowler on his buttocks, and Finn is very ass-less. Before seeing him today I thought he could overcome this; maybe I was wrong. Very few fast bowlers are ass-less to his extent. McGrath was one. If you thought about Finn's ass-less appearance, his eight-year-old boy's haircut, and his height, you would see why he is one of the four bowlers in world cricket being called the new McGrath. I couldn't see it. I also didn't see it in Bangladesh, when he made his debut. That he has talent, I see; that he is the new McGrath I don't.

Jimmy's 'good' day kept getting worse. A Haddin pull went straight up in the air and somehow, defying all logic and fielding coaches, Anderson didn't get a hand on it. He then took 20 minutes to get up. It was back to the bad old days with Anderson's body language. He just looked pissy and angry. You can do that when you are the petulant young bowler; not sure you can do that when you are a team leader of 29.

Then I chatted to Nasser Hussain. It's not really like me to start a chat with someone like Nasser, but he was sitting next to me and I needed to know something. You see Sam and I are very happy with our soon-to-be internet sensation *Two Pricks at the Ashes*. The thing is, with the complete resources of the press box, we wanted to exploit some of these people to make our videos better (more watched). I mean they're there, and they're famous, why not cash in?

The problem is, if you call your show *Two Pricks at the Ashes*, it's hard to just go up to Ian Botham and ask him to come on it. So I thought, before I went up to someone and just asked them, I'd ask Nasser what he thought about the name. It was my first ever interaction with him, and it told you a lot about him, because it was a simple question, but he thought it through on every level.

First he lifted his eyebrow a bit, then he smiled. I doubt that it was the question he thought I'd ask. Perhaps he thought I'd ask about an innings, or the toss at the Gabba that he ballsed up years ago, maybe even for a quote. Yet he composed himself and gave me an insight. Nasser said most of his people (my words, not his) wouldn't come on the show. He then added that many of the people already on TV and radio are not allowed to appear on a rival's programme anyway. So the name wouldn't matter. Then he said something that I really didn't expect.

"If the name suits the show, and people like it, keep it; those who don't want to come on it probably won't anyway. No one's going to forget what you called it." Once Nasser left I ran over to Sam and told him about my conversation with Nasser, and *Two Pricks at the Ashes* went from a name we used because it was too hard to come up with something else, to the name we'd use for the entire Ashes, for better or worse.

England's fielding kept getting worse as Hussey brought up his 150 and the partnership with Haddin passed 300. This must have been some sort of record now: best stand between a left-handed former opener and right-handed 'keeper at the Gabba on a Saturday at the very least. Hussey was in such good form that his Twitter account was following people while he batted. Which was proof it was a ghosted Twitter account, or that his form was supernatural.

Then it was over, as Haddin was caught at slip off Swann. And, as often happens, when one partner goes, the other quickly follows. Finn bounced Hussey out, caught at deep mid-wicket pulling. The Australian tail then took themselves way too seriously, and instead of getting on with it, Johnson took 19 balls over a duck and, somehow, Finn had ended up with six wickets.

Maybe Finn was the new McGrath. Or the new Siddle. Or a registered charity.

When England batted again they were 221 behind. Strauss left the first ball of the innings and was struck on the pad as it swung back in from Hilfenhaus. Australia reviewed it and it was only just a touch too high. Strauss and Cook then did their thing, draining the fun out of the day with a stand that got them to stumps at 19 for no wicket off 15 painful overs. They did their job well; I just wish they could do it in private so I didn't have to watch. At the close, England were a biscuit over 200 behind. That had all come from one partnership, and sucked for them.

But the day had been as cool-as-hell one of Test cricket. That might sound weird coming from me, because I like my wickets, and I'd only seen five. The morning had been all about Jimmy's dream balls, and Australian survival. The afternoon had been all about humiliating England. It had also contained a mini-collapse. Then it finished with a classic wet blanket English opening partnership. This had been a day with a touch of everything.

That night I grabbed a bit of free food then headed off to a bar in the city that sells really over-priced beer. Beer is really over-priced in Australia. They should form a Senate hearing about that. I drank with Big Daddy and Blair, another cousin. I wasn't running a family get-together; it just happened that everyone had been at the cricket. The bar was a German place. I sort of liked that Brisbane had a lot of German places; it made all the Nazi references I had made about the place as a youth seem right. The beer was as good as it was expensive, and a real German served it. It felt very Brisbane.

DAY 4 – THE GABBA

Overnight, I had had drinks and didn't see Sarge's underwear so it was a good one.

Cook and Strauss now became set, the best time – perhaps the only time – to watch them bat. A set Strauss would play some shots; he understands that when you are in, it is the time to pounce on the opposition. Cook had still to learn this. Cook just liked to be in. Separate, they are two handy openers; together, they are a slow-moving unit. Although it was their partnership that had been pivotal in helping England win the Ashes in 09. At Lord's, they had smashed around some of the worst bowling you'd see in international cricket and Strauss had picked up a hundred and Cook had just fallen short.

That had been Strauss' most recent hundred in Tests.

Strauss had been pretty damn ordinary since then. He had missed out on almost certain centuries by opting out of the tour of Bangladesh and instead playing quite a lot of cricket for Middlesex at the start of the 2010 summer. But his numbers were way poorer than his PR, which was almost always exceptional. The worst press he ever gets is talk about him being a conservative captain.

Today Mitchell was having a terrible day, and Strauss and Cook looked like they were up for the fight. I always find it interesting that both of them bat like they are in trench warfare. It's not necessarily correct, it is just head down, get the job done by any means. The funny part is that because of their breeding and schooling, Strauss at Radley and Cook at Bedford, they would never have had to set foot in a trench. It shows that breeding and class privilege have no effect on survival skills.

If the phrase 'bat like millionaires' is often heard in cricket circles, these two bat like peasants. They approach most innings as if they have never made a run before. The closest thing to flashy with either of them is Strauss' cut shot. And even that has a bit of survival about it. Strauss flashes at the ball because otherwise he can't break the shackles at all. Cook has given up flashing altogether; he prods.

Cook's technique was almost the end of him for a while. It is a technique that has slips salivating. Then he added the odd lbw to the equation and suddenly it looked like his career was in jeopardy. Graham Gooch then worked with him for a while, but all he seemed to do was come in and say, "Hey, Cooky, bat like me and be a good lad." It didn't seem to straighten Cook out all that much, and the comedy backlift didn't fit, so Cook and Gooch then just gently realigned his technique to make him less likely to be leg-before or caught at slip.

That is all you have to do for someone like Cook. His main skill is not his technique, it's his Zen-like patience and dogged determination to succeed. He wasn't picked to play Test cricket as a young man because his technique was watertight, but because he had something about his demeanour that said, "I will stay out here for hours and really torment spectators."

Today it was the Australian spectators who had to feel the pain of watching Cook. Strauss was a bit looser, keeping Australia interested, and on 69, he hit a ball from Doherty to Mitch, who dropped it. From then on in it was obvious that Strauss would make a hundred – yet again handed to him by Mitch. Strauss should name a child after him.

Sam and I had child worries of our own. By this time, we had realised that walking into the media lunch area was kind of uncomfortable. It was like a scene from every awkward American teen film – holding a tray of food, looking for a place to sit. Unless by some fluke there was a seat free on a table where you knew someone, holding that tray of food while you desperately scanned the room looking for a place to sit was torture.

Sam came up with a brilliantly nerdy way of handling it. We'd go to lunch together a few minutes before lunch was officially called, pick up some food, find an empty table and occupy it together. Like social rejects from said teen film.

The long-termers all know each other well. They stay at the same hotels, and have had many a hungover breakfast together. They've probably double-teamed the same Jamaican prostitutes. Even if not everyone gets on with everyone else, they all know each other and finding a seat is easy. When you are the new kids, what's the dining etiquette? You know almost no one. Can you just sit at Jonathan Agnew's table? By finding our own, we were probably missing a great chance to bullshit with old cricketers, press our claims to get real cricket jobs and actually meet the vast number of cricket journalists we didn't know. The fear of the tray was what did it.

If the previous day's cricket had been like a video from the Australian golden period, today's was from a similar English period. It was the sort of struggle it had seemed Australia wouldn't have had to have worried about after Siddle, Hussey and Haddin had put them on the road to victory. It all became a bit blurry for me.

Then the Gabba was brought to life. By a flash mob. Few people know what the term 'flash mob' is, so I shall explain it like this: it's a very-heavily practised form of spontaneity, usually a cheap marketing ploy. You know those adverts when a bunch of people turn up at a place and start singing or acting in unison? It is obviously pre-planned but still freaks out the people involved? It's one of them. The night before, our *Two Pricks* filming had been interrupted by them practising. So they did their dance and people cheered because people are idiots. And then they left. Their seats remained empty from that point on.

The Aussies were like a flash mob. They had performed just well enough for just long enough to get the crowd involved, and then left. They were no more in the game than the flash mob were in their seats. They had jumped the Poms with some well choreographed routines that were mostly just for show, and had then taken the rest of the Test off.

This was confirmed to me when Andrew Strauss, who had just got his hundred, got out to Marcus North.

Trott came in and Australia looked just as toothless. Not only had the poor performance upset the local crowd, some of them were still pissed off with the weird Gabba ruling that says you are not allowed to take bags with more than one zip into the ground. It is the sort of ruling that Australia would come up with. People who haven't been to Australia don't generally believe me when I say there are few countries on earth that are as over-regulated as Australia. The zip rule is just more proof of that.

The idea behind it is that letting people into the ground and searching their bags is too much hassle and would slow entry down. Never mind that almost every sporting stadium in the developed world does it, the Gabba says no. Instead, if your bag has more than one zipper, or one compartment, you must store it at one of the docking stations around the ground. I'm a naturally cynical person, but put me with someone else just as cynical, and it's a whole lot of fun. So when I heard about this I started chatting about it with Martin Samuels, the chief sports writer from the *Daily Mail*. It seemed we had a similar sick outlook on life. This is what we came up with.

You're a terrorist, right? And you want to bomb the Gabba. All good. Now you know that you can't get anything into the ground, because this zip policy is enforced by Nazis, but you also know that your bag will be stowed inside the Gabba for you without being checked. So you go to one bag check, with one bag, then another bag check, then another, and another, until you have bags filled with C4, or whatever the kiddies are using these days, all over the ground. You link it all up to mobile phones, get a taxi – that might be the hardest part at the Gabba – and drive across town, call the numbers in the bags and bring down the Gabba stands when they're full of people.

On the other hand, we figured that they could be checking your bags after you have left them. Meaning that pimply-faced contract workers could be going through your tampons, spare underwear, naked photos of your girlfriend, bank statements or whatever else you have in your bag for the day. They could be taking photos of your shit-stained underwear while you support your cricket team. Then putting them up on Facebook.

I then did something I almost never do – journalism – and found out that they never, ever check what you have in your bags if you aren't around. That would be rude. The bags sit there with whatever explosives they have, waiting to be triggered by some nutcase that believes that as sport is the opiate of the masses, he can shake people out of their numb existence and change the social doctrine of the world with only a few bombs and the use of the zip policy.

There is also a ruling that says you can't bring anything into the ground that could be used as litter. I'm not sure if Cricket Australia has been punished for bringing the Australian side in.

None of this put off Cook, and Trott was just as focused. For Australia, it was sickening. Cook brought up his hundred, and the crowd applauded, hoping that he would go away afterwards. Nope. The new ball came out, Siddle dropped a Cook hook, Trott's fifty came up. I tried to think of one shot that had stood out, but I gave up when I got a headache.

What I had no trouble imagining was a cartoon anvil falling on Mitch's head. For years Channel 9 had the duck cartoon for batsmen who'd failed to score. But they should take it a step further. If a batsman gets hit on the head, little birds fly around him. If a captain looks like they are out of ideas, a truck with ACME printed on it delivers them a package. If a bowler doesn't get a wicket, steam from the ears. I'm not rewriting comedy here, just remembering the days before *The Simpsons*.

Channel 9 has so many stupid gadgets, most of which show you what you already know. Such as how much a ball spun. I just saw it spin, it spun a fucken mile, I don't need a protractor on my screen to tell me it was eight degrees. Before I knew it was eight degrees, I didn't know any less about cricket, I just didn't know the exact angle of the spin. It's the same as when a ball keeps low and someone almost gets bowled, I don't need Hawkeye to show it to me, I saw it. What I need is a bit of light relief when Mitchell stuffs up. A cartoon anvil on his head would be perfect for that. It might even loosen Mitch up – that night, he's watching the highlights in the hotel, and he sees the cartoon anvil hit him and thinks, "This is all just a game. I should lighten up and stop taking it so seriously."

England got to 309 for one, which meant they were in front and taking the piss. While the pitch had flattened out the afternoon before, there is flattening out and flattening out. There are very few pitches in the history of Test cricket that are so flat that only one wicket can be taken on them in a day. The one-wicket-day was more to do with very disciplined batting and a very poor bowling and fielding performance. Three catches dropped isn't the reason England were in front, but it was the reason this was embarrassing.

I then started flicking my eyes between the cricket and my email inbox. If you run a cricket website of any note, such as Cricket With Balls, you're going to get PR people emailing you. Everyone wants a free link or story about whatever crap they're trying to flog. Sometimes it's cool shit, like when the PR team for *Out of the Ashes*, the film about the rise of the Afghan cricket team, offered my readers ten copies of their DVD, but mostly it's useless shit, promoting some posh English car company's crappy viral video without getting paid for it. Today I got a ripper, an email from Lalit Modi's PR company.

What I loved about this was that his PR person had taken the time to write a post for me to put up, they'd taken the time to find out who I was, and they'd taken the time to send it to me with a suck-up intro, but, they'd taken no time to type Lalit Modi's name into the search engine on my site. The first two posts would tell you that any effort to try and get me to spin for Lalit would probably end in tears. The first is titled *Lalit Modi Memorial Day* and has a picture of him as the Wicked Witch of the West melting, done by my friend Ceci, and the other is a fake press release saying he is about to take over the ICL.

I posted his PR flunkies column with my notes under each paragraph. Probably not the desired result.

It's a shame that Cricket Australia didn't invite Lalit out to watch this Test – one day of him watching Cook and Trott could have been enough for this man to completely fall out of love with cricket forever. Although, I bet he'd like the cartoon anvil idea.

When my inbox was empty, I went back to editing and was having some technical issues with *Two Pricks*. Running an online social media driven chat show after a day's play is not easy. This night, I closed the press box. Even Andrew Miller wasn't there. Now there is a man who knows how to work late. He might be a posh bastard, but he puts in the hours. So when he isn't around, I know I've done something special. Not special good. I am sharing the ground with the cleaning staff. It's the first time I've ever seen a ground cleaned, and it's not really that interesting, but there are only two other people in the ground. One security guard guarding the square, and one guarding me.

The press box security guard was annoying me with personal boundary issues. And the good news was, I got stuck with him. It meant I got conversations about life, got told about money troubles, about how the freelance security system in Brisbane worked, why I couldn't possibly be left in the press box alone, details about the trip home (including bus numbers) and most lovely of all, some information about chafing.

I suggested that since we were one of only two or three people left at the ground, and on no other night did a security guard need to be here, leaving would not be a problem. I would be fine. No one was waiting for a security guard smaller than me to leave so they could attack me. No, that didn't work, because they have cameras you see, and if they were seen to leave me alone, they wouldn't get any more work. It took about 15 minutes, but eventually I convinced the guard that the chance that there was anyone else in the ground, and that the person was watching a video feed of the press box, was pretty low, and he left.

I continued to wait for my video to upload, then five minutes later the guard crept up (well it felt like that) and said, "How do I get out of the ground?" Scared the shit out of me. I needed a guard to guard me from my guard. I then stole some food, made my way to McDonald's, where the staff had pictures of Warnie on their breasts, and then home to drink with my old man. Who wanted everyone dropped from the Australian side.

The Ashes wasn't going to be the beer and skittles time I assumed it would be. In my future I could see a great deal of time where I was working on my own as the people who I'd convinced to let me stay were asleep in bed and I had a chance to sober up. I'm not sure how I expected my first Ashes tour to be, but I didn't expect it to be finishing work at 2am to sleep next to my snoring father. His snoring is so loud that you feel like you are vibrating. You might actually be vibrating.

DAY 5 – THE GABBA

There was no doubt that Andrew Strauss wasn't going to declare and make this game interesting. That isn't his way. In his mind he thinks he's lucky to get out of this with a draw, and that will do him nicely. The English brain processes draws quite well. They feel a certain comfort in them. You even have draws in club cricket in many English competitions, unlike in Australia. They even have winning and losing draws, because they like a variety of draws.

With England mentally already in Adelaide, they wouldn't dare throw this game open. It was a shame, because it meant that today's cricket was largely pointless. Australia now knew they couldn't bowl England out, and weren't really trying. Only a tasty declaration from Strauss could bring it back to life. Instead we had Trott and Cook continuing to accumulate well. I couldn't pretend to have any interest in this, so instead I edited footage of a Strauss and Cook press conference to the audio from the *Brokeback Mountain* trailer.

The better the opening partnership, the more romance there seems to be between the two men involved. Hayden and Langer, Hobbs and Sutcliffe, Greenidge and Haynes, Taylor and Slater – they all had weird relationships, not sexual, but definitely with a deeper and different level of friendship. The sight of Langer and Hayden hugging showed you so much about both men and how they felt about each other. Cook and

Strauss would probably never hug the way Hayden and Langer did, but their relationship was more one of father and son. At the press conference Cook deferred to Strauss as the captain, and the senior partner. A partnership that transcends the batting crease. While I say father and son, it is really mentor and son. *Tuesdays with Morrie,* the cricket edition. For those who have seen *Brokeback Mountain,* you'll know what I mean when I say that Strauss is the one who spits in his hand.

But the development of the Cook and Strauss pairing wasn't the only relationship I was noticing. The other was between Sam Collins and me. It was rather unusual – the posh Eton pretty boy with the school-leaver ugly Aussie loudmouth. One craving love, one craving hate. Somehow, on *Two Pricks* this seemed to work. Sam and I were also becoming closer friends. We knew each other before this tour, but mostly just catching up at cricket events or friends' parties. Mostly, we talked about how we should catch up far more than we actually caught up.

Two Pricks was not a plan we had both had months in advance. We'd caught up a few days before we were leaving so we could work out if we could help each other out with travel, accommodation and that sort of stuff. During the conversation, we chatted about how I had a camera and wanted to film stuff over there.

Now we were our own sort of partnership. Sam with his stats, research, lists, and careful analysis, me with my improvisation, yelling, piss-taking and gut feelings. Perhaps if either of us had had our ladies on tour with us, the friendship would never have had a chance, but with nothing to do except work and two prick, we found each other in every way except sexually. It was beautiful; I sort of wish Cook and Strauss could have seen it so they could have taken the piss out of us with a YouTube video.

While the English continued to accrue runs, a statistical milestone was notched. England had reached 500 for one. While the majority of stats in cricket, and this book, are bullshit, that number meant much to many. To English fans, it signalled a lack of fear. Even though England had won two of the past three Ashes, they'd still had that fear that Australia at home was too much. The contributions of Siddle, Hussey and Haddin had brought this out in them.

The English are nothing if not naturally prepared for abject humiliation. So many of them set themselves up for a loss at all times in the hope that somehow they'll be wrong. At 500 for one, even the most negative among them knew that this could be their Ashes. It was impossible to think any differently. Their batsmen had looked in such complete control that it looked more like they had been playing against schoolkids in preparation for the series.

On the other hand, the Aussies were finding out what it felt like to be English in the 90s. This was exactly how Australia had played against England for years. Domination of the opposition's minds and bodies while making the whole process look easy and inevitable. Had Steve Waugh and Mark Taylor been out there, with Angus Fraser toiling away, it would have felt roughly the same. I'd seen that before. Now it had swapped over.

It felt to me like inviting all your nerdiest friends around to your house, and after years of being a bit of an arrogant and patronising dick to them, they jump you, tying you up, chatting up your mum and taking turns to wobbly H her. You knew it was fair, because your previous behaviour had probably felt roughly the same to them, but being forced to watch it for hours on end was really painful. If this lasted until 600 for one I'd almost start to pity the English fans for all those years.

But with Cook's double hundred having arrived, thanks to a misfield from Mitchell Johnson, and Trott reaching his hundred as well, England declared on 517 for one. The declaration was not about winning the game, it was about momentum, that amazing elusive concept that gets used in sport because actually explaining the real reasons for a victory or defeat can be too hard. England wanted to get a few wickets in the last couple of hours so they could embarrass Australia on every level and prove that the first couple of days had been a hiccup, and that the new pecking order was in place.

When Simon Katich lifelessly pushed at one outside off stump to Stuart Broad, England had their bowling momentum in the right direction. This brought out Ricky Ponting, and he had the step. When Ponting is really up for an innings, he walks out on the ground harder than at other times. Sure this sounds like something I'm making up, but after watching him for 15 years, you can tell when he really wants to make runs.

His foot hits the grass harder. It's not an overly obvious thing – that I grant you – but you can see it clearly if you look through my eyes, and he had it. Ponting doesn't like to lose or be embarrassed. His team coughing up 517 runs for one wicket at home was as embarrassing as Ricky could handle before imploding. You could tell he would want to prove to the world that it was not his lifeless and ineffective bowlers that were the problem, but the pitch.

Ponting's first two balls were ducked as Broad tried to get at him. The next one hit his gloves and popped safely around the corner for a single. The next over his best shot was a single that KP, in that attention deficit disorder way of his, pinged wildly at the stumps, giving him overthrows and a five. Then Swann and Finn came on and Ponting took flight. It was a Ponting statement innings – not the fuck-you hundred – but a punchy press release about the pitch. Finn was driven and pulled like his bowling was unimportant; Swann was slog swept for six just for the impact. When Ponting wasn't playing the big shot he was scoring singles with ease.

This includes his 50th run off only his 40th ball. If you're going to make a statement, you might as well do it at better than a run a ball. Ponting does like to make a point, whether with the fuck-you hundred or a 400-page diary. Ponting would tell the press that it wasn't just because of his bowlers that England made a kabillion runs, and he wanted the evidence to back him up. As if by doing this, everyone would ignore that Mitchell bowled like I synchronise dive.

On around December 27, this Gabba pitch would start breaking up. They should bring the Aussies back then just to see if it was the pitch, or if they really *were* that shit. By then, they might have won or lost the Ashes. The good thing for Ponting and Strauss was that now neither of them would have nightmares about losing 5-0.

But since Australia were smashing England all over the place towards the end of the match, the momentum was with them, wasn't it? They were momentuming all over England's face. From what I can tell from any number of experts, that is how momentum works. So Australia would be odds-on to win the next Test.

My big problem with this Test, thankfully highlighted by Ponting, was the lack of life in the pitch. There was a lot of weather interference coming into the match, so maybe that threw the groundstaff off their game. With weather, you expect a tough pitch for batsmen, especially in Brisbane. Many a southern state side has been thrown to the Gabba for an early-season slaughtering at the hands of Queensland bowlers on a green top.

But I don't really understand how an underprepared pitch can end up becoming a batting haven. It's the opposite of any cricket logic I grew up with. The real shame is that the Gabba is in general the best pitch in world cricket. It offers runs, wickets, spin, bounce, pace and results. It was the pitch I wanted to watch cricket on the most in the world, and it disappointed me in every way.

I wouldn't be missing the Gabba, but I would leave it with a letter.

Dear Gabba,

I've always lusted after you. You know that, you've read my letters, smelled my intent and let me carry on as a horny fool around you. I think you know that my lust is pure and right, not some sort of passing fad. It has lasted for years. And, right until this moment, I thought it would last forever.

This was my first trip inside you, and I didn't like it. You were boring, plain and depressing, and not how I'd seen you on the TV. I felt like for years you had given everyone else the good stuff, and I was left with just a hollow shell, not the Gabba I always wanted.

My whole life I have watched while many people have been with you, and I thought that when I finally did, it would be one of my finest moments. It wasn't. You were boring, to be honest. Worse than that, you didn't even seem to try to entertain me. I was just another punter to you.

Perhaps we didn't have the chemistry that I expected. It could have been too much anticipation, but you just didn't give me what I wanted. You see, for years when others have been with you, you've had energy, spin, swing, bounce and fun.

I just assumed you'd do the same when I was there. Instead I got some grass clippings and rolled concrete, not really what you'd want after 30 years of fetishising your surface.

You left me wanting much more; now I have to go to Adelaide, which I've never felt any love for, and hope it can fill the massive void you have left. Flat wickets do nothing for me; you could have won me over forever, but no, you had to put out this stupid imitation Gabba wicket, and now I am forced to look elsewhere. Maybe one of the other three will take your place, or I'll just roam the globe looking for some place to do for me what I hoped you would.

Goodbye, Gabba. I thought you'd be the one; now I realise you are just part of my past.

You'll always be the one I wanted to get with and never quite did; we'll both have to be happy with that.

Regards

Jarrod

Not enough films have a proper fight in them. I mean a scrappy, pull your hair, sit on the chest, eye gouging, awkward punching fight. The Gabba didn't either. If this was the opening of your film you'd probably be pissed off at the director for starting with some big action, and then having the main protagonists just monologue in a fairly lifeless way.

Alastair Cook batting for three days is not an art-house slow start, it isn't building tension for an action scene, and it isn't even setting up the relationship for a fall later on; it is simply one man plying his trade well in much the same way you can watch an instructional video on how to build your own table. You can appreciate the skill involved, you might even like the guy in the video, but at the 40-minute mark you want Godzilla to stand on the guy, his film-friendly shed and his stupid little table.

That was the Gabba. Godzilla never saved us from Cook,

Haddin, Trott, Strauss and Hussey. It just kept going and going. If this had been a timeless Test Alastair Cook would never have seen his family again, he'd just be out there, clipping the ball off his pads, hitting the short balls, and keeping out the good ones.

A film, story, play, book, or anything that you are going to sit down through needs Godzilla, a dramatic break-up, a death in the family, an earthquake, or even a tricky moral dilemma. The Gabba gave us how to build an innings by Cook after teasing us with an out-of-place opening scene starring Peter Siddle as the man who could run through brick walls.

The next day I spent entirely Samless. I played golf, ate Moreton Bay bugs, drank booze, things that all make sense in New Texas. I also wore my Victorian Bushrangers shirt while playing golf, which led to me being abused by a Queenslander. I'd like it on the record that I've never abused someone wearing a Queensland Bulls shirt in Victoria. Mostly because I'm always afraid they'll make it violent.

At the airport as I left Brisbane, I saw Sam. He abused me for my red socks, I abused him for his pretentious hat. It all felt right. It seemed that we would never be far apart on this tour.

ADELAIDE

When my room smelled like piss, I knew it was a sign. A sign of what I wasn't sure, other than terrible cleaning from the staff at my motel, but something about Adelaide wasn't right. Even on the flight to Adelaide I was accused of being a Pom, without having spoken a word whilst wearing a Bob Hawke T-shirt. When I pointed that out to the guy, he said that made me sound more like a Pom. We then had a conversation where he said the way that Ben Hilfenhaus had bowled wide of off stump at the Gabba was UnAustralian.

Oh, UnAustralian, what a brilliant word it is. Only countries like America and Australia could come up with a way of questioning your patriotism in such an easy way. If you don't like footy (Aussie rules): UnAustralian. If you're a vegetarian: UnAustralian. If you think the Aborigines have been treated harshly: UnAustralian. If you don't like the Union Jack on the Australian flag: UnAustralian.

It's such an easy word to say. Of course Australia is slightly more complicated than the phrase UnAustralian. In Brunswick not drinking coffee out of tiny little cups and eating Turkish bread could be UnAustralian, in rural New Texas you could be UnAustralian if you believe immigrants should be allowed into the country. I've been called UnAustralian for liking basketball, supporting gay marriage and not liking VB. All the while I've felt very Australian. Whatever that means.

This guy's point was that Hilfenhaus, and Watson, were bowling a defensive, wide-of-off-stump line waiting for a mistake, rather than attacking and trying to get wickets. I pointed out that Bill Lawry calls this line the Queensland line. He cared little for that factoid. He was intent on demanding an explanation from me as to why this went on. I explained that it was merely a tactic that Ponting used when he was trying to build the maidens to put pressure on the batsmen. Then the guy flew off the handle like I'd invented the tactic. I was very glad to leave that flight and arrive at my motel.

My motel was very Australian. It was set up for driving tourists, had a pool with a creepy crawly and the lady at the front counter greeted me with a healthy "G'day". It was in Glenelg, the beachside part of Adelaide. Not only did this place stink of piss, but it was far further from the beach than was advertised. And they didn't have a free room for the Friday and Saturday nights of the Test. I had nowhere else to stay, and was preparing for staying in the sort of hostel that I stayed in when I was 23. A sticky floors and smelly sheets place.

Upon picking me up for some *Two Pricking* Sam smelled the room and concurred that it smelt like piss. He'd also told me that there was a room waiting for me in a house just near the Adelaide Oval and the owner of said house was demanding I stayed with them instead of this place, and that was before she knew of the smell.

It says something about my personality that I stayed in that room and didn't complain. It was a room my wife would never have stayed in. Travelling with her, I had now learnt not to put my bag down until she had accepted that the room was good enough. I, though, just took anything. Deep down I really felt like I deserved a room smelling of piss. That it was my place in life and all the nice rooms I'd been in were not really for me at all.

Then we did the Glenelg thing whilst filming *Two Pricks*. We started with a busker who came up with a theme song for us, went to the beach and filmed the start and then retired to a restaurant and recorded while we drank Australia's best beer, Cooper's Pale Ale. We were joined by Jeremy, an English friend of mine with such skill in the out-of-the-side-of-the-mouth putdown that Steve Waugh would approve. Jeremy is a former indie film star who'd worked with one of those directors who now makes cutting-edge Hollywood blockbusters. Dining with him was like dining with someone who was almost famous, who then insulted you in a gentlemanly way.

This was the first real time Sam and I had been out together, and I instantly realised there was a difference between dining with most of my friends and Sam. With him, the waitresses almost knocked themselves over to serve him. If he moved in any direction the waitress was over asking if he needed anything. I could have had 20,000 bucks sticking out of my pants and not got service that good.

After some steak and beers, I made my way back to my piss-smelling motel. I had to catch a taxi, as it quickly became obvious to me that I had no idea where the hell I was. I wasn't even sure if I was drunk and lost, or just not so observant, but I figured it was safer to just jump in a taxi. The taxi driver asked me what I did for a living. I told him I was a cricket writer, and he said, "I hate cricket." I stopped for a moment and wondered if I should tell him I hate beaded chairs and cars, but there was no point.

The next day I went out to discover Glenelg. It felt like any small town beach community that had sold out. Not in a bad way, just in a commercially viable beachfront way. They were maximising their assets, like a man with good calves wearing shorts. I've never been one for beaches, so I just went around to pick up socks and bourbon. I got a bottle of Woodstock, because a bottle of anything else would have been out of place with the general aesthetic of the room.

That night I ate one of the best takeaway meals of my life, calamari and chips, from a local Greek restaurant, and missed my wife. It had been years since I was in a motel. Since then I've been in plenty of hotels, and I like them. Motels are different; people have their cars right up to the window, and the pool always looks suspect. The people who work there own the place, and everyone else always feels like they've stayed there 93 times before you. The guy who checked in when I did was talking about his prostate condition – the reason he was in Adelaide – and I just figured that at a big, faceless corporate chain hotel I wouldn't have to hear this conversation or take my meal back to a room that smelled like the hallway of a council flat.

My family never flew on planes, we were too poor for aviation. We (and by we I mean my dad) would drive everywhere. We drove from Melbourne to Mackay once, which is about 2,500km or just really fucken long. It took us four days. That was just one of many mental long trips, not including our driving holidays where we'd move from empty charming country town to slightly bigger empty less charming country town.

Motels were a big part of my life when I was growing up. Somehow I'd even convinced myself that motels were better than hotels. I thought only poor people stayed in hotels, that's why you had to go up to a small room without the ability to park your car outside or easy access to a pool. It wasn't even till I'd checked into this motel that I remembered what they were like. People chatting outside your window about the Big Lobster or whatever plastic tourist trap they'd been to, or comparing freeways like they were competing political parties.

At night my room hummed and I could still smell the piss as two families sat outside their rooms and bonded over Aussie rules football whilst listening to bad 90s rock. It might have been a sucky motel in the middle of nowhere, but it was the very antithesis of UnAustralian. Unlike the word antithesis, which is UnAustralian.

DAY 1 – ADELAIDE OVAL

If I'd been a player, I'd have had a shocker at Adelaide. Preparation is key, and so my trip to Adelaide Oval via Sam's friend Mimi's (he calls her Meems, and I feel like I've walked into a 1930 posh comedy) was pretty horrible. It involved buses, taxis, phones going dead, walking, heat, bad directions, angry gate officials and wardrobe changes.

When I finally got to the ground, I found I was to be seated behind a large concrete pillar. I was pissed off, but I think I handled it better than most modern batsmen do when confronted with a pitch with grass on it.

With all that, my start was still far better than Australia's. The first wicket fell while I was standing up and trying to find a better view. It involved Watson and Katich in another stuff-up as Watson hit the ball straight to the right hand of the right-handed Jonathan Trott and took a single. Attempted a single, anyway.

Katich run out off the fourth ball for a diamond duck. Bringing Ponting out to face before Australia had scored. Not cashing in on his momentum from his last innings, he nicked to Swann and Australia were nought for two or, as I'm sure a few said, pretty fucked. Clarke survived the team hat-trick, but faced a short ball from Broad in the next over that seemed to bother his back. Next over he half committed to a three-quarter drive and Swann had caught two of Anderson's victims. Australia were really fucked at three for two.

At Adelaide three wickets before tea is OK. Three wickets before the members have picked up a Pimm's is not. It does feel like an exciting Test match, though, and after two and a half days of competent batsmen batting, it's enjoyable up to a point. That point is probably Australian-ness. The good news is that with this pillar in my way I didn't see every detail of it. The pillar was mid-pitch. I never even saw Trott (neither did Watson) until he threw the stumps down, and then twice Jimmy bowled into the pillar; his magical ball disappeared and then reappeared on the edge of the captain and vice-captain.

It wasn't the only disappearing act for this Test. Australia had dropped Mitchell Johnson and Ben Hilfenhaus. Before the Ashes a few of the Murdochian papers ran a piece about "Magic" Johnson. It was all about how great Mitch was, and I'm sure it wasn't meant as an insult to one of the best basketballers of all time. Of course, now that Mitch had disappeared, it was prophetic in its own way.

Replacing the steady as a train Hilfenhaus and Magical Mitch were Doug Bollinger and Ryan Harris. I like both these guys, both are wicket-takers who try very hard, and I probably would have had both in my Gabba side, but I was so fucking sick and tired of the selectors screwing over Australian bowlers. The Australian batsmen find new ways to fail and collapse on a Test-by-Test basis, and they never seem to get dropped. As a bowler you only need to string together one bad game on the trot and you might be shown the door.

I mean I was hot, my shirt was uncomfortable, I had a pillar in front of me, I had a fight with the taxi lady after my bus never arrived, my phone went dead when turning up to Mimi's place, and the bastard at the gate wouldn't let us in even though the actual media gate was nowhere near where our press box is. All of this bugged me far less than the way Australian batsmen were allowed continually to fail and the bowlers were shafted at a moment's notice.

Look at them out there, flailing around like a cricket ball is something new to them. Ponting was like a dodgy shopkeeper who was manually changing his use-by date, Clarke was half crippled, Watson and Katich didn't trust each other, Hussey had spent years doing nothing, and Marcus North was not worth my bile. At the Gabba they might have made a big total, but that was the work of two men. I felt roughly the same in Adelaide then as I had on the way back from Headingley last year…

> …*The smell of shit in this bus has just hit me. I've been travelling on it for ages, and I'm about a third of the way from Leeds to London. The bus didn't smell so bad before because the roof vent thing was open, but it just shut itself when we went over a bump, so now we have stuffy hot air and the faint smell of some bastard's defecation.*
>
> *I'm on my way back from Leeds because Australia have just lost a Test in three days, one hour and five minutes to Salman Butt's Pakistan. It was Pakistan's first Test win against Australia in 15 years. (Although that record was helped by Australia not touring there too often). Pakistan played brilliantly, shambolically and nervously. Australia got bowled out for 88. What this means for the Ashes I don't know. I know I would have preferred Australia to last longer, but mostly that is because I had a train ticket booked for later tonight.*
>
> *For those that love this sort of stuff, Australia drawing the series with Pakistan means that England now have the Ashes momentum. England had it after winning the World T20 and the three one-dayers against Australia earlier in the summer, but Australia snatched it back by winning the last two. Now England have it, again. Of course England could lose it again if they draw with or lose to Pakistan, and Australia could then lose it if they get it back by losing to India. Is that clear?*
>
> *Momentum aside, Australia do have some holes to plug. Marcus North is now struggling with an average of 30 in his last 10 Tests, Michael Hussey is not the superhero he once was, Mitchell Johnson has never truly recovered from the Ashes of 2009. His Harvey Dent routine continues to let Australia down.*
>
> *Then there is Ricky Ponting. Australia's one true champion. Perhaps the most competitive man left in world*

cricket. *An old-fashioned guy in a new world. Former world number one batsman. A true Aussie battler. Holder of the flame. One hell of a sonofabitch. Other clichés and platitudes I can't think of now.* There was a time when Ricky Ponting coming out at number three was an event. While all the other best batsmen from around the world hid themselves at number four, Ponting refused to move. He wasn't going to have some inferior player taking the spot he was born for. Perhaps he would go out to the new ball more, and perhaps it wasn't the right move for team harmony, but Ricky Ponting at any other position didn't have the sense of purpose.

He was *number three.*

Those days are no longer here. Ponting is now no longer an event, just an ageing professional sportsman who believes in himself enough to keep coming out day after day. His brilliant record is slipping. He is far from the run machine he was in his prime. His newest claim to fame – the fuck-you hundred – is often brought out for big matches and important moments, but Australia now have a lot of important moments. The top order is in much the same situation as this bus.

Technically it has all the parts it needs. Whether it is the poor air ducts, dud air conditioning, barely flushing toilet, horrible suspension or squeaky brakes, something isn't right. I also suspect this bus has broken down more than its fair share of times. I can imagine it breaking down in the worst possible places like on a London motorway, so people can't get out, have no way of opening the windows or air vent and are just trapped inside this modern-looking, ancient-acting bus; the people inside trying to stay cool and not take a smell of that aroma and shit wafting around.

Ponting, as the driver, knows that all these things are wrong. He just doesn't have the tools to fix it. He knows that Shane Watson is always one straight ball away from an lbw. That Katich is going to fight as hard as he can to get to 75, but then get out. That Michael Clarke is better than he has ever been, but still not really the man. That Michael

Hussey is holding on to his Test career because of how much he wants it and nothing else. That Marcus North is not quite consistent or good enough. That Brad Haddin will give him a few big hits before making a mistake.

Ponting knows all this, and, perhaps, a 28-year-old Ponting could smooth over some of it. He could counter-attack, take the advantage away from the opposition. Ensure that when these men are in there is less pressure on them. Now, he has to use all that effort just to remain at the crease. Early on his innings is 70 per cent lunging. The trigger movement of a man not in form. Ponting has always searched for the ball early on, but now he gropes for it almost blindly. He never comes in looking like he is comfortable. No early drives through mid-wicket anymore, now it seems it is all about survival.

Even his former friend, the short ball, torments him. Not that he constantly gets out to it, but it is no longer that ball that he sends on its way with a macho thump. Now the ball goes off the splice or edge, he misses a few, he spoons others, and Kemar Roach almost tore his arm out of its socket at the WACA. Pakistan had the audacity to try to bounce him out in Melbourne. In this series they didn't even bother. He seemed to have so much trouble with the swinging ball that they just kept the ball up and waited. They didn't have to wait long.

In a press conference Ponting refused to concede he was struggling with the bat. He also refused to step down the order. This is a proud man, and this is his team. This isn't a team he inherited from Steve Waugh or was built by Mark Taylor or Allan Border. This is a new Australia, a team that Ponting has built for himself, one that he wants. He doesn't just want to be remembered as the guy who won with Warne and McGrath, and then couldn't handle a team without them. He wants this to be his legacy. That he took over when on top, saw them lose some champions and then rebuilt on the fly.

It could still happen. But, like the rancid smell that has just come wafting down from the toilet, it could all be shit. Ponting's side is not that good; it is inconsistent and erratic. They play their best cricket followed by their worst. They fight like Ponting, but they don't have his class. They say captains build teams in their own image. Ponting seems to have done that, but it is the image of himself now, not the great Ponting he once was...

...That was how I felt in the shitty bus, and not much had changed. Except Mike Hussey. While he should have been dropped before the Gabba Test (in fact, well before), he was now making more runs and making the others look ordinary. The problem is, even if Hussey makes runs, he's still a 35-year-old in an old batting line-up. When you have a team that needs an overhaul, he is a dangerous man to have.

With Watson, though, he helped Australia rebuild after their disastrous start. Anderson's swing lessened, Broad grew tired, and Finn wasn't as tight or deadly. Watson's front foot goes so far down the wicket when Finn is bowling that it is like a shorter batsman charging at him. There is no doubt that if Australia had their way they'd ask to face Finn every day of the week. Compared to Broad and Anderson he looked like a net bowler floating the ball up, and both batsmen tried to get at him when they could.

At the other end Swann started well. Unlike at the Gabba, he looked every bit the cocksure off-spinner as he dropped the ball on a dime and made both men defend him. Australia said they had no plan to attack Swann, but suddenly, after bowling three overs for only three runs, Watson hit him 110 metres for a six, suggesting otherwise. From then on Hussey and Watson looked eager to try to put England on the back foot a little. It wasn't cavalier counter-attacking, but some risky shots on the up and in the air through gully, especially from Watson. And that's exactly how they got him. Anderson gave him room, Watson tried to flay it away, and instead he was out, yet again struggling to get through the 50s.

Australia's small rebellion had ended, and I doubt there was a person in the ground that expected Marcus North to survive. Least of all me.

I'd invented a betting system on Marcus North's batting

that was so foolproof it was more like an investment than a betting system. It broke down like this: North at one stage in his career had more scores in single figures and triple figures than he did in double figures. This might not seem like brilliant information for a betting system, but it actually is. One way of betting on cricket is to gamble on whether a batsman will reach the runs line that the bookies give him. For those not into cricket gambling, when a batsman walks in, the bookies will give you a line to bet over or under, say 24.5, and you can bet either side of that. If you know that North is going to fail to make his runs line, or go well past it, this is special information. All you need to do is bet on him going under the line; if it gets out, you cash in. If he goes over it, you keeping betting over the adjusted run line the longer he bats. Once North is in, he generally makes big runs, giving you the chance to cash in three times after your initial loss.

If you had followed this system every time he batted, you'd be richer than you are now.

Unfortunately, today he couldn't even be relied on for betting or making runs for Australia. He made 26, not enough to make a difference or save his career. In my notes, I write that it's a fucken-wank-shit, useless puke-in-a-toaster shot. That his wicket is lost to Finn after the pitch has settled down and his eye is in suggests to me that I have seen his penultimate innings in Test cricket.

Sometime during the play Channel 9 interview Shane Watson so he can apologise to Katich for the run-out. Oh, we're in the cuckoo's nest now, interviewing a player while his team-mates are out batting. It's another innovation of Cricket Australia and Channel 9, made to make their players more likeable I suppose. It made me want to find Watson and beat him with the camera.

Perhaps I'm removed from normality – it's not a big stretch to assume I'm the crazy one. I just don't see how an interview while Australia are trying to stay alive helps Australian cricket. It doesn't make Watson more likeable, it won't bring any new people to the game and it's surely time that Watson could spend in the changing rooms, bonding with Katich.

Watson's box office persona didn't put off Hussey and Haddin, though, as they got a chance to rekindle their Gabba mood. In the press box we celebrated as an Adelaide Oval employee came into the box saying, "Who ordered pies?", which would have been funnier had Mitchell Johnson been bowling. No one wanted to admit to ordering a whole box of pies. Personally, I suspected Stephen Brenkley; I was happy to be wrong, but he had a twinkle in his eye when the pies came in.

Sam asked if I wanted to share a pie with him. For once I am too shocked to make a sarcastic reply. I eat my own pie. Like any Australian man should. I might be losing my accent and love for motels, but I'll be damned if I ever share a pie.

The pies seemed to jinx Hussey, who got an edge to Swann. Out in the 90s two Tests in a row: 93 and 195. Hopefully Greg Chappell would see this failure to convert as a big problem. Ryan Harris came in, a man who was once rumoured to be an all-rounder, now dreadfully high up the order. He lasted one ball, lbw to Swann, although he referred it, and it was probably not out as there was the faintest of inside edges on hot spot, but it's given out anyway. I feel like it would have made very little difference to anyone's life even if it was given not out.

Haddin then survived one of those reviews that made no sense the moment it was made. I may have been behind a pillar, and not anywhere near straight behind the bowler's arm, but you could feel it wasn't out. One of the differences between the two sides was the reviews. Ponting reviews so fast that sometimes the ball in question hasn't even hit the batsman yet. He's instinctive as hell, and a lot of the time he doesn't even bother asking anyone else what they think. Strauss is the opposite. He is calm, measured, and wants to ask every player in the side their opinion.

Somehow, Ponting still seems the better at it, which is a bonus for those who believe captaincy should come from gut feelings. The problem is that England's system will eventually come together. Matt Prior couldn't spend five Tests telling Strauss that everything was worth a review. Either Strauss would ignore him (I would), or Prior would get it from his team-mates until he changed his excitable nature.

Haddin continued to hit out at the other end, even if Xavier

Doherty got run out while it was happening. Haddin brought up his fifty and was then the last man out, Australia having made a hugely under-par 245. It wouldn't be under par for all grounds, but Adelaide is full of runs like few other grounds, and those runs are generally first-innings runs.

England had played well, better than well; they'd played with organised pressure and cricket sense. It bores me to write it, but that doesn't mean it didn't happen that way. Anderson had something going on, and once Watson ran out Katich, he pounced with top quality swing bowling. On good batting pitches you have to swing the ball, otherwise you spend days in the field watching the opposition cash in. Anderson took only the four wickets, but the Poms hunt in packs.

Hunt is not really the word; they stalk, or maybe not even stalk; they are less than menacing yet hard to escape from. Swann still looked far from a weapon, and that applied to Finn too, but everyone plays their role. Broad bowls dot balls and uses his height, Swann attacks and adds variety, Finn bowls balls that you feel like you should be hitting further and Anderson adds the class when required. It's not unbeatable, it's just really good. Really, really good. And sometimes, when you're facing a weak opposition, really really good is really really fucking fantastic.

Based on England's form, Australia's frailty and my gut feeling, there seemed no way Australia could win these Ashes. And that wasn't some half sentiment, like, Australia can't win them but England can lose them. Come my birthday, January 7, England would be bathing in the glory of winning an Ashes, and Australia would be making excuses, finding scapegoats and planning how to win the ODI series.

Luckily I was briefly cheered up by the fact that Lawrence Booth had been forced to buy a Cricket Australia polo shirt to get past the members' strict clothing guidelines that also went for the press. He tried to hide it from me so I wouldn't tweet about it. So far Lawrence had been a Twitter soap opera story with him crashing a computer, pouring coffee on another and now switching sides mid-tour. Lawrence pretends to be down with technology, but when he becomes the global emperor, he'll ban Twitter. Gideon Haigh also bought a collared shirt to get in and proudly stated he would wear just the one shirt for all five days.

The press conference that evening was mostly about how there were words between certain players as they came off the field. It looked like good, clean, dirty fun to me. The Australian team were obviously trying to win the series verbally, because their cricket action didn't seem to be working.

After our *Two Pricking*, Sam and I went to a famous local fish and chip shop, called the Blue & White. It had something called an AB, which is short for Abortion, I think. It looks like an abortion, but tastes great, which is probably unlike an actual abortion. It contains chips, lamb kebabs, BBQ, hot chilli and garlic, mayonnaise and tomato sauce. I think. In the shop they claimed the food had a Wikipedia page. Even though this was the local meal of choice, I insisted Sam try Dim Sims.

Dim Sims are perhaps the greatest culinary invention in the history of mankind and, completely unrelated to that, they were invented in Melbourne. Sam had to have these mysterious dumpling-like Melbourne creations. I knew he'd like them, not because of our newfound bond, but because it is impossible to dislike them. Everyone likes Dim Sims, they're extremely Australian.

I was so excited as he took a bite that I stopped my fish and chips to watch. The results were not so good; he thought they tasted like vomit. It was a blow to our friendship, which had now moved on so much we were sleeping in single beds only a couple of feet from each other. If I didn't sleep in an eye mask we could gaze into each other's eyes as we drifted into dream land. I finished off the Dim Sims he didn't want.

DAY 2 – ADELAIDE OVAL

Sam and I got up, showered, breakfasted and walked to the ground. Some of those things were not together. On the way to the ground I went to an op shop (charity shop) and picked up some shirts for the rest of the Test, not wanting to end up like Lawrence or Gideon. I also needed shorts. Before leaving for Australia I'd lost about 12kg and all my shorts no longer fitted. I figured that I'd be able to get some good shorts in an Adelaide op shop.

It turned out that all they had was jorts (jean shorts). They had many different varieties of jorts. I am fundamentally opposed to jorts. I like jeans and I like shorts, but the meeting of the two has always felt wrong to me. You don't want to abuse a whole city for what one op shop has, but I couldn't help but think that Adelaide was a place that embraced the jort. Why, I don't know. Why would I want heavy and hot shorts? The whole idea of shorts was that it was hot outside, and I wanted to cool down; denim would not help with this.

But I had no other options. I had two pairs of shorts, one of which didn't look very smart casual, and might have got me into trouble with the Adelaide members' police, and another pair that wouldn't get through three days of a Test, let alone five. And at Adelaide, you can bet on five. The two shirts and jorts cost me about 12 bucks, so I couldn't really complain. When walking up to the gate past those who were queuing, I couldn't help count that 14 men had jorts on.

To start the cricket Douggie Bollinger bowled Strauss with a straight one that he left. Leaving a straight one is never fun. Douggie celebrated like he had completely outfoxed Strauss. It was followed by Xavier Doherty missing a run-out and Michael Hussey not even getting his hands on a catch from Jonathan Trott. Australia were not far away from where they needed to be, but a dropped catch and a missed run-out at Adelaide when you've had an early breakthrough can haunt you for two days.

By my notes, which are wonderfully unscientific at the best of times, Australia had now dropped eight catches in seven days of cricket.

Catches win matches.

If ever I had the chance to change the English language, or cricket language, to make sure these two words did not rhyme, I'd do it. I hate those guys. Giving you a whole sport in one piece of rhyme. Like you and every other cricket fan hadn't noticed that a) catches were important, and b) that taking them would help you win. It's like saying bombs win wars, or money wins court cases: it's hard to argue with, but annoying when repeated.

Hussey's effort was pretty ordinary. The ball went straight to him, and while it went quickly, it didn't break any speed records and he barely moved. Just more proof that he should have been dropped. Sure he top scored, but catches do actually win matches, Hussey, shit, haven't you heard that before?

Then we got more of Trott and Cook. There were few attacking shots; there were nudges, open faces and a lot of runs off their pads. The Australians needed to work out a way to dismiss these guys. Not so that they can win the Ashes, but for Cricket Australia's bank balance. How can you talk up how exciting the Ashes are and just have a nudge-a-thon every Test? They were practising smart batting. Using the pace and line of the ball to accumulate.

It was very similar to the way England bowled; this was the batting equivalent of getting it in the right areas. England's game plan seemed to rely on the simple strategy of playing good shots and assuming that the bowlers would lose their line. It would be an interesting experiment to see whether the

English bowlers or batsmen would win if they had to play each other. Both camps do the basics really well and wait for the opposition to break. It was admirable cricket, but it wasn't Dale Steyn v Virender Sehwag.

The only reason I didn't kill myself was that we were given free oysters for lunch. Some cricket writers were quite held back, not heading in straight away, and only taking a couple. I had about ten. My parents never exactly had a saying that went, "never walk away from a free oyster". However, I was taught by my mum to take as much as you can of anything that is free. When I was a kid I'd come home from somewhere with more useless free merchandise than I could comfortably carry. My mum would carry the rest. I felt much the same way with the oysters, except without my mum there to carry the extras. There was not a statistician counting, but I think I was only beaten by Derek Pringle. I was Trott to Pringle's Cook.

After lunch Cook and Trott were scarily efficient, both men bringing up their fifties. Cook's was chanceless. It was Trott's that really got me thinking. There was no doubt that watching him was like watching a documentary made by the American Government on the steel industry, but it was also hypnotic in a largely unentertaining way. Every ball was a chance for Trott to play off his pads. Not in the way an Indian player would extravagantly flick, but more a safe push. Some would fly off the bat, most would ease off for one or two. You knew he could smash it off his pads if he wanted, it was just that his entire Test career was about doing something with the absolute minimum chance of a dismissal.

I thought that he might struggle in Australia in the channel outside off stump, but that now didn't look likely. The ball just outside off stump or on off stump could be placed capably on the leg-side for a single. Balls further outside off stump could be left or defended, until they were wide enough to play square. Which was not a weakness, even if it wasn't a strength. Anything on middle or leg stump would generally be flicked away on the leg-side for runs. The only shot he played that I'm sure he admonished himself for was the drive on the up through the covers.

He did it so rarely, but he was almost on the move when he played it, and there was always a chance that away movement, pace or bounce could undo him. He didn't seem to have to play that shot.

Trott is the only current player in world cricket who I honestly believe flagellates himself with a homemade cat of nine tails if he gets out to a bad shot. I've never seen his thigh or back, but I think there would be welts there from the occasional poor shot. While we were eating lunch, he was probably flogging his thigh (I assume he uses his back for the wickets) for the loose drive that Hussey should have caught. Trott even has a bit of waddle in his gait, which is probably evidence of this self-flagellation.

His actual batting style is so simple that if you shaved a primate, bought a whiteboard and gave him some encouragement, you'd feel like you could teach it to him. Then the primate would get bored, stick his finger up his ass and sniff it. And you'd be left with a limited batting primate with no real patience. Trott had nothing but patience and a limited game plan. Steve Waugh once said that to make it as a Test batsman you had to eliminate risk. Trott had done this, and then eliminated anything that could be perceived by anyone as risk, then cut back a bit more and was left with flicks on the leg-side, the odd shot square through the off-side, hook shots and defence.

Without patience it just wouldn't work. Trott had it. Oh, did he have it. When he batted you could see the whole crowd start to shift in their seats from boredom, fiddle with rubbish and talk about what kind of children's shows their kids liked. They didn't even have the patience to watch him. It made him special. One day he will be the first batsman ever to score a hundred all on the leg-side, and no one will be awake to see it.

To wake a few of us up, and get some journos to look up from their Twitter and Facebook pages, Cook was given out for playing a hook shot off his arm, but the review system worked for him, perhaps because Prior wasn't involved. It was moments like that which proved the UDRS was worth it. However, no one could doubt that this game needed a farcical dismissal just to get the juices pumping again.

People might hate bad umpiring decisions, but if years of

bar talk about cricket has taught me anything it's that bad umpiring decisions give people a lot to talk about. It gives the team who has received it an excuse for losing, and the winning team a reason to mock the losing team for holding on so tight to one insignificant part of the game. Sport needs hard luck stories. And being that cricket cannot have a technology system that is perfect, I'd prefer the anger of mistakes anytime. Cook probably disagrees with me.

With that disappointment Ponting went chasing a wicket. Harris came round the wicket to Trott and Cook was given a 5-4 leg-side field. Siddle was told to bounce them out. But Siddle was now a long way from his six wickets at Brisbane. Ponting had often used him for grunt work. Bowling long spells wide of off stump to bore the batsman, or short heavy lifting spells where, on a flat wicket, he was forced to try to bounce out the batsman. It's probably the reason he went and got fit. Bowling he could do, pointless spells of bowling as fast and short as he could were too much for him.

In the whole time I'd seen Siddle, these short, bouncer-only spells had barely worked. To the odd tail-ender it had done its job, and South Africa's J.P. Duminy had never really recovered from Siddle working him over. In general, though, it was just a way of slowly killing Siddle. I've never seen Ponting bet, but I bet he's a chaser.

For a few years of my life, I was a local at a pub Big Daddy worked at, the Court House. It was one of about ten bars in Melbourne with that name, and it was like many grotty inner city pubs – all about punting and locals with no money or livers. On one side were the pokies (slot/poker machines), metal family-killing units that were mathematically designed for you to lose money, and on the other side was the TAB (totalised agency betting).

Being there that often, and going through a particularly low point in my life, even I had my problems with betting, but compared to one kind of punter, I was fine. They were the chasers. People will spend all day trying to get back their losses from early in the day. They might have lost their money early betting on a major race meeting at Flemington where they knew something about the horses, jockeys and form, but by the end they would spend their money on greyhounds, pacers and trotters from places like Cannington, Globe Derby and Albion Park.

Then, if they somehow managed to have any money left, they'd spend their last dollars on the pokies. It was a sickness, and different from the normal degenerate punters who could lose with a certain dignity. These chasers just kept going until they had nothing left, always believing that the one win was what they needed.

And over the years Ponting had started showing this kind of look. Now he was clearly a chaser of a captain. Trying to prove to himself and to others that his wins at the start of his captaincy career could come back. So he kept going, and no matter how much it was obvious to everyone else that a win, let alone a string of Test wins, was almost impossible, he would just keep going, and it was the bowlers he was prepared to gamble with. Their bodies or their minds.

Xavier Doherty was another one. A poor version of Nathan Hauritz who looked completely out of his depth as Cook and Trott milked him. When he was hit for three consecutive cut-shot boundaries by Cook, he couldn't have looked less like a Test bowler. Ponting knew cricket, and he must have known that. This was not the man he needed in his side. Doherty looked like a kid, and he'd been given this Test because he had been given the last.

There was no other reason. At the Gabba he had proved that he was not as good as Nathan Hauritz. The selectors could have easily dropped him and brought Hauritz back. Instead they went with Doherty again to prove they had not made a mistake at the Gabba, whilst really just reinforcing their mistake. They weren't chasers like Ponting, they were trying to cover their backs. Australia had now played in two Tests and their best XI still hadn't been picked.

While Doherty was licking his wounds, Haddin dropped Trott off Harris. Trott's innings wasn't as convincing as it had been at the Gabba, and this was a poor attempt at a hook shot. I made a quick mental list of Australian wicket-keepers in Shield cricket that could have taken that catch with ease (Chris Hartley, Graham Manou, maybe even Tim Paine) and then went off to meet Greg Matthews.

Sam had interviewed Matthews by phone during the Gabba Test, and they'd agreed to have a beer while they were both in Adelaide. Sam took me as well so we could try to convince Matthews that he should appear in *Two Pricks at the Ashes*. It was clear straightaway that trying to get a word in with Matthews was hard enough, let alone asking him to do something.

When Sam and Matthews went to the bar to get drinks, I stayed back with Matthews' partner, who seemed a lovely, normal person. Matthews, meanwhile, seemed to inhabit his own world. Just to emphasise that, as Matthews came back from the bar he was apologising to Sam for almost getting into a fight with someone who had bumped into him when queueing. I'm quite an angry person at times, but I can't think of a time I've almost ended up in a fight because I was bumped in a crowded queue.

Over the next few minutes Sam and I tried to have a conversation with Matthews, but that seemed all but impossible. He was either talking about himself, mocking the fact I had a T-shirt under my shirt on a hot day, or looking really bored. I've met a lot of people in my life, but he was the closest I have ever met to a cartoon character.

Any writer could follow him for a day and write an animated sitcom about his life. Sort of *Family Guy, American Dad* and *Duckman* rolled into one, but painfully Australian. Even when he called people "cats" in the American jazz way, he was not UnAustralian. When the conversation reached a lull I thought I'd actually try to ask him a vaguely journalistic cricket question about Xavier Doherty. It was a stupid question, because I didn't really care about Xavier Doherty, already knew he was getting dropped next game and knew that Matthews wasn't going to be positive about him. However, having already been shot down when talking about the weather ("I've been in hotter days") I thought it was worth a try. He didn't think much of him, so I thought I'd offer him an alternative view, "I'm mates with Eddie Cowan [the Tasmania and former New South Wales batsman], and he thinks Doherty is…"

That was as much as I got out. Then Matthews, who'd played club cricket with Cowan at Sydney University, took over. "Let me tell you about Eddie," he said, and he did. It was a story involving two black American mates of Matthews who were 300lbs each and how he should have got them to fuck Eddie up to get some sense in him. Matthews left after that. He probably wasn't going to appear on *Two Pricks at the Ashes*.

Trott continued flicking Ryan Harris to leg. In this Test I realised that I had a mancrush on Harris. Harris' rise in Australian cricket coincided with mine nicely. In the days when I was a film-maker (unemployed) I watched quite a bit of him playing for South Australia, and I couldn't believe how good he looked. At this stage he wasn't statistically a demon, but he was easily the second best fast bowler in Shield cricket after Dirk Nannes.

I talked him up for a while, even in Pepperonis, a café where Big Daddy, Sime (another mate of ours) and I would discuss the world of sport. I told Big Daddy, as I ate an Aussie pizza and he waited for his salad wrap, that Harris would play for Australia; he mocked me. Not long after that, Harris signed to play for Queensland because South Australia would only offer him a one-year deal, and I doubted myself.

If South Australia had let him go so easily, maybe in that one season I'd overrated him. But he seemed so strong, clever, able to move the ball, and fast. Very fast. He bowled what people like to call a heavy ball. That season for South Australia he was basically bowling with a past-his-use-by-date former superstar Jason Gillespie at the other end. I sort of forgot about him while he was in Queensland and I was in England, until he finally did make it to the Test team – and he looked the goods straightaway.

By the time the Ashes were about to start, it looked like he would hardly play in the summer at all. He had the bad knees. Not bad knees, but *the* bad knees, the ones that can never really be fixed, and when he missed out at the Gabba because of them, it seemed like he might just miss out for good. Luckily for him, Mitchell Johnson was rested and Ben Hilfenhaus was left out because of injury. That his injury was less serious than Harris' was hardly mentioned at all.

When Harris got Trott out for 78, even if it was a soft

dismissal rather than a brutal delivery, it felt good. Harris was the newest member of the Ponting working-class bowling troupe. He had what we called a hard head. Was built like a man who'd done years of manual labour and powered in all day even on pitches like this one, where batsmen fall over each other to get out there. He was clearly too big for fast bowling; he should have entered The World's Strongest Man contest instead.

KP arrived in the middle to increase the excitement factor. His praying mantis style of batting is always worth watching. Australia brought Doherty back to bowl to him straightaway. I suppose if you pick someone just so he might get one batsman out, you might as well try it. KP started with an aggressive four, and just for a moment you wondered about his supposed problems with left-arm spinners. Then he jumped down the wicket to Doherty and scooped the ball straight up in the air, for it to drop safely. It was ugly and awkward, but in KP's mind it all made sense.

Ponting ignored the new ball as Cook accumulated with his eyes closed and KP scored with ease. Ponting tried a weird field of three shortish catchers on the off-side to Cook as North bowled wide of off stump. It was a strategy worth a shot, but it didn't work. Cook easily kept himself in check and with KP scoring more quickly England piled on the runs. The day ended with them on 317 for two, KP having skipped to 85 and Cook, whose hundred felt more inevitable than newsworthy, having moved to 135.

If Cook had just made two fairly ordinary low hundreds by this stage in the series it would have been amazing. That Cook had two completely fucken awesome scores and a plucky half-century three innings into the Ashes and looked like he could never be dismissed was just too much to handle. He was an impenetrable fortress. I could only hope that someone somewhere was starting on a comic book of this series to make him into a superhero. This was the guy who had spent the entire English summer making batting look really complicated. And who might have been dropped if, when England looked in the cupboard of openers, they hadn't only found Michael Carberry.

To see Cook succeed, and Australian batsmen with better techniques and overall records fail, told you something about these two sides. England prepared for this series with every resource, Australia played Sri Lanka in a one-day series that people forgot as it was happening. If Cook had been an Australian batsman he might have gone the way of Marcus North.

At the press conference England's vice-captain was still in form. He answered questions almost as well as he'd batted. And now that he had been in three or four press conferences I realised that Michael Clarke, his Australian counterpart, had not been at one so far. Sure, form is involved, but Brad Haddin was pushed out to talk by the Aussies when perhaps Ricky's deputy should have been selected.

For our next episode of *Two Pricks* we convinced a security guard to let us film from out on the ground. Then I went home to edit and drink while Sam met a friend working for the ECB. With as many support staff as they have, it's a surprise everyone doesn't know an ECB support staff member.

Sam called regularly to give me more ideas for *Two Pricks* and check on its progress. Then he came back fairly early. I think he missed me.

DAY 3 – ADELAIDE OVAL

Before going to the ground I played some music while we ate our breakfast. Sam and I have fairly similar tastes in music. It's things like this that make a relationship bond.

In the Adelaide Oval members' area a statue of Jason Gillespie was unveiled. There is no doubt that Dizzy deserved a statue at his home ground. I did find it interesting that the statue was in the members' area, which is not the sort of place that would have let Dizzy in all that much, even with 200 Test wickets to his name. It should have been out in the public section, where his mullet would not have felt so alone.

It seemed that somehow, perhaps by accident, word of *Two Pricks* had spread far and wide enough for the press elite to speak to us. We still had little to say other than various grunts and noises, but Stephen Brenkley, of *The Independent*, encouraged us to get various cricket writers on to the show to speak for about 20 seconds. He didn't add, "and then take the piss out of them", but it would have been rude not to.

Some stared blankly at the camera and had no idea what we were filming or where it would end up. Others, like *The Guardian*'s David Hopps, used it as his audition for the Rotherham Amateur Theatre Guild's production of *The Sunshine Boys*. It meant that, while we were not being let into the cricket writers' club – and it is a club – we were at least known around the club. And that was good because, as great as it is to travel and cover an Ashes series, the idea is that you do such a good job that people pay you to do it again.

Two Pricks was now a fairly consistent nightly wrap-up of the day's play with cameos, edited footage from press conferences, crowd vox pops, and fights between Sam and I. The hits were up to about 2,000 per show, and people would email me if it wasn't online a few hours after play finished. We'd created a fun, furry monster.

It was also good because networking has always been something I'm really bad at. I once tried to chat to a publisher about releasing my book in Australia and ended up being castrated mid-conversation as I fumbled around for words. *Two Pricks* having our faces in it meant that people could come up to us and have something to talk to us about. It also meant a fan could do it. In my mind I always thought the first fan to come up at me would be a Zooey Deschanel nerdy brunette with a cool 80s cartoon backpack and chequered shirt. Instead it was a drunk guy with sweaty hands.

KP's hundred came up, and with a batsman you can often tell if he's only got a hundred on his mind, or if he wants *real* runs. KP wanted real runs. You couldn't blame him. His form had been questionable for a while, and now he saw a zombie attack coming in to him. In his mind he was probably eyeing 400.

During the morning session I had a few things to do on the phone, and it's easier to do that out the back of the press box than in it. This meant I missed Alastair Cook get out. Now, in general this is not a big thing. People miss wickets. But for me it was huge, as I wasn't sure I'd ever see Cook get out again.

The previous night I'd had my first Cook-related dream. He was buying vinyl in my local record store (Rat Records in Camberwell) and we both fought over the same album, something by Gil Scott-Heron. It wasn't sexual and it segued into a dream about having breakfast, which I did shortly after. It did show that Cook was now part of my world, probably forever. This was my first complete Ashes series, and since it seemed like Australia would never get him out again, I had to live my life knowing that at any stage Cook could turn up whenever I slept.

I could be at Cannes, walking down the red carpet for my new film with Natalie Portman at my side when Cook pops up and starts asking what my inspiration was. There is a chance it'd be the one where I'm on stage singing my political folk classics, and I look down and Cook is reviewing it with an annoying pen light. Or it could be the one where everyone in the world suddenly turns on each other and I make it to the countryside, survive, take in strays, fall in love, and start to rebuild society when I see Cook walk up the road on the hottest day of the year without a drop of sweat on him, asking for a place to stay.

Because as weird as the dream was – and it was – it is far weirder that Alastair Cook doesn't sweat. He said so in a press conference, but he didn't have to. It was plain to see. I'm always studying players to see how much they perspire. If Shoaib Akhtar is like a waterfall, then Cook is like a desert. It was hot in Adelaide, not humid, but when you're playing cricket, hot is hot. Still Cook didn't sweat.

It made me think about David Icke, as most things do, and his brilliant theory that the world is actually run by reptilian half-breeds from Anunnaki. Icke was once a sports journalist, like I sort of am, and now he teaches people about hollow earth, blood drinking and Kris Kristofferson's alien tongue. It's that tongue that reminded me of Alastair Cook. In press conferences, Cook licks his lips an amazing amount of times. Way more than is ever necessary, even after a day of batting against an average Test attack.

A quick visit to YouTube will inform you that if you want to tell if someone is reptilian or not, constant lip licking is important. Like lizards do. Another is that reptilians don't sweat. Like Alastair Cook. Now add to that Cook's posh upbringing, which might not have been part of the Illuminati but was certainly more affluent than most, and his new-found form, and I don't need to tell you that we've just tumbled down the rabbit hole. David Icke was probably watching Cook bat in this match and editing his next book, *How Reptilian Software uses Jewish Midgets to Keep Us in the Matrix,* to include a bit of Cook's batting in it.

I would certainly never think of Cook as human again. If Cricket Australia had thought about this, they could have issued a press release saying our cricketers were still good, but they couldn't take down reptilians. Perhaps they were filing it away, waiting to use it if Australia did lose the Ashes. I suppose Cricket Australia was one of the few places left in the country that thought Australia could win them.

The Cook reptilian theory made it to YouTube that night via *Two Pricks*, and hopefully the truth would help people make sense of Cook's form. I've always liked that Icke, Hunter S Thompson and Rael (the leader of the Raelians) all started as sports journalists. In the future I could only hope my career would become a combination of these men. I think it is days like this when your side is being crushed by a machine that you start inventing an alternative to your reality, or take bucketloads of hardcore drugs.

Collingwood was not a lizard, and he looked more like himself today. He wasn't brilliant and was still lucky to be batting in the top seven for this side, but he was batting consciously enough to manoeuvre the ball around off one injured bowler, one non-Test bowler and two tired bowlers. KP treating Australia like a team of tax agents didn't hurt either and by lunch England were 449 for three.

The Adelaide press lunch tent was right next to the nets. On most days Monty Panesar was there. No one trains more than Monty. Almost every time I'd passed the nets Monty would be out there bowling to Mushtaq Ahmed or some other coach. Trying desperately to make himself better and learn something. Today Mitchell Johnson was also out there doing some bowling under the eye of Troy Cooley.

Usually I'd watch this intently, but it was free beer day in the press tent, so I might have looked at it more casually than usual. Something did catch my eye though. Someone had hit the ball into the corner of the nets and got it stuck. I noticed this when Mitchell spent the next five minutes trying to get it out by throwing other balls at it. He took far more time doing it than I would have thought possible, and I looked up half expecting to see some sort of special one-of-a-kind cricket ball that needed to be saved. It wasn't. It was just a ball.

After Johnson had tired himself out, Cooley had a go. He threw gloves, drinks bottles and other balls at this trapped ball for at least another five minutes. Our lunch table was now completely engrossed by it all. Wondering why everyone needed to get the ball down so bad. This ball had suddenly become their quest. They had to get it down. Cooley almost got hit on the head trying to get it. This was serious.

This wasn't a ball they were trying to get out; this was some Don Quixote shit. The ball was Mitchell's talent. Mitchell spent some time trying to find it, but mostly got frustrated as he was usually too wide with his attempts. You'd have to say he never truly put in or even worked out the best way to get at the talent. So he called in his mentor, and Cooley then spent longer, devoting more resources and analysis to getting this talent out. Eventually he left, dejected that the talent might never come out.

One day I'd like to get Cooley really mental on absinthe and try to convince him that Mitchell Johnson only exists in his mind. That all this time he has been trying to help Mitchell he's just been fucking around with a tongue-pierced windmill, and there is no Mitchell Johnson. I couldn't tell him now, because I had no absinthe. Perhaps all this bonding over the ball would help Mitchell when his "rest" ended.

After lunch, it seemed as if Kevin Pietersen was batting at both ends. By that I mean Paul Collingwood got out to Watson leaving everyone to marvel at KP's demolition of Australia. KP was not a machine like Cook or Trott, but more the camp supervillain. Before this Test he'd been out of form or, more importantly, out of runs. During the preparation he'd switched counties, been dropped from England's ODI side and gone back to his South African homeland to see his mentor, Graham Ford, to help rediscover his mojo.

Perhaps I had too much reptilian stuff in my head, but I couldn't picture Graham Ford without seeing KP as some tall, slimmer version of Luke Skywalker carrying Yoda around on his shoulders in a swamp. Ford probably didn't need to do a great job with KP for today. Harris couldn't break through, Douggie looked fat and tired, Siddle was being used in the oddest ways and Xavier Doherty was looking for the Test to end.

KP might have been able to take this team down even in poor form. With Trott and Cook having taken the edge off them twice KP was in full flow. He can be such an annoying cricketer that you forget that when he is really flying it is beautiful to watch. Even if, because it's against your team, it feels like watching a great lover fuck your lady. On TV his technique looks forceful and aggressive, but in real life it looks more like he has extra arms and legs: a giant bug with multiple limbs all going in different directions at once. There is no smoothness to it, yet when he is on fire, it looks like there is no way through him.

When English fans had told me he was out of form, and should be dropped, I sort of ignored them. He is a match-winner, and when he's needed, he'll win matches. So I never really looked at how bad his form was. In the T20 World Cup he looked pretty good as he smashed everyone around, and I just figured he'd do the same in the Ashes. I never trust the bad form of match-winners like KP. It always comes back to bite you. I'll revel in their bad form if it's come to the end of a series against my team, but I wouldn't dare do it midway through a series – that's a jinx.

Before the Ashes, it seemed that for the first time in his career, KP had doubted himself. Hence the sudden change of counties and finding his mentor. It's safe to say that the effect of losing the captaincy had far more impact on him than I had ever noticed. If you take the confidence out of someone with a dodgy technique and eager batting style they find ways to get themselves out. Which may be part of his problem with left-arm spinners. I doubt they would have affected him the same way if he were the big swinging dick KP from before the captaincy shitstorm.

Yet that captaincy shitstorm with him and Peter Moores getting fired was the best thing that could have happened to England. It had brought them a home Ashes win, and was now doing the same for an away series. With a confident KP in charge they wouldn't have been anywhere near this good. KP brought up his double hundred, one of the easiest I'd ever seen.

Collingwood's latest failure didn't gain anyone's attention.

Australia's bowlers had fallen into some sort of horror film hole. Siddle is in *Saw*. Ponting is Jigsaw, giving him more and more self-harming activities to do, with the promise that they might free him; they don't. At one stage he is bowling four feet outside off stump, and he even appeals for one ball – the wide is given anyway. In one-day cricket appealing on a wide ball is seen as a tactic; in Test cricket it's painful to watch. Siddle also has to try to bounce out KP on the cricket ground with the shortest square boundaries in Australia. Surprisingly that fails.

Bollinger is in *Seven*. He is the slothful one. He looks fat, slow, unfit and really shit. For a natural trier like him this must be hell. His speeds are now down so low that all he needs is for the 'keeper to stand up to the stumps for the ultimate embarrassment. You can't help but wonder why he was picked at all if this is his fitness level. Mitchell Johnson might have bowled just as badly, but he would have been faster.

Harris is in *Night of the Living Dead*. He is the one competent one who probably can't believe some of the stuff the rest are trying without him. Whilst he hasn't been leader of the attack before, no one is, so he just steps up. It's all in vain though. There doesn't really appear to be anything he can do at all. He'll get shot through a window by the end of this test.

Then there is Xavier Doherty. He's in a Gornography film, something like *Hostel, Audition* or *Haute Tension*. His career is being dissembled and tortured. Sometimes KP or Cook will look to end him quickly, at other times Trott just peels back his skin ever so slowly. He's locked to a chair; there is no getting out. Xavier Doherty is going to die a slow painful death, and we all have to watch it.

While KP and Bell effortlessly bashed the Australians around I wrote the easiest piss-taking column of my career, stating that Dizzy Gillespie's statue was the best bowler for Australia today. It would be funnier if it weren't true; his statue has a brilliant follow-through.

To make it easier for the Australian journalists it happened to be the free beer day for the press. At the Gabba they had hardly tried to woo us, just a bag of free goodies from Cricket Australia and free sweets from a Queensland tourism stand. Adelaide was going all out. Oysters one day, free beer the next. I was won over, and when the rest of the beer ended up in the fridge of the press box (conveniently right behind me) even more so. The first beer was almost ceremonial, it was James Squire I think. It came at a great time for me, not just because of the cricket – England ended the day at 551 for four – but because I had now completely run out of patience with Sam's constant mouth noises.

That's when you know you've spent too much time with someone – the constant smacking of their lips, chewing on their fingernails or tongue hitting the side of their mouth makes you want to smash a bottle of beer and cut their throat out. I think Sam has an oral fixation. There is always something in his mouth or on his lips, and when you spend this much time in close proximity to someone, you notice every flaw. Sam and I had moved beyond the honeymoon stage in Adelaide, and I was now annoyed by his very existence. And he might have felt the same that night when I was washing my underwear while chatting with him.

Washing your underwear while sharing the spare room of someone you only met through your hetero mate is when you know that you've not quite made it yet. I doubt Vic Marks has to wash underwear in a sink while drinking cheap bourbon. He's probably in a million-dollar suite with champagne on tap and his feet being massaged ever so gently to wake him up in the morning by a woman named Penny who has been training in foot massage since she was three.

All I had was Sam's constant mouth noises and he had my snoring/farting. We were still a long way from making it.

DAY 4 – ADELAIDE OVAL

If there is a phrase I have heard more than any other it is that Adelaide Oval is pretty. Such a pretty ground, welcome to beautiful Adelaide Oval, it's another amazing night at this picturesque ground, I've never loved a ground like I love Adelaide Oval, sometimes when I think of killing myself I look at a picture of Adelaide Oval and I know what beauty really is so I uncocked the trigger and put the gun down. You know, that sort of stuff.

This was now my fourth day there, and I couldn't say I really got it. Just because something has grass and trees around it doesn't make me go all gushy. It's really just a ground. There are some OK-looking stands, great grassed areas out the back, and it's a lovely walk down to the Oval, but none of that makes it pretty. The thought that a cricket ground can be pretty is odd to me anyway.

When I was a kid I was always told Melbourne University's ground was pretty, that it would blow my mind with its grassy banks and well-maintained trees. When I got there it was just another ground. This experience of Adelaide has been much the same. It's like a university ground with a modern, tasteful grandstand. Hardly something I'll always treasure.

Adelaide is more appealing to your eyes than the Gabba or WACA and it makes Old Trafford look like a garbage dump, but that doesn't make it actually pretty. It isn't somewhere

I'd visit if I wanted to see something pretty. It's just a cricket ground with grass around it. You'd drive past it without even knowing it was something special unless the taxi driver said, "And on our left is Adelaide Oval, known as the sexiest cricket ground in the world." Then you'd look at the taxi driver wearily and slowly turn to see a lot of grass, some grandstands, and trees.

The first shot of the day was pretty, and dangerous. Smashed on the up through the covers by KP. There was a sweeper on the cover boundary. It still went for four. The fourth ball of the day KP smashed another one. This time it was into Douggie's shin as he followed through. I doubt it hurt more than the first ball. This wasn't going to be a good day for Australians. Or Douggie.

Channel 9 showed Douggie's speeds. It was not a pretty sight; they're declining so quickly that shortly he'll be bowling slower than Xavier Doherty. Douggie does try, though. There is almost little else to him. Pace, occasional movement, and effort. So much effort. There are professional cricketers who have made it to the big time by preparing, working hard, fixing their flaws and cutting out risk. And then there is Douggie, who has made it because he has choked every last bit of life out of his talent when out on the field. He probably isn't as fit as most international cricketers, and he doesn't look like someone who would spend hours worrying if his diet was right. It's all about the effort he puts in out on the field. So to see him bowling at speeds I believed I could face was quite sad. While it hasn't been announced, it seems injury is his problem. I can't believe he is the sort of person to just stop trying on a batting pitch. I can't believe he'd ever stop trying when playing for Australia.

It was his injury that cost Australia a Test in India. Douggie had taken three for 32, and was looking like a demon when taking Tendulkar and Harbhajan Singh's wickets. The score was 124 for eight when Douggie finished his last over, the one in which he removed Singh. From there India got to 216 for nine to win the match. Douggie then spent a few months out injured. Whether the injury was made worse by bowling more was unknown, but it was that spell that very nearly got Australia over the line. Now he was bowling again when he wasn't right. It could have been a lack of overs coming in. It could have been a flare-up of his injury. It could have even had something to do with his crazy schedule of flying around the country in the days leading into the Test. But it wasn't pretty at all. Although, neither is Douggie.

KP and Ian Bell went for the full frontal attack. Bell was charging down the wicket and KP was trying to beat Australia up; sorry, not trying – succeeding. He passed his Test career-best of 226 and looked like he was about to really let fly when he got caught at slip by Katich for 227. Xavier Doherty got him, probably his last Test wicket. That was nice, because at least he can say he got KP in top form. Even if he did contribute to that form earlier.

Katich was at slip because he was now properly injured. When you start to see Katich in the slip or gully catching positions, you know something is wrong. He isn't a man that likes to admit defeat or get a free ride. Some players would probably just be off the field at this stage, getting their injured heel worked on and the coaches to move them down to number seven. Katich doesn't have that in him; he'd prefer the pain even if it leads to a lengthy injury.

Prior came out and had some fun, and Bell brought up his fifty. Prior got hit straight in front from Siddle, and was given out. Unlike when he is keeping, he decided not to review it. Bell had to convince him to review it. It could be that Prior had finally worked out that not everything was worth a review and sometimes you had to think about, or it could be that he knew they were going to declare. It turned out the ball was missing the stumps, and they returned to their beating of Australia.

Then the whole Australian outlook was revealed in one ball.

While Prior was trying to get some quick runs he took a liberty too far with Xavier Doherty and top-edged him straight up in the air. Ponting and North charged at it, and then left it, and the ball dropped between them.

It reminded me of the time that Steve Waugh's face broke Jason Gillespie's leg in Sri Lanka.

A similar top edge went up and both men went for the ball with furious intent, colliding before the ball hit the ground, both breaking bones. Steve Waugh's desperation was amazing. Even if he didn't know Gillespie was there, the way he went back for the ball was the act of a man trying to do nothing but take a catch for his country. When the clash happened Sri Lanka were 139 for three in their first innings after Australia had made only 188. Waugh knew he needed Mahela Jayawardene out.

Ponting's non-effort was completely different. You could say there was no reason to have a kamikaze catch attempted while England were so close to declaration. But perhaps the act of Ponting storming back, willing to break something for his country, would have inspired the Australian team. Perhaps seeing him bounce off Marcus North would have been what the Aussies needed to know about performing for this man, their one legend, and get him a draw. Instead, it was like two old ladies in a nursing home encouraging the other to eat the last cookie, only for a nurse to knock the plate and drop the cookie on the ground.

England declared at 620 for five, a lead of 375. It might as well have been a lead of zatrillion. Australia don't bat for the best part of two days for a draw.

And they came out all guns blazing in the first few overs. After the non-catch incident, it was pleasing that Australia still had a bit of fight in them. It also meant that in no way could they draw. The fact that Australia cannot play for draws is perhaps one of my favourite qualities about Australians. The English love a draw, but we just don't get it. It's a beautiful part of the Australian psyche, although in situations like this it does us no good.

Katich batted like he does – an old man who hates birds – and he was also hobbling. In the first innings it looked like he could sort of run (although Watson still tested him), but now he was limping around the crease in a painful way. There was then talk that he hadn't even asked for a runner. Now, he may not have got one anyway. It was obvious by the end of the Gabba he was injured. But it said a lot about Katich. He'd rather suffer than be happy. Which explains his batting technique.

However. Coming up to lunch (free wine day for the press, but I don't really do wine) Australia lost all their attacking instincts and got nervy. But even with a lead of 300-odd Strauss is quick to defend. An edge from Katich flew through fourth slip, but there wasn't even a third slip there to try for a classic catch. Strauss is quick to defend, but hesitant to attack.

It didn't matter much after the interval, because Australia lost their first wicket with the score around 80. Again. Swann had got Katich with a bit of spin. Everyone started pencilling in a Swann five-wicket haul. When he got Ponting shortly afterwards, they started to carve it into their skins with a knife. Ponting had barely batted at all in this Test. There had been an odd sweep shot, and then he edged a straight one. It was about the same as him not going after that catch. He never really looked like Ponting. He'd certainly lost something, because that was about as limp an afternoon as I'd seen from him.

When Watson left, Australia were naked on the bathroom floor, at 134 for three. Hussey and Clarke came together, although it may not be fair to call what Clarke was doing batting. It was a sort of artistic interpretation of batting. To my eyes, as one who also has a dodgy back, his back was still hurting him. His batting got better, though, and with Mike Hussey needing to make up for dropping Trott (and the Ashes), they put together an English-style partnership.

I don't mean old-time England. I mean this NuEngland: professional, safe and smart. Clarke and Hussey did little wrong. Hussey didn't really look like getting out – threatening him with being dropped was the best thing the Australian selectors could have done – and Clarke even looked calmer being with Hussey. Which was weird, because Hussey is the sort of person who would make me nervous. They built for a while. I didn't want to jinx either of them by seeing how they could get out, so I decided to waste my time in better ways.

Being that the Ashes is a chance to meet up with people, I'd been quite shit at that. In Brisbane a few people contacted me, and I just didn't have the time; in Adelaide I made the time. I met up with Sunny, the guy who runs the Sehwagology Twitter and Facebook pages, and we had a shit beer under the grandstand. While we were bullshitting I saw Broad come into the nets. I also saw Greg Matthews coaching Monty, but that was too much to even think about.

Broad came into the nets with a bandage barely covering what looked like a massive bruise on his stomach. He looked stupidly positive. David Saker and Andy Flower did not. England have a training drill for their fast bowlers where they slam medicine balls into the ground and bounce them back to a coach. It's a lovely masculine endeavour. For *Two Pricks* we already have hours of it, as Sam seems to have a thing for it.

Broad was given the very smallest ball. He barely got it to knee height. At full strength he can get the very biggest up to about chest high. Flower's face went from its normal grey to a London grey. Then Broad tried to bowl in the nets. It was painful, slow and uncomfortable. He wouldn't be bowling again in this Test, or perhaps this series. I was certain of it.

Being the sort of journalist that doesn't need scoops like this to fill inches of columns, I gave it away. David Hopps, Lawrence Booth and Andrew Miller have all helped me out in the past, so they were all informed of what I'd seen, and what I thought. Sam was told as well. I probably didn't need to tell him – we were now practically like those weird couples who finish each other's sentences, or those twins who feel what the other twin feels. I didn't even bother writing about it myself. If I'd used cricketwithballs.com to write a piece about how Stuart Broad might be injured and not bowl again, I'd be pelted with eight-bit tomatoes. Unless I talked about how the injury might have come about from auto-fellating.

After Broad's attempt at bowling and medicine balling, he was back out on the field. He even dived to stop a ball. And just for a second I almost thought about doubting myself. I gave a panicked look over at Andrew Miller, but he hadn't seen it. That is the one good thing about all cricket writers, you can bet on them missing at least 90 per cent of play, on a good day. Even Miller, the hardest worker in the press box.

The Broad injury was a shocking thing for a professional sportsman to deal with. However, since I'd taken two bets with Test Match Sofa's Tom Clark, and Bell looked like winning money for Tom. Broad's injury would mean I came out even with him, as Broad hadn't scored a run in this series. I'm sure knowing this would help Broad feel better. Now if I could only get Hilfenhaus to take some wickets.

Clarke's back still looked like a problem. Usually he plays half pull shots; today he'd turned those into quarter pulls. They were working, and he even survived a wicket when he referred a short-leg catch that had been given out. All in all, Australia were powering in a professional way towards stumps. I didn't think this meant they'd get a draw, but I did think it was a positive thing. Clarke needed this. Australians don't do excuses; you're either fit enough to play, and need to perform, or should get out of the way and stop being a nancy. By getting to the 80s, he was doing two very important things: setting up Australia's innings and getting the pressure off him.

Michael Clarke gets a lot of flak from fans. Some of it is warranted, some of it is not, some of it is from me, some of it is not. In his career he has been the dominating superboy, the man afraid of being dropped, a batsman capable of long innings when not under pressure, the automaton of batting and now the injured veteran looking for form.

Through all these periods in his life, one thing seems to have remained the same: the boy gets out right before a break in play. About two years ago the press made a big deal of it, then it died down, perhaps it went away, perhaps no one cared anymore. Well it happened today, and I think people cared. I'm not nerdy or bored enough to look up exactly how many times it has happened, but it happens a lot. Today Australia had done what they needed to do: built a base and hoped that the ball spinning viciously would miss the stumps. They didn't panic, or worry too much when England were bowling well. They just batted, for the time, for the rain, for the draw perhaps. It wasn't the most Australian of pursuits but when the opposition had bent you over for three days there was little else you could do.

Clarke did this better than any other Australian. His batting was the best of his three Ashes innings, because it was his only real Ashes innings so far. He made runs, he kept out the good balls and together with Hussey built a draw-making platform for Australia. But then he got out. Not to anyone, but to Kevin

Pietersen, a man with four Test wickets before that moment. And not at any time, but with four balls left in the day.

Australian fans are wild angry dogs on a good day. Most of them would have been so pissed off they wouldn't have seen beyond those two points, but it went further. Marcus North now had to start the next day with four balls from the deadly KP, and then get through the new ball. Being the starter that he is, that might not be that easy. Clarke had picked the worst possible time to get out, as if he did it just for shits and giggles.

You might think that if he failed to score more than five, game after game, that would be worse. It wouldn't be, because those sort of failures would get you dropped, even from the Australian team. His failures come on the back of a good or at least an average Test match innings, but they give the opposition the biggest boost imaginable.

They are also the very opposite of a captain's innings; he is like some evil anti-captain who does everything he can to make the team think he is helping them only to Judas all over them at the last minute. He's probably a double agent, and he's infiltrated the ranks for years to scuttle Australia's best-laid plans. And for the chicks.

This won't end. Everything in Clarke's life seems to change, but not this. I'm sure that when he was born it was inconvenient – perhaps his father was just about to go to the footy, and then he got the call, or maybe it was the day that his mother and father had tickets to the *Evil Dead* opening night. He shall just forever be this way, it's bred into him. One day, Lara Bingle might be more loved in Australia than Clarke, because at least she was dismissed at the right time.

Of course, that is just the rage of someone who has had to live through this sort of thing too much. Michael Clarke is a class batsman who on the odd occasion gets out when Australia need it least. But it makes me want to wipe out a small village and then cut the hair off a young girl who has been growing it for years.

But as if that wasn't enough, he took it further. Way further. He fucken wrote a Twitter apology for the other bullshit that I haven't even mentioned yet. You see Clarke wasn't given out, no, his bad timing had way more than that to it. KP had been brought on for the last over as Swann looked stiff and unlikely to get a wicket if he had bowled it. KP can get a bit of turn, and although he hasn't got many wickets, he started as a spinner, so he got the chance.

He bowled a ball that bounced slightly more than Clarke anticipated. Some tried to use this bounce to protect Clarke, as if the ball spat up at him like a mega shark in a shark/octopus exploitation film and there was nothing he could do. Actually it just bounced a bit more than that which Swann had got, and Clarke turned it into his thigh pad, and then to Cook at short-leg. KP went ballistic. It was like he'd never got out a Test vice-captain with the fifth-last ball of the day before. Clarke turned to walk off. Then he stopped.

Whether he stopped because he thought he'd wait for the umpire's decision, or because the umpire had given him not out, I'm not sure. England reviewed as quickly as Strauss could get his hands into a T sign. This wasn't a review based on them talking about the dismissal, this was a primal referral based on the fact they thought he smashed it. There Clarke stood, waiting for the decision he had to know would be given out, because he had smashed the ball. I can only imagine what went through his head at this time. Finally the verdict came through, and Clarke had to walk off.

My problem wasn't with him staying at the crease – when I was young we were told it was UnAustralian to walk. Of course that is bullshit; walk, don't walk, who the fuck cares? That is your decision as a cricketer. It is the umpire's job to make the decisions. However, if you know that the technology is going to make you look like an idiot in 90 seconds' time, you might as well walk. My problem was that he started to walk, and then stopped. Like he didn't even know what he wanted to do.

But I'd forgotten about that when I saw his tweet, because it was annoying, but not a big deal. "Just want to apologise for not walking off the ground tonight when I hit the ball," he wrote. "I was just so disappointed, my emotions got [the] best of me." What? Are you kidding me? Has your brain been replaced with a Kinder Surprise toy? You're Australian, you're trying to save a Test match, don't fucken apologise for not walking. Just walk or don't. Who was he apologising to anyway? No one had had the time to complain, surely.

Clarke was apologising before it became an issue, trying to take the steam out of the situation, and accidently making it worse. I felt for Clarke, he seemed to triple guess himself all the time. Yet again he'd done something he thought would placate people and only got people more upset. I almost felt sorry for him, until I read the tweet again and realised just how angry I was. Now I wanted an apology for the apology.

And, if you are going to do a bullshit apology, don't do it on Twitter; man up and appear at the press conference.

At stumps, the score was 238 for four. Australia would need a flood to get them a draw. Swann wouldn't rip through Australia without help, but now they were four wickets down he wouldn't need much help. John Howard had once prayed for rain to break the drought, which it didn't; surely to him this was more important.

Michael Hussey came out to do the press conference. Again. While he was talking you could hear the English players in their dressing room laughing and carrying on. I have no idea what they were doing there, yet I was convinced that no group of 38 men and one woman had ever been happier than they were right then. Over the hooting and hollering, it was hard to hear Hussey say Clarke was disappointed. It sounded like they were barn dancing. Australia's dressing room was equally close to the press conference, not that I'd heard a word from in there.

That night we vodcasted long into the night. So long that my one attempt at a beer and a steak in Adelaide was very nearly missed. There is no time when you are trying to film and edit a whole webisode after play, and if it wasn't for Andrew Miller, I would have missed out on the steak. Being the gentleman that he is, he ordered us steaks as the chef was closing the bar. We were at a pub somewhere in Adelaide; I really had no idea where it was, but Sam had suggested that it would be good if once in the Test we went out and met people. He never added, "as a couple", but it was implied.

After last call Andrew Miller put cheese in my last pint of Coopers. This was a risky move by Miller. I was massively under-alcoholed on this trip, and a move like that could have provoked punching. Instead I stole his beer.

DAY 5 -ADELAIDE OVAL

Stuart Broad was out for the series. I'd been right. Even I was shocked. Apparently I knew a bit about this cricket. I should have cashed in on this brilliant knowledge. After my great success, I would have bet my house and CD collection on Mike Hussey outlasting Marcus North. Instead, Hussey got out.

You could actually hear women weeping, nerdy women, who usually hide their emotions. Finn had taken quite a few wickets in the series, but he was still Hussey's bitch. Every time he dropped short, Hussey seemed to have time to lick his lips before smashing it away. This time he spooned it generously into the air, and although Australia still had zero chance of a draw, the end would come way quicker. So far Australia had relied almost exclusively on Hussey, so his betrayal was more than enough reason to be dropped, surely.

Haddin and Harris had hardly bothered walking out before the new ball had them, then Marcus North followed. He'd made 22, which may have been slightly over the betting margin, depending on when you had laid your bet. It was sad to see him go, even though I had done everything in my power to get him dropped. I thought that because I started the call for him to be axed while others were still calling him "organised", I should have been the one to say goodbye.

I'd called North a toaster, waffle maker and a cockroach. I'd mentioned his loss of nip, talked about how I would kill

116

him, said I'd love to drink bourbon with him, made a very good betting system on his batting, and said that he was Australia's best spinner before he even played for Australia. I'd been kind to him, dreadfully mean to him and I'd let him know how I felt at all times with my kind of bullshit honesty.

I thought this was the end for him. I couldn't see how he would ever play another Test; not even the Australian selectors would stick with him now. If your average is 35 after 21 Tests, talking about your conversion rate of hundreds is like talking about Josef Mengele's services to the health industry. He was 31, and Australia couldn't look back now, not even if he could be a very good captain.

My favourite North innings was his first hundred, because I was still full of hope for this averagely talented batsman who could bowl a bit. My favourite spell would have to be his bowling to Pakistan at Lord's – six wickets of pure ass should always be celebrated. I also loved it that he found it funny that the same media who was talking about how he might be dropped then wondered in the next breath if he might be the next captain.

As much as I'd called for his termination, I still liked the guy, and I hope he helps Western Australia become a better team. Any man who makes hundreds on four continents in 21 Tests should be respected, and I was free to do that if he was no longer to be the weak link in the middle order.

I once heard Mike Atherton say that he would have written savage reviews of himself had he been a writer watching himself play. I think North could be a good writer. I'm basing this on nothing that he has written; he just seems to be a terribly self-aware guy. He is an honest player who tried to get the most out of himself, and you could never truly dislike someone like that. Well you could, but you'd be an asshole.

Once Swann got North, he took the last two wickets as well to end with five. It was just like I said, Swann couldn't rip through Australia on his own, and by the time he came on he didn't need to. That was England, they didn't need to rely on one player, because everyone did their job pretty well. Finn was their weakest bowler – and the leading wicket-taker in the

Ashes. England won by an innings and 71 runs. Innings is such a harmless little word, until put into this context. It basically means an ass slapping till it is red raw.

England had outplayed Australia in every part of the game except referrals. Their batting looked calm and calculated, their bowling had sensible plans that were easy to maintain. They fielded well as a unit. And they seemed to be enjoying what they were doing.

The time they spent preparing for this tour they weren't all sitting around watching Adam Sandler films – they actually learnt that shit. In my life I didn't think I'd seen a better performance from an England side. I might have seen more talented England sides, but I'd never seen all 11 players pull together at one time to play like this.

It's easy to apply the professional tag, because that is what England were. But when I call them professional, it's more than just a phrase. I grew up with professional cricketers. By the time I was a teenager Australia had become a professional cricket outfit and used that and Shane Warne to become one of the best teams in Test history. Gilchrist, McGrath, Hayden, and Gillespie all had exceptional talent, but it was the professional nature of Australian cricket that turned them into Test cricket's best.

Now England were the most professional team in world cricket, but they were using that professionalism to beat the team who had brought it to cricket; there's a movie in that. Although, looking back at the last sentence, not an exciting one. England now looked like the prototype for modern teams. They were still not the most talented, but they played thinking cricket. For all of the talk that cricketers are an intellectual bunch compared to other sportsmen, most cricketers are still thick. There are probably even players in this side who are thick. But their cricket was not stupid. They thought their way through situations. Strauss may have been defensive in the field and their cricket not that exciting, but it was still quality cricket.

Minutes after play David Saker was out on the square with the back-up bowlers. While Strauss, Ponting and KP were at the presentation, Saker was taking the back-up men through their paces. England had just won by an innings, and their back-up bowlers were bowling through Strauss' interview. Australia might have had their players in the nets at the same time, they might have been planning for a victory in Perth, but it seemed like they were being out-professionalled on the same day their team had not even made lunch with six wickets in hand.

From here on in I won't call England "NuEngland". They deserve better than me using a cheap piece of right-wing abuse for a poor Labour Party. Even at this stage of the Ashes they looked like a more competent unit than the English Labour Party was under Blair or Brown.

Strauss said whatever he said at the press conference. Ricky said the word "execute". We didn't execute our skillsets, we didn't execute our plans, we need to work on better execution, and we need to execute our executions better whilst learning to execute the executable. It just kept going on. He then said the rain wasn't ever in their thinking. Now that is a positive thing to say. You can't rely on weather. You just have to get out there and play.

Of course by 2pm it had started raining, hard. So hard that even though it was refreshing, you still had to run to get out of it. By 3pm it was the hardest rain I had ever seen. It was biblical. God, or the Aliens, had sent this rain to mock Australia.

"Foolish Australian Earthlings, if you had only managed to bat like a competent Test line-up instead of a bunch of drunkards on a buck's party, you could have drawn this Test and gone to the one ground you should be favourites at with a clean slate. You are stupid, stupid little creatures, and this is why we have made it rain so hard, so every drop is a reminder of your failures. Every lightning bolt is a reminder of just how bad you fucked up. You are pathetic mammals. We use the rain to spit on you."

The rain came so hard that by 4pm parts of the ground actually looked like a lake. The members' side was completely under water. Twitter was suddenly chock full of cricket journalists trying to update everyone on what could have been for Australia. It was so wet, that a pasty English redhead went for a slip and slide out on the surface. This was perhaps the biggest failure of my career: I saw the complete slide, and was amused by it. Had I picked up my camera and filmed it I would have got Paul Collingwood (allegedly, all the ECB would tell me is that it wasn't Ian Bell's body shape) doing a victory slide on the ground that had brain-fucked him four years earlier.

Instead, I left the Adelaide Oval with no viral video to break to the world and was wearing full length garbage bags with Sam. It wasn't how Adelaide was supposed to end, but walking out of there with those green bags on to keep my clothes dry seemed about right. When I got to the street I took mine off, just as Gideon Haigh walked out of a random restaurant having just given one of his 17 press phone calls of the day. I didn't say anything to him, I just turned him around and let him see Sampson Collins, of Eton and *Two Pricks*, walking down O'Connell St wearing a bin bag.

It was perhaps the only victory Australia had in Adelaide.

Adelaide Oval gets Test cricket. I'm not sure how or why, but it brings out dramatic events on what is a pitch that is made for batting. Quite often Adelaide gets cool on the last day; it gives you a slow-paced German drama for ages and you can almost fall asleep waiting for it, but then at the end it has nun prostitutes with AK47s attacking an army. This time, Adelaide flipped. All the fun and sex was at the start.

Australia's first day was like showing the horror at the start of the story and then letting you see what happens, afterwards. It wasn't always pretty. England tied Australia up, left them in a basement and just went down from time to time to use sandpaper on Douggie Bollinger and drop Xavier Doherty into the odd vat of acid. Although Katich's injuries were all due to self-harming.

There was too much exposition from Alastair Cook; having finished making his table at Brisbane, in Adelaide he went about making all the chairs as well. Then KP came in for a long scene-chewing cameo. It was a bit much, but the chest wound of Stuart Broad led beautifully into Michael Clarke's scene-stealing performance as the man who wouldn't go and then couldn't apologise quick enough. The final act was brilliantly handled by England, brutal and quick and then the way they let the rain end it all, that wonderful biblical rain, it worked well.

Paul Collingwood after the credits was amusing, but you had to wonder if it was done just because he'd had no real role in the film, or because he was still angry about how the Adelaide story ended last time. His reaction certainly proved it's more fun to be the extra in a good film than the star of a shocker.

Back at Mimi's place I thanked her for letting me stay and she showed me pictures of her Gin Palace she was designing down on the coast. I now knew someone that had a Gin Palace. My life had changed. Mimi told me I could stay there the next time I was in town. I must admit I really wanted to, just so I could say to people, "Yes, this year we're summering in Meems' Gin Palace."

That night I flew out to Melbourne and had an unexpected person on my flight, Jimmy Anderson. Between Tests Anderson was flying home to attend the birth of his baby. He was sitting in the gate lounge the same as I was, well not the same, he wasn't staring at himself wondering, like I am, why no one is talking to him. Perhaps Anderson doesn't look enough like a cricketer, or the English team – KP aside – just aren't well known faces in Australia, but no one has walked up to him yet. I was in a sport store recently and they had a special Ashes twin statue of Ponting and KP together. The reason those two were picked was they share the same sponsor, but I doubt most Australians could pick Strauss out of a police line-up anyway.

After a while I forgot about Anderson and just spent time talking to my wife via Skype. I was spent after two straight weeks of cricket. Back-to-back Tests may be a formality to modern cricketers, but I have no idea how they do it. I spend most of my time just trying to survive them, and that is without two days straight of batting or bowling bouncers on a flat track. Talking to my wife is good. After the next Test, which was now the way I counted time, I'd be seeing her again, which would be good. For now it was good just to talk nonsense with her.

Unfortunately for Anderson, eventually English fans started to invade his space, and whilst it must have sucked, I was glad. The man had bowled some serious spells in these Ashes, and looked the best bowler in the series by a distance. That sort of skill level should result in more hero worship. He may not be able to do it in the next Test. If he was more tired than me, which I assumed he was, he'd be flying to the UK and back while dealing with the birth of a baby during his week off.

That didn't seem like rest to me.

MELBOURNE

To properly celebrate being back in my home town, I went to the bar at the Trades Hall Building to listen to Gideon Haigh and Martin Flanagan, another sports writer, chat about their craft. In front of me was a six foot tall bald black woman, a guy wearing an Essendon T-shirt, three Asian students, an elderly couple and two hipsters who had spent hours trying to look like they spent no time on what they wear at all. It was very Melbourne. I've never met a city that tries harder to be cool while doing everything in its power to maintain the image that it doesn't care what you think. It was as if these people had been positioned around me by a film director.

A friend of mine was once seeing a woman who stopped him when he was putting on socks that were the same colour as his T-shirt. "Don't make your clothes match, that isn't cool," she told him. "You should always make sure your clothes don't match as that's cooler." That's why everyone in Melbourne is a film-maker and everyone in Sydney is a DJ.

Flanagan and Haigh are both brilliant Melbournites, which means neither of them are actually from Melbourne. They are the Nick Cave and Warren Ellis of sports writers. And if you don't get that reference, it's OK, it's a Melbourne thing. Haigh is the thin wiry intellectual type, the sort of extra you want in an arthouse coffee shop or old dusty library. Flanagan is the bar-room pontificator. All beard and belly laugh. The sort of lefty intellectual that only looks complete when he's also drinking a beer. On stage they bounced off each other with anecdote and opinion like two old men on the bus. It was magical.

Later on I found myself in the pub with them both, and was slotted in next to Flanagan. He asked me who the Australian team could bring in to win the Ashes; I said even Chuck Norris wouldn't help. Then I was worried about my remark. Had he thought I meant the Chuck Norris of recent times, the Chuck Norris facts era (when Chuck Norris breaks the law, the law doesn't heal. etc), because I actually meant *Delta Force* era Chuck Norris.

Flanagan didn't really seem to worry; he was more interested in Julian Assange. I'm sure you know of Assange, I'm sure it made news in places other than Melbourne when the head of WikiLeaks dropped the US Cables and then found himself in hot water accused of rape in Sweden. It just happens to be that Assange is from Melbourne. Not born there, but I think he got his dress sense and haircut there. Assange was Flanagan's Alastair Cook; I didn't ask him if he'd dreamed of him, but I assumed he had.

The Australian papers were not sure how to handle Assange. On the one hand, he had exposed governmental hypocrisy the world over and was a local boy. On the other hand, he could have been a rapist. It was hard to make too much of a martyr out of him. Flanagan was obsessed with Assange, and wanted to know my views. I had almost no views on Assange. Not because I had no views on Assange – I have views on everything – but because I was trapped in the Ashes bubble. I'd hardly read a website, glanced at a newspaper or even scanned Twitter for news stories.

All I knew about Assange was that he had barracked for North Melbourne (Ricky Ponting's Aussie rules team), was involved in WikiLeaks, and was facing a rape charge. I gave some vague answer about supporting his right to out the truth, and then listened as Flanagan gave me the small details on a story of which I barely knew the big details. This brought in the guy who ran New International Bookshop at the Trades Hall. He had met Assange years earlier before WikiLeaks even existed. It was a similar story to when I met then Carlton full forward Brendan Fevola (yes, Lara Bingle's Brendan Fevola) before he was famous. Because the important thing about Melbourne is that no matter what the conversation, there is always a way to bring it back to Aussie rules.

I'd been away for a while, but I still knew how to survive in Melbourne. I was certainly not UnMelbournian, even if on that very night my accent had been questioned again, as if I was trying to sound British on purpose. I spent all my time trying to sound intelligent, and I couldn't do an accent to save myself.

It wasn't just Assange – the news was full of Melbourne boys. Some time around the first ball that Xavier Doherty bowled in Test cricket, a website devoted to people donating their money to bringing back Shane Warne was started. It amazes me that human beings can walk upright, talk and operate any kind of mobile phone device. We are so fucken stupid as a species that I for one cannot wait for the day our alien masters come here and make us into food, pets and handbags for the bored middle-class aliens who don't have to work because they have designed machines to do everything they need to do.

Writing this is stupid. Painfully so. Because this isn't even the first time I've written something like this – I've done them for Warne, Gilly and Hayden. Probably for others as well. I get sucked in by the stupidity of others and just feel the need to comment when I really should be doing something more meaningful with my time like cutting off my nipples to sew them onto a mouse.

Great players retire, get dropped or die. It's a simple concept. Most of them retire. They do this because they no longer want to play the game at the highest level, no longer can play the game at the highest level, or are just sick and tired of training. Warne retired at the right time for him. The fact that he and McGrath had left at the same time created a chasm bigger than Paris Hilton's, but they both had to retire, and at that stage Australia had Brett Lee, Stuart MacGill and Stuart Clark. It wasn't as if they'd left Australian cricket with a homeless guy who yells at tourists.

Now, four years later, some people wanted Warne back.

Actually, it isn't four years later. They've been saying it on repeat every single day since he left, because people are morons. Warne made them feel warm and fuzzy. Well, they felt warm and fuzzy when he played. That was because he was a major part in what was a brilliant cricket team. As good as he was, though, it wasn't just Warne. Australia had three of their best ever bowlers for years in one side, and they also had a bunch of great and very good batsmen, some capable back-up bowlers and a cricket-changing wicket keeper.

This team had made these people feel warm, fuzzy and mostly satisfied. Now that feeling was gone, and these people, like the simple morons they were, wanted it back. Well, you couldn't have it back. Forgetting the fact that Warne was 41, hadn't bowled more than four overs a game at the top level for years, had an average of 36 at the WACA in his prime, had nine other jobs, was working on what seemed to be a crappy chat show and wouldn't want to tarnish his name by coming back, he just wouldn't come back.

At the very least he'd have to make himself available for Victoria, come back from London, and make sure he really could bowl 30 overs a day. None of these things were going to happen, regardless of whether he ruled out coming back or not. He just wasn't going to play at the WACA, and even if he did, he wouldn't be winning the game for anyone other than England.

Asking your very retired players to come back every time your team struggles is about as stupid as you can get. It is the sports version of having a bad night with your girlfriend, ringing up your ex in a drunken horny state, then appearing at her house at 4am professing your undying love for her. The chances of it being successful are very slim; the chances of you ending up looking like a complete assclown are odds-on.

Just writing about this had made me dumber. Because I knew this was a nonsense media and idiot-related issue, and yet I still wrote about it. Just reading this has made you dumber as well. Because you also knew that he wasn't going to play and that this whole thing was just a colossal waste of your precious time. You could have spent your time reading about something important, taking your nan flowers, helping a young person get off drugs or clipping the toenails of orphan dogs. You've let down your community, family and species.

Instead of making a difference you spent your time reading this stupid ranty nonsense, written by some idiot who calls everyone else an idiot, about something that was never going to happen in the first place. It's non-issues like this that keep us all so distracted we let the world become the sort of place that allows reality TV stars and cardboard cut-out politicians to take over.

You and I are the problem.

Plus Warne – he is definitely part of the problem. When the talk of him coming back started, he could have just said, "I'm flattered, I won't be coming back, so please don't donate money to that particular cause, spend it on helping Aids babies in Zimbabwe or on a surround sound system for your car."

He didn't do that. Instead he lapped up the praise and casually mentioned the name of another player who he just happened to play with once in the same club side. No one pimps his team-mates like Shane Warne, hence why his original list of the 50 best players he'd ever played with had Darren Berry in it, and why the names of Tremlett, Watson and any Victorian are so often spoken by him.

Warne gave the world the name Michael Beer, someone with 19 Twitter followers and five first-class matches to his name. Another Melbourne boy in the news. But not a real chance of playing for Australia, surely, as before Warne mentioned him his name had never been brought up as potentially playing for Australia, and as much as I didn't rate Nathan Hauritz, he was tearing up Shield cricket with his best batting and bowling performances ever. He was making hundreds and taking wickets, so any talk of Beer playing for Australia was really far-fetched. Except actually it wasn't. This was how I recorded it on cricketwithballs.com:

Australia picks new spinner from bus shelter.

Having run out of cricketers in Shield cricket due to injury, T20 contracts and general uselessness, Cricket Australia has made a shock decision to pick a player from a local bus shelter in Perth. Michael Beer is this lucky man's name. Beer, 26, a tall blond chap formerly of the Democratic Peoples' Republic of Victoria, was waiting for the number 87 bus to go down to the beach when Greg Chappell was driving by.

Chappell, an amazing judge of cricketers, saw something in Beer as he was tapping on his legs waiting for the bus to arrive. Those seconds of tapping were enough to show Chappell that Beer could be the spinner that Australia have been waiting for. Chappell said, "You can tell a great spinner by his fingers, it doesn't matter if he is bowling or not, it's just a case of looking at them and feeling that they have the magic in them. Beer's fingers certainly felt magical to me."

It was only later on that the Australian selectors actually found out that Beer was actually playing Shield cricket. Chappell apparently saw this as a sign that his eye was keener than most, but Beer had been wearing his full Warriors kit when at the bus stop.

When presented with the fact that Beer had played five first-class games and taken 16 wickets at an average of 39, Chappell said, "So, this isn't the Matrix, numbers mean nothing, my eyes are all that matters, there is no spoon." Later on Andrew Hilditch was informed of the selection, and said, "Look, I didn't have that much to do with this selection, but Matthew Beer is an exciting prospect, Warnie told me about him."

Nathan Hauritz's shoelaces have been taken off him as a precaution.

Australia were losing the plot. Shield cricketers didn't even know who the chairman of selectors was. Warne was picking players. Greg Chappell was doing all the talking as part of his role as National Talent Manager (either a phrase borrowed from the Third Reich or an elaborate way to explain wanking). Andrew Hilditch was saying Beer had been picked for his local knowledge. Beer had only played in four matches at the WACA in his life, far fewer than Xavier Doherty or Nathan Hauritz. Hilditch obviously knew nothing about him. Which for once meant he had something in common with the rest of the Australian public.

The most sensible thing Hilditch had done all summer had been that walk around in circles at the Gabba. His selection policy, before Greg Chappell, was to use old players, take few risks and try to keep the Australian team at the top of the tree by doing this. Now Chappell was involved, and it was Russian roulette. Hauritz had copped a bullet and Beer was given the opportunity of a lifetime.

It was Hauritz who I felt for.

Hauritz is the sort of guy who would be perfectly at home as one of the nerds in a teen comedy. Not the main guy, or even the main guy's friend, but as someone in the background who ends up with a cooler girl than his status deserves. He'd be the butt of jokes for much of the movie with just one scene where he redeems himself in the eyes of the audience. None of his lines would become catchphrases; no one would really remember him being in that film.

In real life Hauritz is the luckiest unluckiest cricketer there has ever been. A perfect combination of club cricketer, mouse and plucky fighter. A man who is picked from club cricket to play for Australia should be lucky, but when he spends the rest of his time being used and abused by the Australian selectors, that luck seems to have faded.

On August 16, Ricky Ponting had been asked if Hauritz was a lock-in to play in the Ashes, and he said, "I think so." But before the first Test Hauritz had to go up against Xavier Doherty for that position. "I think I am (a better bowler) definitely," he had said, "but my opinion doesn't really matter unfortunately when it comes to picking the side." This was perhaps the biggest statement of Hauritz's career. Publicly saying he was better than his main opposition was something that wrestlers did, not mousy off-spinners picked from club cricket.

Hauritz is undoubtedly a fighter, but not the person who starts the fight. The worst news for Hauritz is that when he seems to have no confidence in himself, he gets picked, and when on those rare occasions he finds a bit of self-belief, the Australian selectors bin him.

Before the Ashes of 2009 Hauritz offered to write a blog for the series. His blog on the eve of the first Test was rumoured to be so timid that Tim Nielsen, the coach, asked him to rewrite it. It basically said he thought he had let his team-mates down during the warm-up games and that he wasn't sure that he should be playing Test cricket. Three Tests later, he had outbowled Graeme Swann but was left out of the final Test on an Oval surface that would have suited him.

Part of Swann's skill, like Murali, Warne, Kumble and Mushtaq before him, is his tremendous self-belief. You need to believe you are a world-class spinner before you are. Hauritz wouldn't think that ever. He probably wouldn't even be bold enough to dream it. Yet, even after a predictable mauling in India, he was the spinner who should have been picked if Australia were only going to pick spinners like Doherty and Beer. They were more or less the same bowler, but with less experience. Getting rid of Hauritz for these men was like upgrading your '87 Volvo with an '84 model.

The list of Australian spinners since Warne was not pretty. Beau Casson was still missing. Xavier Doherty was shaken. Bryce McGain was waiting for a comeback. Cameron White had recently bowled medium pace for Bangalore in the Champions League. Stuart MacGill didn't finish a Test. Marcus North pretended to be a batsman. Jason Krejza was obsessed with the number 12. Brad Hogg would prefer to be a postman. Steve Smith wanted to bat at six. Michael Beer was a moment from pain. Cullen Bailey and Dan Cullen missed the twilight of their careers. Simon Katich and Michael Clarke invented injuries to get out of bowling. Andrew Symonds became a hard drinker to survive. Nathan Hauritz was now selling his pain – well, if a factually inaccurate piece in one of the Australian newspapers was to be believed. It said he was selling some of his Australian kit saying he wouldn't need it anymore. It was just old jumpers and not his baggy green. You're not allowed to sell your baggy green – it's like an Oscar. If you try to sell one, the baggy green code of conduct means you have to give it to Steve Waugh for a dollar. That's not true, I think. But who knows what the truth is with Hauritz?

And what's weird is, I'm his biggest critic. I've never wanted him in the Australian side. I thought it was a mistake to begin with, I took the piss out of him with reckless abandon, I have mocked everything about him since he made the side, I explain away his victories, talk up his defeats and use him as a punchline when I'm bored. But in picking Michael Beer the Australian selectors were way harsher on Nathan Hauritz than I ever could have been.

Beer should have been the biggest story in town, but Warne was about to trump him again. The man was still way bigger than cricket. When photos of him and Liz Hurley making out hit the news, not even Michael Beer and Nathan Hauritz becoming a couple could have topped it. Some tabloid had been staking out Hurley and Warne for a while, just waiting for those million-dollar photos. Hurley and Warne both released statements (which seemed to have been written by the same person) about how they'd broken up with their respective partners earlier.

The papers went wild. The news was either about Warne and Hurley, or Oprah Winfrey. Oprah was coming to Australia because her Scientologist friend John Travolta was a Qantas ambassador or something. They gave him a plane, I remember that much. Now he does things like flies around in his retro plane outfit to promote the company. Oprah's coverage in Australia was amazing; the Pope hadn't got as much. It was like Australia had never really existed before she arrived, and we'd just been a hollow shell of a country floating around in the Pacific hoping that one day a talk show host would arrive and make us whole. One news programme only seemed to have news about her arrival on it. Then the sport and the weather, and the weatherman even mentioned her.

The purpose of her trip was to bring over various fans of her show to see shit, Australian shit, and then there was to be a show and probably an onstage LSD orgy with her, Travolta and some lucky audience members. Warne missed out. He was in the UK for most of this time, with Liz. Or, he was with her for at least one kiss. Had he been in Australia and got it on with Oprah he could have completely taken over Australia. They would have had to rename the country after him.

With Oprah and Warne sucking up every available slot in

newspaper, radio, forum, Facebook, blog, Twitter feed and TV station, the Julian Assange story just disappeared. Assange was clearly the Marcus North of the news. North had been dropped, but no movie stars were involved.

Steve Smith and Phil Hughes were also lucky winners in the Hilditch and Chappell lottery. Smith was selected to bat at six, although despite a plucky, entertaining 70 against the world's best bowling attack from Pakistan, Ponting said he couldn't see him batting at six. Hughes was coming in for the injured Katich because he'd made an 80 not out against New Zealand in his most recent Test. He hadn't seen a run in the ten months or so since then. That was mere detail. He was picked because potential rivals Shaun Marsh, Ed Cowan and Liam Davis hadn't piled on the runs.

Luckily for me I was spending my week in Melbourne because England were playing Victoria. It meant I could visit the first love of my life. The G. Now that I live in London I'm removed from my spiritual home. Growing up in Melbourne only 40 minutes from the MCG is something I took for granted. Every year I would visit the ground at least 30 times. Most cricket supporters from around the world would love to visit it just once.

My first cricket memory was a state game between NSW and the Vics. Mike Whitney stormed in first ball of the day and slipped over. That's when I fell in love with the game. Later in the day Simon O'Donnell hit out, and was eventually caught hooking. That's when I fell in love with Victoria.

The first Test I saw was against Pakistan. Wasim Akram was the fastest thing I had ever seen, and then Dean Jones came out to face him and was given a Victorian hero's welcome. There aren't too many things like a Victorian doing well at the G. All the Australian players get cheered, but when a Victorian comes out the crowd seems to double in an instant. At that stage Deano was God in Victoria, and because he had got out for a golden duck in the first innings, everyone was willing him on in the second. Ten runs later and he was sent back by Akram. Later on, a Pakistan player picked the ball up from the fence and someone hit him with a flag. The

Melbourne crowd always have an extra bit of mongrel in them.

The first one-dayer I saw was with my uncle. My dad wouldn't go, as he hated one-day cricket and Kerry Packer. The game was against New Zealand, and the only thing I remember is getting told off by some middle-aged woman who thought I was standing up too much. Oh, and a lot of sheep jokes. One of the best moments there was when I went to the David Boon memorial game, and spent most of the second innings chatting to Devon Malcolm on the fence. He was a very nice chap – good sense of humour.

I saw Warne's hat-trick. No, really. I was in the underneath section of the old Olympic stand at the back of the first level. Just my dad and me. We actually thought it would be a good day's cricket. Second ball, Craig McDermott got a wicket off a full-toss, I think, and I remember saying to Dad what a waste of time it was coming down. Other than the hat-trick, I was right. My dad still won't forgive me for going to the fourth day of a Test, against the Windies in '92. We saw a scrappy day's play, where Damien Martyn made 60-odd, I think. My dad wanted to go on the fifth day, when Warne ended up taking his first seven-wicket haul. Whoops. But I blame him. I knew too much about cricket: he said, let's go to the fifth day, and I said, no, the cricket might not last all day on the fifth. I wanted to see a whole day's play. I was right. It didn't last all day.

When I was a teenager we used to take plastic containers full of bourbon into the ground strapped to our bodies. Even then, I knew drunk was the only way to truly enjoy a one-dayer. We never really got that drunk, to be honest, and it was so hot you usually sweated it all out. By 2001 we were old enough to drink legally, and on the way to the G for an ODI, my mate Big Daddy and another guy got run over in front of me. I'm talking the full deal – knocked up in the air in slow motion. I thought they'd both be dead. Instead it was the car that was smashed up, and they were both fine. Big Daddy's shoe had flown about 30 metres. The ambulance took us to the hospital. They decided that both of them were OK, so from there we went straight to the cricket, where Big Daddy continued to take the glass out of his hair for the whole game (and for the next few days).

I remember the state games when Justin Langer would be abused by the Victoria fans from the moment he walked out on the field until the close of play. I also remember him swearing at them, threatening them, and one day squaring up to a guy who was standing next to me. The guy was 6ft 6ins but he backed down before Langer did. I remember the state games when Greg Matthews would sledge the crowd non-stop. Between every ball, and at the end of every over. In fact, the only time he slowed down was when he was bowling. I saw Glenn McGrath flip the bird (the finger) to a Victoria supporter one day.

Of the three best innings I have seen at the G, only one was not by Matthew Elliott. That was Jacques Kallis holding off Shane Warne on a fifth-day wicket. It was amazing. He was beaten so many times, but he just never wavered.

Almost every time I'm at a cricket game with my dad, he mentions the story about the day he was working the bar at the G, but no one wanted a beer. Sobers was playing for the World XI. My dad watched the whole thing for free. Sobers made a double hundred. It isn't just my dad who talks about that innings to this day.

I sledged David Hookes the day he was king-hit and ultimately died. He was Victoria coach at the time, and as he often did, he was walking around the boundary while we were struggling. I said, "Think we've got enough all-rounders playing, Hookesy?" He smiled and said, "Yup." We had about six all-rounders playing that day, and Darren Lehmann was smashing them everywhere. That was the last time I saw Hookesy, as the game turned, and the all-rounders took a bagful of wickets.

Later that season I went to four out of the five days in the Sheffield Shield final. I was on the ground when the great Darren "Chuck" Berry announced his retirement, and someone yelled out, "Oh fuck, no" as he said it. I was also at the one-day game where Warne did his shoulder and Berry had to go out and field. As Warne walked off it was as quiet as I have ever heard the G during a one-day game.

At a football game on the way out, I walked past the Keith

Miller statue at the ground. He looked like a superhero, which he practically was. I remember standing there and just staring at it; people must have thought I was mental.

When I was young, I attended a Bushrangers camp where I bowled with Damien Fleming and Craig Howard. And Chuck Berry gave me 'keeping advice. All of this happened on the G. It remains the only time I have played cricket on the G. But thanks to the football season I spent quite a bit of time out on the sacred sandy surface.

Even my first public hand job was at the G.

The last Test I saw there was against India. On one of the days, Big Daddy and I got amazingly hammered, but we were still trying to focus on what might have been the last time Sachin Tendulkar and Rahul Dravid would bat at the G. On that day Sachin's batting sobered us up, and Rahul's made us rush to the bar.

It's amazing how a piece of real estate can feel like a family member. I felt more comfortable sitting in the grandstand on my own than I felt at any job or social situation in my whole life. It was just an everyday part of my life. Now it isn't.

On the trip into the ground I counted down the stations on the Epping line. I even managed not to get angry when we stopped at West Richmond station and as normal no one got off or on. I am one of literally 3 other people who got off at Jolimont. Then I looked up. There she was. The same as when I left her. I practically ran through the car park to get to the ground. The minute I stepped in it felt like home.

I did the journalist thing and rushed up and found a desk. In front of me was some other journalist looking at porn. For a minute I thought I was dreaming. I kept staring at this guy, waiting for him to at least huddle over the computer to try to protect those of us who could see his screen, but he didn't. So I looked around to see if I was the only one who could see it. Andrew Miller was smiling at me with a knowing, "yes, someone really is looking at porn in the press box" grin on his face.

The G was clearly welcoming me home.

Had Cricket Victoria planned for Moreton Bay bugs, steak and oysters for lunch, I still wouldn't have eaten them. Actually

I would have, but beforehand I would have gone downstairs and gotten a pie. A pie at the G is mandatory and folklore. You have to do it, so at lunch I practically floated down to level one. Then, it all went wrong.

There were no pies at the MCG. When someone said that you can never go home again, they weren't kidding. This was mental; the G was formed on pies, and the overcooked ones were used as bricks during the Great Depression. It's a tradition that goes back to the first time I ever ate one, perhaps even before that. Pie and sauce, or if you feel the need to make it longer, dog's eye and dead horse. They go together like homophobia and the religious Right. And here I was, back in my spiritual homeland, the only place I've ever felt a truly religious experience, and I couldn't have my holy communion pie.

I was reared on pies the way most kids are reared on breast milk. I can't confirm this as fact, but I believe my mother had no milk and instead squeezed out fully formed four and twenties from her teat. Not the full size ones you can get at the milk bar, but the smaller ones they sold at the G for twice the price. Sure, the pies were often dreadfully overcooked, the pastry harder than Steve Waugh's nerve, and worse-tasting than David Boon's box, but they were ours. Meat, gravy, pastry, and one time I found a fish bone.

It wasn't gourmet, or even that pleasant; it was just what you ate at the ground. Ritual and sacrifice (especially at that price). Going to the ground with food showed you as an outsider, whether you were some toff in the members' with the crusts cut off your sandwiches or an Indian family with a fully cooked meal. It wasn't right. Not eating a pie at the G was UnAustralian according to some, but it was bloody UnMelbournian, that I could be sure of. On a cold southerly-inspired July day they were the only way to get warm in the top tier.

Now I had come back to my ground after approximately 866 days, 17 hours, and 12 minutes, and all I needed to complete the experience was a pie. It shouldn't have been tough. Even for a stupid tour match between second string Victorian and English sides there should have been pies. The first place I went to, there was one pie, some gluten-free monstrosity. I don't really know what gluten is, but I wanted it in my pie. What am I, some kind of animal? I just want a typical G four and twenty pie.

I waited for five minutes as a South African woman told me she had just arrived in the country and still had jet lag. She couldn't work the coffee maker. I wanted to ask her why she had come to the ground straight off a plane – she's probably married to one of the English players, I thought, but any conversation and one of the other pie vultures might have swooped in and got my meal. Because I wasn't the only one waiting. I ignored her in the rudest manner I could, until she left with her overpriced coffee. Eventually I was told that there was a problem with the pies, and they wouldn't be ready for a while yet.

No problem, this was the G, not some one-pie outfit. I walked out of the members' and into the public area, found another food store, and waited for a pie to come out. None did, so I asked, and they had none ready either. I continued walking to the remaining two food stalls – no pies. Madness. At that moment I wanted a pie more than I wanted to play for Victoria. Where the hell were they?

Apparently my whole belief system was based on the fact that the day I returned to my country there would be pies waiting for me at the G. Now, nothing was certain. Australia had changed in my absence. It'd gone gluten-free. Pies were no longer easy to obtain. When I left we had a weak dollar, pies everywhere and a cricket team that wouldn't lose an Ashes Test by an innings at home.

Not helping the whole hunt-for-a-pie situation was Sam. He was in Perth, and felt like it was his daily duty to come up with a cool new idea for *Two Pricks*. He called me, Skyped me, emailed me and texted me all the time. It was our first week apart since *Two Pricks* started, and I talked to him even more than when I sat next to him at the games.

This was the not fun part of the relationship, because while I wanted *Two Pricks* to do well, I really wanted a week off and to spend a bit of time relaxing at the G and talking to my wife, who I really miss. Sam I could happily go three weeks without conversing with; with my wife back home in London it was driving me crazy. I knew it would be hard being away from her, and I think I could handle it if we were in a compatible time zone. But getting her replies to texts ten hours after I'd sent them was not making for great conversations. But in just over a week I'd see her.

I handled missing her a lot more easily once I got a pie. A proper four and twenty pie. I finished it in 12 seconds and headed down to watch Monty bowl from behind his arm. Philip Brown, the photographer, was there, and he was eating a burgundy pie because he couldn't find a plain old four and twenty one. I'm not exactly sure what is in a burgundy pie, but it doesn't taste right. You could tell by the look on his face that this Canberra born and bred man just wanted a real pie. To take his mind off the disappointment, we just stood there, constantly moving for the sightscreen and shooting the shit. I'd like to think our conversation helped him overcome the pie horror.

Victoria were actually quite good in this game, and both teams were keen on setting up a result on the last day. That result could have been a Victorian win had the weather stayed away. Clint McKay was probably not among the eight best bowlers in the country, yet here he was making the English look a bit shaky.

There were many rumours floating around about England in Victoria: Graeme Swann was getting too big for his boots, the players had tried to visit every late night bar there was, they were letting their eye off the prize. None of this, real or otherwise, helped Victoria get the win. England were probably happy to get the draw.

The highlight of the game for me, other than just being back at the G, was Jayde Herrick. Herrick looked like an extra from a Vin Diesel action film. He was bald, wore a headband, had two massive stars tattooed on his elbows, earrings, evil eyes and a soul patch. He looked every bit the angry fast bowler. If I'd had Warne's phone number, or any contact with Warne at all, I'd have told him to mention Herrick. Not because I thought he was good enough to play Test cricket, but just because he'd make it more fun.

Being in my home town I also had to meet up with family,

friends and everyone else. That was all fine, but every time I met someone new they asked if I was Australian. Apparently I now sounded English to them. Not to my family and friends. To them I sounded like me. But to new people. I met one person, who'd been introduced to my mother and father before chatting to me, who then asked me where I was from. I said Melbourne.

"Oh, just you have an accent."

"I live in London now."

"Why didn't you keep our accent?"

"How would I do that?"

He just stared at me blankly. I knew what he was doing; he was calling me UnAustralian, the fat-faced fucker. It was then I realised that in the UK I was Australian and in Australia I was British. He wasn't the first to say it, and he wouldn't be the last. After telling one person I was Australian, she looked me up and down, like she was looking for proof of my ethnicity. What was she looking for, Australian brands, a bulge of Australian penis, my strong British hips? It was weird. Just before I left for Australia I was at a buck's party and was called the most quintessential Aussie ever. My Aussie friends said I sounded like the same asshole I always did. I'd much rather be known as that asshole. I've earned that. I wasn't born an asshole; it took years.

The week back at home was spent with my mother. She had brought me up to be a very independent kid. I was taught to cook and clean at an early age. I had to make my own way to whichever sport I was going to, and I started buying my own bats at 12. Now that I was back, though, all this was different. It was much closer to the sort of treatment Big Daddy gets from women. Had I known that all I had to do was move to the other side of the world to get it, I might have done it sooner. I caught up with no one in Melbourne other than my parents and Gideon, so I travelled out to the suburb of Lara to spend time with Big Daddy, his fiancée Nicki and his two little girls.

While I was there I dreamt about Alastair Cook only once: he was a postman who delivered to the whole city and I was doing a documentary on him. It was even less exciting than his batting.

PERTH

When I'm on planes I think about how the plane will crash. It isn't a fear of flying thing, as I don't mind flying. I just think about death so that if something weird happens on the plane I won't have to think about death. I'll have already made peace with dying and leaving my wife, family and friends. I think about what I have achieved, what I have tried to achieve, at least one really kinky sex story and then work out how the plane will crash.

I have no favourite way; my wife makes me watch those air crash investigation programmes, so I have many modes of technical or man-made disaster to choose from: faulty hatches that rip off and slice the plane in two; engines catching fire and taking off a wing; some sort of gas knocking out the crew whilst you slowly float until you crash; the pilot making one of those fatal errors when he forgets to flick a switch over; a problem during take-off that means you crash soon afterwards; the rudder having a mind of its own and death-spiralling you to the ground. Or my personal favourite: the mid-air collision. I think that if you are going to go down, that is the one. If for no other reason than it will look great on *Air Crash Investigation* when they recreate it digitally.

This might sound morbid and wrong. Fantasising about your own death is rarely seen as a positive experience. But it just makes things simpler for me. I can sit down with a book or listen to podcasts and not worry about the bumpiest of flights, or about any sudden problems that might occur. On this trip I'd made an art form out of only flying during storms, and without my system I might have had some moments of occasional worry. Turbulence couldn't hurt me, though, when I'd already thought about the plane breaking up into a thousand pieces.

After Adelaide, I assumed that many Australian fans felt the same way as I did about their team. It was an unfortunately English way to think about things, but after two Tests the Australian fans must have come to understand why the English fans had been so negative for years. With the selection stuff-ups, failed promotions, terrible planning, bowlers and batsmen out of form, and fielding becoming a serious problem, a few of them would be bracing themselves for the worst outcome: a summer where Australia did not win a Test.

Although Australia were an emotional mess, I thought they could win at the WACA. Not the series. The Test. England hadn't looked quite right against Victoria in the tour game. They were off, not quite there and they looked like they were all hung -over from Adelaide. Stuart Broad was their most economical bowler and he was going home. Finn was taking wickets but going for hundreds of runs, Swann would not be a factor at all in Perth and James Anderson had been around the world and given a press conference where he said he wasn't tired whilst he looked really tired.

Add to all of that the fact that Australia could now pick four quick bowlers without any fear. Sure, Hilditch had said that Beer would play, but he hadn't cleared that with Chappell yet, and the WACA was finally looking quick.

The WACA is like an old rock star. It's from another era, falling apart, rough, ugly, but people still flock to it, and it lives on past glories. This Test I was hoping for the sort of WACA pitch that I now feared we had all made up in our minds. Blood and carnage. I wanted giant cracks to open up and be filled with blood and broken bones once again. That is how I and many people remember the WACA, but that wasn't what this ground was like anymore. It hadn't been like that for a long time.

The talk before the WACA Tests used to be about fast bowlers and death. Now all you hear are the same whispers before each Test of how the pitch was now quicker and more like the WACA of old. It was a sly admission that they let the pitch get slow, but then a positive smiley face on the fact that it was quick again. I'd heard about this new, quick square for so long that I no longer even believed there was a new square. I think some cricket administracrat just started talking about it so that there would be positive publicity going into the match, meaning more ticket sales, and then they would produce the same flat, dull, shitty excuse for a WACA pitch in the hope that on the last day they might get an extra 1,000 people there.

This is a pathetic way to deal with a legend.

In music, rock legends end up making jingles, playing at birthdays, endorsing butter in stupid ads, or in Vegas performing to people who were too afraid to see them when they were young, virile, and dangerous. The WACA has suffered that same sad fate.

The pitch was now friendly enough at certain times to allow old ladies to face random quick bowlers at lunch to win a weekend away at a day spa. I hoped for the best, because Test cricket needs pitches to start showing their individual flair, but until I saw old ladies getting hit, I wouldn't be convinced that the pitch was getting quicker.

The night I arrived in Perth, I met Sam at a traditional soccer match between the Perth Glory staff and the English cricket writers. The Glory staff won easily. I arrived just after everyone had showered, and they all looked so very tired. Dean Wilson saw me and claimed I should have played for them. I didn't think that was a suggestion that my accent had gone, but more a recognition that I was probably a tad fitter than some of the others. I assured him that having never played in a football match, I'd have been no use at all.

I was there because Sam had a rental car and had promised me a candlelit dinner with just me, him and Oli Broom, who had completed a 14-month charity bike ride from London to Australia. Instead we ended up at the Little Creatures brewery in nearby Fremantle with a bunch of English fans and expats. The steak was good, but after one night out it was quite clear that Perth was the most expensive city on earth. A pint of the beer they make there was nine bucks. It was OK, but I'd never been a huge fan of Little Creatures beer. Or any beer that costs nine bucks.

One beer, and poor Oli couldn't even afford a dinner. Clearly he hadn't been dipping into that charity money for his cross-continent ride. Silly him. He did start to tell me a story about two Dutch lesbians on his train ride from Adelaide to Perth, but, there were too many people around, and I never got to the bottom of the story.

Then there was a problem. Apparently I knew two people who live in Western Australia. One lives in Fremantle, south of where I was at that point, and one lives in Kingsley, North Perth. I confused the two people and thought I was staying with the one who lives in Fremantle. I wasn't. Sam took this the hardest, mostly because he thought he'd have to drive me to North Perth. Then we just decided that I'd stay the night with Oli, on the spare couch, as he was staying in a expat share house with the world's poshest man – so posh that when he said the word "auctioneer" it seemed to take 15 minutes to come out.

We called up the people in charge of the house, and asked if we could stay there, and it was all OK. So Sam drove me there, and then we got a call back. They thought Sam was trying to pull a swifty on them, and that the one night on the couch would really turn out to be a full week. It wouldn't, but trying to explain this to people at 11 o'clock at night after everyone involved has been drinking was never going to work, so I caught a taxi, which cost me about a million Australian dollars, to North Perth. I told the taxi driver my story; he couldn't believe it. He told me I should punch the guy.

I liked him. He was Sudanese and angry. It was a good trip as he told me about every person, mostly women, who had done him wrong over the years. It wasn't worth a million dollars, though. He knew nothing of cricket, but had had Ricky Ponting in his taxi before. So had one of my taxi drivers in Adelaide. My friend Astrid was awake when I arrived, so I talked to her and her mum for a while before falling asleep on a blow up bed that I'm sure will deflate, thinking about what percentage of Australian taxi drivers have carried Ricky Ponting.

DAY 1 – THE WACA

The air mattress stayed up, a good sign because it was the first time in my life I'd stayed on one that has. Astrid dropped me off at the station. I was desperate to get there early to get a good seat in the press tent. Perth has a very good rail network, and without sounding patronising and like I expected them all to be travelling by stagecoach, it's way better than what most cities of that size would have. It got better when I arrived at Perth central and there was a free bus straight to the WACA. You've got to like a city that gives you a free lift to the ground.

When the bus arrived I felt like I was standing in front of a ground from another era. I was born in 1980, but this ground felt like the 1970s to me. I half-expected men with proper moustaches, stubby shorts, terry towelling hats and singlets to walk past me. There was no smell, but it should have smelled of stale beer and piss. Now I see why the WACA had such a reputation; it's where I'd be filming my Aussieploitation satire one day, I was sure. I couldn't believe a Cricket Australia ground would be allowed to stay this old-feeling.

One of the few modern touches it had was a painting of the Western Warriors logo. It didn't make the ground feel any more modern; it just looked odd. There are some who will tell you it's quaint that the WACA has remained largely untouched by the modern world. I doubt that many will say that when they're using the toilets or trying to find food.

It's not structured quite like a stadium. Everything looks like it is about to fall apart, the light towers are a weird design and kind of dirty-looking, and the whole set-up reminds me more of a country show than an international cricket ground. When I finally made my way to the press tent, I still didn't have my name on a seat. Luckily it was quite obvious that no one would want to sit in the front row, as it was in the sun.

The good news was that Australia had picked four quick bowlers at last. If they'd picked four quick bowlers earlier, they'd still be losing 1-0, but at least it would have been a step in the right direction. Strauss inspected the pitch, listened to the hype, and sent Australia in. It seemed odd. The pitch was not that green, and Hauritz had taken eight wickets here a few weeks ago. Strauss' decision could have been based on the fact that Australia had no spinner.

In the first over, Shane Watson was given out. He referred the decision, and it was overturned. Perhaps I was, as Gideon Haigh described me in a Test Match Sofa interview, just someone who loved chaos. But it felt wrong. Had Watson been given out incorrectly before the review system, it would have been great theatre, a wicket in the first over on a bad call – welcome to the WACA, bitches. Instead the correct, and boring, decision was made.

Phil Hughes was at the other end. Phil and I had a history. I was his defender. Often his only one. Whilst the whole world crapped on about how he couldn't play the short ball, I'd defended him. I thought Hilditch dropped him because of pressure from the media, and that his Test record was still quite good, and that he didn't have a problem with the short ball. I should probably rephrase that – he didn't have any more of a problem with the short ball than he did with any other ball. Because his technique was like a collection of tail-enders and small children all playing shots at once, his problems seemed to come from short balls, wide balls, full balls and straight balls. He'd also got out to balls down the leg-side. He didn't appear to have any deficiency against spinners, but he hadn't had to face them that much in his career, unless you counted Paul Harris. And no one did.

The talk of Hughes and the short ball went back to when Steve Harmison bounced him out in the game against the English Lions before the 09 Ashes. He was then bounced out by Flintoff in Cardiff. Both were nasty throat balls, played by Hughes as if he had never seen a short ball before. Since then Hughes had got out to one short ball in seven innings in Test cricket, and that was a short ball down the leg-side he was trying to pull.

Hughes had got out driving many times. But, and this is the special thing about people who play the short ball in an ugly way, it still got blamed on the short ball. People said, "Sure, that was a length ball that he tried to slap through the covers, but if it wasn't for the short ball that rattled him, he would have been further forward." Of course, that could happen to any batsman, short balls push you back in the crease even if you're a good player of short-pitched bowling. But that just doesn't fit the narrative.

So let's look at the over. The first ball was short of a length, and was defended in Hughes' typical awkward style. The next ball was about the same length; Hughes dropped his hands on it easily. The third ball was way too short, and Hughes got under it with time to spare. The fourth was fuller, and a cracker; it squared Hughes up, and he edged it past gully for two. The fifth ball was full again, and a real cracker, and the only thing Hughes could do was miss it.

And then the last ball. A full ball again, and Hughes played the sort of shot even Christian fundamentalists would abort. It was a weird, ugly drive-like shot that he never got close to, and he was clean bowled. His weight was on his front foot when it happened.

Hughes' biggest problem seemed to be that he no longer believed his technique was right. Whether that was because of Harmison and Freddie, the media, or even the way he was dumped after failing in two Tests, he just didn't seem to be the same Hughes who smashed Makhaya Ntini, Dale Steyn, Jacques Kallis and Morne Morkel around South Africa. In the Shield match before the Test, Hughes had made four and a duck; before that, in first-class cricket going back to September when he played for Hampshire, he had scores of 10, 48, 81, 2, 39, 12, 5, 4, 11, 38, 1, 11 and 2. The 81 had come in Hobart against the English second-string attack that included Chris Tremlett. That, and the undefeated 86 he'd made in the ten-wicket win over New Zealand the previous March, was almost enough to put a case forward for him. But if you'd dropped him against England because he handles the short ball badly, why would you recall him to play against them at the WACA? It didn't make much sense.

Almost immediately, Ponting was out caught by Collingwood – an instant classic. How I'd love to field in the WACA slips one day so I could dive like that; sure, I wouldn't catch it, but it'd still be worth it. Ponting had played an angled bat shot to a wide ball on the WACA from Anderson. I think that would be ruled as a suicide, like running into the middle of a freeway.

I tried to think about whether Ponting's shot was a continuation of his slide. He could argue that he was unlucky to get out to such a catch. You could say the older he got, the unluckier he got. It seemed to be less about luck and more about technical error. Clarke was out shortly afterwards, playing a similar angled bat off Tremlett, and Australia were 33 for three at drinks. Every time I said, typed or even thought of an angled bat, I heard the words in Ian Chappell's voice in my head. It's not a good way to live.

Watson was busy planting his front foot down the wicket at Finn when Finn found a yorker, and the top order had departed with only 36 runs on the board. Finn had been bullied by Watson all series, but I got the feeling that Finn was a smart guy. Even if he did once tweet about ghosts. And he knew that with Watson's leg planted he'd be able to hit it once or twice early on. Watson referred it but there was no need.

Australia brought up their fifty and the WACA crowd all but gave them a standing ovation. It was quite sad to hear.

Steve Smith came in at six. He and Hussey nervously moved the score forward. To help them out, Strauss brought on Collingwood. It was mental. I'm sure Strauss had his reasons: he was hot with the catch, he might swing the ball a bit, Collingwood was looking yummier today, or it was a hunch, but it just wasn't a good move. With Smith struggling to stay in, it being the second last over before lunch, surely he should have attacked. Get Hussey or Smith, and half the team were gone. I liked surprise part-time bowlers, but when you were this on top it seemed like the action of a captain who was trying to be unpredictable instead of going for the throat.

Collingwood's over went for two and Australia got to the break only the four wickets down. But then another disappointment: lunch was a large cardboard box filled by a company big on airport food. Unlike many others, I didn't stick around to whine; I went and paid for chicken and chips.

After lunch Smith continued to look unsteady. Even though there was always the chance that Smith could bat at six, with the score the way it was and Australia having being sent in, I'd have thought Ponting would have opted for Haddin. It was Ponting who'd said Smith couldn't bat at six, so, you know, I had some reason to think he might not actually come in then. Smith didn't last long; his technique may be stronger than Hughes', but it still wasn't right. Smith pushed too hard at one and, in my head, Ian Chappell chastised him.

When I see a technically poor bit of batting, I'm almost tempted to turn on the Channel 9 commentary to hear if Chappell is giving his normal sermon. The only thing stopping me this time was the thought of my radio being stuck on Channel 9 from then on. Those little ear radios they sell at the game, or give out for free in the press box, are the most fucken annoying things on earth. I'm glad I've never paid for them, because I've never had one that would allow me to flick between the coverage, or that could be reset by anything other than slamming it on the desk.

With Smith in difficulties, it wasn't too much of a stretch to think of Usman Khawaja. The man who started the Shield season with a double hundred but was being overlooked because he lacked the all-round skills of Smith. Some might argue that Smith lacked the all-round skills of Smith as well. Fewer people would argue against the fact that Usman had the skills, technique and temperament to bat for Australia at number six.

Usman was the new face on the scene, and because his face represented Asians, Muslims and gritty left-handers, he'd got far more press than Callum Ferguson who'd played almost 30 ODIs and averaged over 40 in them. It was pretty safe to assume that Usman would be the next batsman into this side. Some of the first reports of Usman were about how he was going to be the first Asian to play for Australia. Then someone remembered Dav Whatmore and the script was changed to first Muslim.

Whilst his religious beliefs would be the story if he got picked, perhaps the story of the moment was that while Hughes and Smith seemed to have trouble with composure and technique, Usman seemed to have problems with neither. Unlike Smith or Hughes, he'd had to wait a bit longer, but he'd performed in Shield cricket as well as either of them. He wasn't flashy, but looking at Australia's top order and its recent collapses, perhaps they needed a guy who could hold them together in a time of need. The selectors were seemingly the only people around who believed that Hughes and Smith were better options than Usman at that point.

Usman's non-selection might have had nothing to do with racism, but it could have had something to do with his playing style. On the face of it Hughes and Smith are typical Australian batsmen: they attack and take risks and back themselves to succeed. Usman was not a typical Australian batsman. He was not a natural attacker; he was more of a defensive-minded, if fluid, player. This had nothing to do with his nationality, and everything to do with the way he plays. For Usman, think Hashim Alma or Shivnarine Chanderpaul. He wasn't the sort of batsman that Australia had needed for a long time, but they might just need him now.

Australia had now lost five wickets for the first 69 runs. It was another collapse. At least they were consistent.

With Smith's dismissal, Tremlett had three wickets. Tremlett was, as they love to say, a confidence bowler (unlike all those bowlers who hate confidence). He had moved to Surrey from Hampshire before the last county season, at roughly the same time Surrey had asked me to write a column for them.

Tremlett had had a great season for Surrey, taking 48 wickets at an average of 20. My column lasted two editions and I was discarded after an Andre Nel joke (nope, not about his penis, infidelity or even attempted suicide; it was about his batting/suspension). It did mean that I saw a fair bit of Tremlett during the year, as Surrey still let me in for free, and I live five minutes' walk from the Oval. If you'd told me that Tremlett – however well he'd bowled, especially during the second half of the year – would be a factor in the Ashes, I would have slapped you.

Yes, he took a bunch of wickets, but it was in division two of the County Championship, and he was never all that inspiring. I expected Tremlett to come to Surrey and eat everyone in his path. Instead he failed to take a five-wicket haul in the whole county season. I've never checked this, but I think even I took a five-for playing division two in May. Everyone does. It's division two, and look at him: he's a fucken monster. No man has ever looked more like he was carved from stone. I was walking past the Oval one day, and he was walking the other way, and it was like I was being passed by a giant wax dummy of a 1950s John Ford cowboy. The man is huge, and it's not just height. Anyone can be tall. He is substantial, like a building or an HGH-using transvestite. Put some make-up on him, and shoot him from underneath, and you've got yourself one good-looking Hollywood villain.

You just expect him to be a kick-ass batsman-killing machine, or maybe I do because I've seen too many Westerns. I don't expect lots of small clumps of wickets, but I do expect massive breakthroughs and eight-wicket hauls where the other two batsmen have refused to come out. However, that isn't how Tremlett is. Inside this mammoth wax rock formation is a line-and-length merchant. Whether it is for Surrey, Hampshire, or England, he puts the balls there and thereabout. The wickets come, but not the big hauls.

Even today, with Australia at 69 for five, although he had been the most impressive of the bowlers, his three wickets seemed to be more of a complement to Anderson and Finn rather than those of a man who had broken the Australian top order. It was a polite three-wicket haul. Some say he is too polite; Shane Warne spent years at Hampshire trying to fire Tremlett up. You'd like to think that when Warne got really desperate he started hitting on Tremlett's mum or following him around the streets sledging him. Nothing ever seemed to fire Tremlett up. He was just more of the same, and perhaps that was the reason he had been in the wilderness for so long.

Instead of accepting him as the gentle giant capable of always chipping in with wickets, he was cast away from Test cricket for not being aggressive enough. His face and shoulders were aggressive enough for me. And we're all fucked if David Saker passes on the secret of Rodney Hogg's lunacy room (a secret fast bowlers' chamber that brought out the anger). If Tremlett started acting like Rodney Hogg or David Saker he'd take over the whole planet.

With the Australian top order collapsing after England had sent them in, you did start to question the pitch. There was talk that Michael Clarke had seen the pitch, complained about it in front of Phil Hughes or Steve Smith and was dragged off into the naughty corner by Ricky Ponting. I didn't see it as the pitch. I knew some people would say the WACA was back. Unfortunately for Australians looking for excuses, the wicket had very little to do with it.

Yes, the signs were good. It had nice pace – not scary WACA pace – and decent carry, not throat-chomping bounce. There was some help with the new ball, not just from the pitch, but from the batsmen. Clarke could get bounced by Alastair Cook in the second innings and he'd still be flinging his bat randomly at the ball looking like he is being chased by a bunch of scary flying robot snakes. Watson's dismissal never touched the pitch; Smith got a good delivery that left him, so he pushed at it like he was trying to send a rich elderly relative down a set of stairs. And Hughes was bowled by a ball that was inspired by a bouncer. The pitch was a bit quicker and bouncier than usual, as had been promised for years, but I think Australia had the ability to collapse on a far better batting pitch than this. Oh, they already had. In Adelaide.

There was a time when Australia collapsing on a surface like this would send me foaming at the mouth, batshit angry. Now

I was kind of used to it and it was no longer a problem for me; it was now more like a hug from a family member after a long flight. Luckily, another familiar feeling was to be had: the Haddin and Hussey partnership.

They looked so comfortable that I went to have a piss. As any man knows, a piss tray or collection of urinals at a sporting event is the only way to go. But on my side of the ground there was no piss tray. I had two options: portaloos, or lining up for an hour and waiting for a cubicle to become free. And as any person knows, a portaloo on a hot day is no way for a human to use the toilet, so I queued up.

While I was away it seemed that Haddin and Hussey had scored at a decent rate. There was even a moment when positive types started thinking about that partnership at the Gabba. Then that man who wasn't supposed to make an impact took the wicket of Hussey. Swann against Hussey is an interesting contest. The cool guy with the shit job versus the overachieving accountant. Hussey seemed to think he had Swann's measure, and Strauss certainly thought so from the fields he set, and yet Swann did get Hussey out.

It left Australia on the verge of something shit – 137 for six with the non-batting all-rounder to come. I actually rate Johnson's batting; I just wouldn't rely on him to get to five against anyone other than Paul Harris. Johnson's batting seemed to be at its best when he didn't think about it, as with his bowling. The trick was to stop him thinking. Maybe Australia should have a Zen coach.

Considering Mitchell was "rested" (I acted out those quotes with my hands after I wrote them) for Adelaide, and then held back from a Shield game to spend more time in the nets, his batting should have been very good. And it was. There was no working him out; all you could do was just sit back and watch. He batted the way he can, waiting for the ball to be in the zones he likes, and hitting them cleanly.

It wasn't a normal innings from him. He didn't hit a bunch of balls for fours and sixes. Instead, he mixed singles and boundaries, with one huge six off Swann. It could have been one hell of a clean-hitting partnership if Haddin had stayed with him. Instead, Haddin went for 53 and Johnson was left with the tail. 189 for 7 didn't feel great.

Johnson played a shot down the ground off Anderson that was so good the press box sighed as one. Anderson bowled a length ball on the stumps that was angling across Mitch. It was the sort of ball you left at the WACA (© Ian Chappell). Mitch just eased it down to long-on for four. It was amazing.

Siddle even joined in the party. It was as if they wanted to mock their own top order. Johnson was happy enough with singles and just sitting at the other end as Siddle handled England with ease, with a little help from the review system. Johnson crept up to fifty, finally bringing it up with a pure punch through the covers for two. Eventually he went for 62, and even he looked shocked.

Siddle kept going; clearly he enjoyed being the leading man. In one over he smashed a drive on the up and followed it with a dirty slog. Hilfy was just as annoying, hitting fours and looking settled. It was anti-climactic when he went out caught at short-leg off Swann. I was hoping for something a bit more extravagant. They'd put on 30-odd, and with Siddle's undefeated 35 Australia had managed a below par but far from terrible 268. The last five had made 166 of them.

I wondered what the Australian bowlers made of their batsmen. The bowlers were the workhorses of this side, as is often the case. Test after Test they watched their top order simply fall over, and yet remain fairly safe from any kind of demotion. The bowlers were just as inconsistent, yet they could get yanked for one bad Test. They had none of the security of the batsmen, yet were a younger and more promising unit. If it wasn't for them, today Australia wouldn't have got to 150 and the Ashes would have been over. It would have been nice if the batsmen had paid for the meals that night if nothing else.

England came in to close out the day. There wouldn't be too much angled bat work, pushing at the ball, or crazy attacking shots from Strauss and Cook. They'd just punch in at the gate, do their 12 overs and get to stumps. Harris tested Strauss, and there was a whisper that Johnson had swung the ball. I ignored all that. I knew they'd get to stumps without a wicket being lost, so I started editing *Two Pricks* and got ready to abuse Sam for talking about Phil Hughes and the short ball. At stumps England were 28 without loss, 240 behind.

Alastair Cook had cut a six. Even with all his runs and his current form, you just didn't expect Alastair Cook to cut a six. You didn't really expect him to dream about cutting a six. I don't even think he dreamed. He just came into mine and performed way better than you could expect.

After ranting at Sam, and finishing *Two Pricks*, I was looking for a night out. That night the clan who I was staying with had talked of going out. Astrid's brother David was coming back into town after years of living in some Western Australian town that I couldn't pronounce without him laughing. They seemed to be set for a big one. I was wrong. Instead, it was to be an early night in Perth; they were all yawning when I got into the car.

It did mean I'd spend time with Astrid's family, which was nice. Astrid was a unionist supporter of Kevin Rudd. She was young, smart, and Left. She had a friend named Ruth who was pretty much the same. They were great to chat shit with, which is what you need at the end of a day's cricket, even if you're not at a pub. Eventually the best thing we could do was a Hungry Jacks burger. So I ate my Hungry Jacks and chatted with them.

Life is better with Hungry Jacks, which is actually Burger King. But that's a whole other story.

Astrid's family is amazingly Australian – so Australian that even I noticed. Especially given that her father is English. They were also very easy to talk to and made you feel like you were one of them, even though I'd met almost all of them the night before for the first time and had only met Astrid once before that. They all seemed to genuinely like each other's company, and the fact that they were a family was a bonus.

When Ruth made a noise with her mouth that sounded like a tap dripping water (it really did) it started a 45-minute conversation where June, Astrid's mum, actually seemed proud and intrigued by Ruth's noise. Then it moved to other party tricks. And suddenly everyone was talking about weird noises or things they could do. I might have been in a strangely expensive early-to-sleep city, but at least I was with a family of excellent bullshitters. Plus we googled the term "Hot Carling".

It made me feel very at home.

DAY 2 – THE WACA

On the second day, my desk now booked for the Test, I slept in and caught a lift into the ground with Astrid and her family. I thought driving into the ground could get us caught up in traffic, but they seemed to think it would be fine. Two minutes in I knew why. There was no traffic. I can see why people wanted to live in this expensive city now – because no one else does. I can't say I've ever been in a city where you can drive into it on a weekday, at any time, like it's New Year's Day.

On the trip in I chatted to Astrid's dad, Michael, who has a very strong English accent and yet hates the English. He's not UnAustralian at all, yet he was born in England. He reminded me of a taxi driver I had in America years ago who was Indian, had a Ravi Shastri-type inflection on his voice, and yet talked about America like it was the only country that ever existed. By the end of the trip it was clear that Michael would be supporting Australia, and not only that but actively cheering against England. Australia has a lot of racial problems, but when Australia gets into your system, you can be from anywhere and be 'Aussie as'. It would almost have been worth getting Michael drunk so I could hear a Pom accent abuse the English while everyone around him looked confused. It was also weird that he seemed to see himself as Australian but had kept his English accent quite well, and I was happy to stay Australian and was reportedly losing my accent.

On the field there was also confusion. Harris took the edge of Strauss' bat but the ball flew between slip and the 'keeper. Watson took most of the abuse for it, even though it was clearly a 'keeper's catch. Why Haddin would sit and watch this one was beyond me. His batting may finally have found its happy place, but his 'keeping was still stuck in the naughty corner. Coming into the Test, I felt Australia could win, but perhaps they had suffered too much damage.

It meant that England could just ease themselves towards 800, or whatever they planned on making this Test. Cook and Strauss were in stiff upper lip mode, and they looked like they were setting up another platform for the rest to cash in on. It wasn't as if Australia weren't bowling well. Harris and the others were coming up with good balls, but England made it into the 70s without losing a wicket, and Australia couldn't find the breakthrough.

The magically wonderful, odd thing was that Mitchell was swinging the ball. I like to think it was like the old days when someone behind the bowler's arm noticed it first, and then it fed around the whole ground through Chinese whispers. He was definitely making it move, and not so small you need HawkEye to prove it, but real Alan Davidson hoop, the sort of old timey swing you see on cricket videos from the 1950s. For all the talk about Mitchell Johnson and swing, few have ever swung the ball less. I'd venture that Shane Warne and Shahid Afridi have swung more balls than Mitch has.

But even with the swing, England were still scoring with ease, and were just 50 or so runs away from snapping this game like a twig.

Then...

Mitchell Johnson on song is a savage accident. It is Lennie Small with a small puppy.

When you cast for an amateur film, you get many actors who come in and want to show you their range. Quizzical, scared, bored, amused, confused, horny, upset, happy, and everything else they can think of. They run through the roles while going through some heavy monologue that sounds stupid when read out of place. All these actors would be better off imitating a spell from Mitchell Johnson. The one thing I always love about Mitch is that he hides nothing.

If he is working on his action, you can see it in his face, in his arms, in his body language. The same can be said of his confusion when he aims the ball in one place and it goes to another. It starts at his forehead, trickles down his face, reaches his shoulders, and then spreads throughout his whole body. Mitch has so many tells (a facial expression that gives away that you're bluffing) that it's impossible to list them all, but if he's looking at the big screen, fiddling with something, or not looking the batsmen in the eyes, it means things aren't working for him. You can accuse him of many things, but being false isn't one of them.

Ben Hilfenhaus is the opposite. Perhaps the most visual representation of old school working-class values in Australian cricket. Hilfenhaus will deliver a cricket ball, then turn, walk briskly back to his mark and come back in and deliver the ball. When he is upset or feels unlucky, he will take a slightly wider walk – only a metre or so – back to his mark. Obviously needing those couple of extra steps just to keep his emotions in check and get ready for the next ball.

If Mitch is feeling unlucky or upset, there is not a person in the ground that doesn't know it. Now, when he is struggling, this is a horrible trait, because whilst it shows how much he cares, it also tells the batsman that he has him. The opposite is true when Mitch is playing well. It's a brilliant trait to have because *he* knows he has it, *the batsman* knows he has it, and that plays on the batsman's mind.

Today he had it. I'll never know where it goes when it isn't around, but today Mitch was chatting with the batsmen, looking them in the eyes, and looking happy. None of this was a good thing for England.

As bad as Mitch can be, he can also be that good. There is no working him out – just cut him open and weigh his organs.

When he got Alastair Cook out, the score was 78; when he got Jimmy Anderson out, the score was 187. Six for 38. The man is not real. He's a cartoon character, Inspector Clouseau with a slingy action and tongue ring. It's easier to believe he didn't do this on purpose, because if he did, what the hell has he been doing the rest of the time?

It didn't start with Cook's wicket; it started before then. And if England didn't spot it, it's only because they hadn't seen it before. Kiwi and South African batsmen would have seen it. If they were watching the TV and saw him bowling, they would have known what was coming.

The wicket of Cook was because Mitch swung the ball and did it fast. Perhaps Cook was just tired of batting and appearing in my dreams – in the latest one he was a parking officer who took me out for a drink and pointed out all the flaws in my work – but he was slow on it and drove to gully. Then Trott came in, and he did what he had done for two Tests – moved across his stumps and looked to work the ball through the leg-side to suck a bit more on the great flabby teat of Australian bowlers. Out plumb this time.

Two balls later KP was out, trapped the same way. Collingwood didn't last long, and England had been slaughtered by this smiley, nice, tattooed man; the man they laughed at and mocked; the man about whom they had all wondered why he was picked at all. In a few overs he'd shown them what he could do, and they were reeling.

England had been OCD-organised for this tour. They'd worked out every tiny detail in advance, and when something new came along, like Siddle's six-for, they came up with a plan for that as well. It was a brilliant machine. The thing is, you can't plan for Mitchell swinging the ball, and you can't handle it like a professional when he does.

You can build a solid brick-house, have security cameras installed, build a panic room, have a good alarm, put bars on the windows, get metal doors, have an impenetrable roof, and do everything in your power to make sure that no one can break in. But you can't stop someone burning the bastard down.

And that was what Mitchell did. Plans are useless – all you can do is try to put out the fire.

For me, Mitch's spell stirred something deep. It started before I even saw him. The use of the words "once in a generation" made me keen to know more. When I first saw him I didn't think much of him; he was just a dumb kid and he wasn't what I was looking for. Unlike the rest, I never fell for the left-arm types; I don't care what arm you use as long as you use it well. Then he disappeared, and I must admit that I barely gave him a second thought. When he came back I thought it was a bit weird, but then when he made it to the top level it really annoyed me. This dude had been driving a van for a plumber instead of trying to please me; why would I want him around? It didn't matter by this point; he was in my life whether I wanted him or not.

This, and his constant wide deliveries, really got to me. Every time Lee or Clark put the pressure on, this young buck with a stupid piercing would come on and let it all off. Then he got better. He still bowled wide, but he took wickets as well. Without noticing my feelings change, suddenly it became apparent that I really liked him. The two old guys meant very little to me; it was all about Mitchell.

By the time he took South Africa down on their own soil early in 2009, he was the only one I wanted. Leading into that year's Ashes I wasn't worried about too much: just that Mitchell would get injured. I couldn't stand the thought that he'd get hurt. Then it all went wrong. During the Ashes all I wanted was for him to *get hurt*.

That followed with a year of him being vile to me. Really fucken nasty at times. I tried to be nice to him, but when he goads you like that, you just can't help yourself. It was sick and wrong. We were entrapped in hatred. That is how these relationships go. You can't live with each other and you can't kill the other person by drowning them in a toilet.

This went on for the longest time, until everyone was sick of him. Finally, he was gone. The cycle of hate could end.

But he wasn't really gone. He was still around, but just not in front of me. It seemed like I could move on, find new people, and become happy without him. But it just didn't happen that way.

The other men were just as miserable as him, and he was quickly back. Way too quick for me. Then he did *this*. He'd given me so much in one day that I could barely contain myself.

Whilst I might have hated him for all the shit he brought me, when he was kind, he was very, very kind. The problem is, as good as I felt today, how would I feel in a week, a month, a year? These moments of bliss wouldn't last. He'd quickly become abusive to me again. It would turn ugly. I'd abuse him. We'd try to make life as painful as possible for each other.

The cycle was set to continue. I spoke out because I feared I was not the only one.

Of all the wickets, Collingwood's was the one that stood out. It was amazing that a man that could take a catch like the one that dismissed Ponting, which required such quick reflexes and amazing athleticism, could then look so old when batting. It felt like he played his shot a good minute after the ball was bowled. I wasn't sure I'd seen a top-order batsman look that slow before. There was no doubt in my mind that he couldn't handle the pace of Test cricket anymore. Perhaps he'd stick around and make some runs against some other teams, but I couldn't see how he could make a run against South Africa or Australia in a Test.

He just looked old. It was a shame, because as frustrating as Collingwood could be to watch, the man was grit. I wish I didn't have to watch him bat, but I admired everything about the way he had made himself into a Test cricketer by just being more determined and gutsy than everyone else. He's going to be one of those cricketers that future generations ask old bastards about and say, "How did he play this long and why do people talk about him like he's good?" This was it for him though, whether he knew it or not. He'd always struck me as a proud man, but if he watched the replay of this wicket he would feel sick to the stomach. It was no way for a fighter to get out. It was hard for me to watch.

It was also true that England had outgrown Collingwood. Much like the way the Australian team outgrew Geoff Marsh years ago. When you are fragile and unsure of yourself, you need someone like Collingwood. England were no longer either. There was no team in world cricket that knew itself better than England, and even though they had collapsed here, they were surely not the fragile team that they had once been. Having

Collingwood in this team was insurance you were paying for that you might never need, and which might not cover you anyway.

That Collingwood continued to bat ahead of Ian Bell was just obscene. Bell's rise had mirrored England's. He was dropped after the "quaker in Jamaica", when it looked like he was being strung up for his part in England's total of 51. Since then he had become more professional, smarter, better, and as complete a batsman as there was in world cricket. Few had been harder on Bell than me. And perhaps that is why I refused to believe that a middling series in South Africa had changed him. He had changed, though, because as England fumbled and bumbled their way around on this pitch and against a fired-up Australian attack, he looked cooler, calmer, and more like a Test player than any of his team-mates.

Matt Prior, meanwhile, was done by Siddle in an embarrassing way. Siddle had again been forced to bowl to a stupid plan by Ponting. It was similar to the decision to bowl Collingwood before lunch. If you have them struggling, don't resort to odd plans – trust your bowlers. This one was a round-the-wicket, short-ball-at-the-ribs plan. They then changed it to an over-the-wicket, short-ball-at-the-ribs plan. It worked – mostly due to luck – but so could Siddle bowling at off stump and trying to get a bit of swing. Instead, the ball bounced off several parts of Prior's body and ended up hitting the stumps.

This was when the talk really heated up. You could see Australia starting to chat to England, and getting more and more aggressive as the wickets fell. Prior and Hilfenhaus seemed to exchange words. You could also see Australian fielders do that familiar aggressive clapping and walking towards the batsmen, as if they could smell a victory. If they still knew what that smelled like.

When Prior was out, he and Siddle were involved straightaway. Siddle, happy that his plan had accidently worked, was in the ear of Prior, who turned on his way off the field to tell Siddle of his displeasure at the words being spoken to him. Then Ponting went over and tried to settle the situation down. But, as only Ponting can, he made it worse and the whole thing looked ugly on TV.

Once the tail was exposed, Australia brutally wiped it away. Swann made 11, Tremlett 2, Anderson 0 and Bell fell for 53. Harris helped as well; his wicket of Strauss stopped Strauss from performing any sort of sensible rearguard partnership with Bell. His three wickets were all with sensible balls moving away from batsmen. It wasn't as glamorous as Mitch's thudding into the pads for a series of leg-befores, but he deserved some reward after Adelaide. It also looked like he could repeat it again, unlike Mitch. England's 187 put them 81 behind Australia, which was not the end of the world. No one ever jumped off a bridge for an 81-run deficit in the first innings.

What was more noticeable was the collapse; it was Australian, very Australian. None for 78 and you don't make 200; had I seen that scorecard without England's name on it I would have just assumed it was Australia's. The innings was like two different stories: calmly, calmly let's accumulate, and oh shit, they're bombing us, run for the hills.

Australia's second innings started pretty quietly. Watson was introspective and Hughes bouncy and full of useless energy. While Hughes was batting, Brett from The Roar, a well-known Australian sport website, had alerted me to a tweet. Brett was a good guy, and, it should be said, a far better first-time user of the press box than I was even after all this time. Brett had just decided to follow the Ashes and had convinced the website to let him write a column during it.

Brett would get around the press box, introduce himself to people and chat to anyone. He wasn't a full-time writer; he was just a guy who saw an opportunity to travel around with the Ashes and eat lunch with Michael Holding and Ian Botham. Brett was rarely cowering on the corner table with Sam and I. He was even using frequent flyer points to get around. It was all class. Now he was giving me a story, which was also class.

While Hughes had been hopping around the crease and the other journos had already written the story of how the short ball had got him out, Brett had seen what Steve Bernard, the Australian team manager, was tweeting. You see, if you're following someone on Twitter, you see all their normal tweets, but if they tweet directly to someone you aren't following, it doesn't come up in your timeline, so you can easily miss it. It is public, though, and easily readable from their public timeline. Why Brett was reading Steve Bernard's timeline I have no idea – his tweets were coma-inducing on a good day. Perhaps he just needed something to bring him back to earth after Mitch's bowling.

The tweet was:

"stevebernard37@shanebrien this will be a stern test for Hughes. His form has been poor, but he's trying to work his way through it at the moment."

Brett, like me, found it weird that while Hughes was out in the middle batting, the Australian team manager was pointing out that he was in bad form. Although what was weirder was that someone in Australian cricket was admitting that he was in bad form to begin with. That comment was completely out of character for the Australian team bubble, where everything was fine and would be forever. The good news for Hughes was that his problem wasn't the short ball at all; it was his shitty form.

How nice that the Australian team had decided to give the kid a chance to reclaim his form while playing Test cricket for his country. Perhaps when Australia was a more hostile and harsher country, we would have told Hughes to fuck off, and picked someone else, but instead they'd hugged Hughes to their loving bosom. Hughes' scores coming into the Test certainly showed that he was in shit form. It was a dick move.

And then Hughes got out to Finn, edging one to third slip. The ball before had been a bouncer – case closed for most writers. Finn's return to the attack also woke Watson up and he smashed anything that wasn't perfect. With Finn, that was a lot. Like a few of the New McGraths, Finn didn't have the control of Glenn McGrath, mostly because he was human.

Watson's pull shot is like an 80s action film. I think Jean Claude Van Damme would play it. It's masculine, but somehow also a bit effeminate. Perhaps it's the pose at the end, or the way Watson looks at the ball as it sails away. It says, "I can hit it hard, but I appreciate its beauty." Much like Van Damme in *Bloodsport* when he finishes kicking ass to then tell his hetero friend that he loves him before whispering something sweetly into his ear. The shot is just wonderful to watch. The English bowlers were certainly testing him on it, but he hit it so cleanly you'd doubt he could ever get out to it. At times it seemed as if Finn was bowling just so that Watson could smash it, so that Finn too could just sit back and watch it.

Ponting's innings was more like Steven Seagal's career after the mid-90s. He failed to believe it wasn't working. His first shot was ropey, he fended at balls with his bat hanging away from his body, got hit on the body and then had the ball brush something down the leg-side that England were convinced was out. Ponting was unmoved, but when the review came through it showed he'd got a bit of glove on the ball.

Just unlucky I guess.

It was at this point that you saw the complete difference between Michael Clarke and Ricky Ponting. Ponting had gloved a ball at a key time; he must have known he'd touched it, yet he stood tall, and waited for the review to come through. Afterwards he didn't tweet to apologise – there was no apology at all – and the fact he didn't walk and wasted all our time instead was never mentioned in the press. I couldn't see Ponting ever apologising for not walking, or for waiting for a review. He was out there to win a Test, not friends.

Clarke started with a four. The man was under pressure, his back was still sore, the world had turned on him, his apology had made him a joke and with Australia losing the last Test because of how quickly they folded, his wicket to KP was one of the most significant fuck-ups of his life. This meant he was nervous and keen to do well, so he came out all guns blazing after years of trying to bat more calmly. He punched through cover and mid-off, cashed in down the leg-side, a smashing shot square of the wicket, and he even played a slightly out-of-control hook shot, which he is not known for. He was scoring at more than a run a ball, but the English weren't worrying. He couldn't keep this up, and even with this good start, he didn't seem to be that comfortable.

Off Tremlett, he tried to punch another one through the covers – well, I think that is what he was trying to do. Instead he just helped the ball back onto his stumps while looking like he'd just dropped his mum's favourite vase. He'd managed to be 20 off 17 balls, but I didn't think his strike rate would help him with the media. It was sad to watch him leave the field, but this was the innings of a man with a bad back who was afraid to fail again. While he walked off I tried to think of a time when Ponting might have looked as guilty as Clarke did on getting out.

They really were two different species.

Hussey came out, and Australia had their two form batsmen at the crease. But he was circumspect while Watson went about his business. Then Swann came on and, as it had been all series, Swann was Hussey's aphrodisiac, the left-hander instantly attacking him. He just looked like he wanted to beat Swann up, in a cricket sense.

England weren't looking as confident as they should have. They should have been striving for that extra wicket that would ensure that they would only have to chase a small total. Instead, they looked a little pissy with each other. When there was a good bit of fielding, they weren't running the full length of the field to line up and pat that fielder on the ass. Their ass-patting manual was being ignored. Perhaps it was just tiredness, or anger after the collapse. I mean, who really wanted to pat the ass of a player for good fielding when earlier in the day that same player had walked across his stumps to give Mitch such a target?

Watson and Hussey looked hungrier and more focused. It could have been that England expected Watson to get out in the morning anyway – I don't think anyone really believed he was going to get a huge score – and they'd given up on getting Hussey out. At stumps Australia were 119 for three. Hussey and Watson had turned it around quickly and Australia were now 100 runs from putting this game into the "too hard" basket for England.

Sam and I *Two Pricked*. I talked about cutting Mitchell Johnson open, you know, just to see what was in there. I also threatened Sam with a punch to the throat if he fucked up my opening monologue. A member of the cleaning staff walked through the shot between us and the camera, confirming to us once and for all that we really didn't look like a real production.

After some hasty editing we walked into Perth in search of that rare beast, the cheap late dinner option. Somehow we found a café that had good beer, affordable (for Perth) meals and was open. The call went out, and soon Oli Broom (his ass finally recovered from his cycling across the world) and Jon Norman, a producer with Talksport, turned up. They were followed quickly by Andrew Miller, while I ate barramundi and chips. The place shut so early that we had to work out Miller's order before he got there. It was payback for him doing it for us in Adelaide, but at least it was late there; here, it was only about 8pm.

It was a good night, but Perth still had its way with us. After a good couple of hours we were suddenly told by a huge bald man with a hare lip that the café was shutting. It was only ten. But when we looked around we realised that Perth had shut. Astrid had already texted me to say she was going to sleep. I then went looking for a taxi, which I figured should be easy as everyone else seemed to be asleep as well, and it was. Unfortunately, in the taxi I remembered that I hadn't done my Cricinfo column with professional humorist Alan Tyers.

I started to write it as the taxi driver (I never did ask him if he'd ever driven Ricky Ponting) jumped through what seemed like red lights. Eventually the laptop hit the door hard, just as I'd emailed off my poorly-written barely-thought-out copy. The laptop went black. I should have been upset; instead, I was over the moon. I felt like a real journalist. Drunk in the back of a taxi writing some bullshit I wouldn't remember the next day and breaking my computer. It was like the moment you got your first sex injury and suddenly realised that you were a pervert.

The downside was that *Two Pricks* wouldn't be able to go up that night. I texted this information to Sam. I figured that if I called him he'd just cry and I'd feel bad. I still sort of feel bad – it was the first time I'd really lied to Sam.

DAY 3 – THE WACA

The next morning, the computer wouldn't turn on for a while, which suggested that whilst I had used it as a bit of a fake excuse to get out of work, it was actually hit very hard the night before. Damn fake alibi coming true. It was a good day though, as Australia could square the series and make the Melbourne Test relevant. Astrid was driving in again, and there was also the excellent realisation that my wife would be arriving in Melbourne in about 36 hours, and this Test was definitely not going to last five days so I could fly home early.

All of this passed through my mind until I saw the freeway we were travelling on: the Graham Farmer Freeway. Graham, or Polly as he was known to me, was an Aussie rules legend who could handball (punch) the ball further than people could kick it. The legend goes, and this is all that is important, that when he was playing in Western Australia, a representative from the Geelong footy club wanted to get in touch with him, and was told all he had to do was call the switchboard and they'd put him in touch as everyone in Perth knew Polly. I always liked that story as it made Perth sound like a small hamlet where this one giant Aboriginal bloke walked around like a god. Now they'd named a freeway after him. He still owned Perth, almost 50 years on. Although he didn't really own Perth; Bill Gates probably couldn't afford to own Perth.

When I arrived at the ground, I set up the camera for a

time-lapse shot of the crowd filling up on the grass bank. After a few minutes there was a head peering over my shoulder. It was Philip Pope, one of Cricket Australia's media guys. After we established that it was my camera and I was indeed filming, he told me I wasn't allowed to film the crowd. I accepted this and turned the camera off. Then seconds later his head popped back on top of me again, even closer, so I had to sort of crane my head away when I talked to him to avoid kissing him.

"You're obviously part of the family, but we don't want the others seeing what you are doing and thinking they can do it."

Other than the general weirdness that comes when a man you know professionally whispers gently in your ear that you're family, this could have been the end of *Two Pricks*. It was impossible to think that they hadn't seen us filming beforehand. We'd filmed in the press box, on the ground, in front of the media centres, behind the media centres and no one had come up to us. Not to mention that Pope and other Cricket Australia media staff had sat next to me in the press box while I'd edited footage, and we have two cameras on our desk at all times. It seemed weird that three Tests in they suddenly told us not to film. In all our videos we'd never shown a ball and surely Channel 9 didn't care about two blokes strolling around the outer and getting the odd shot of an Australian rain dance or a dude dressed up like a Swann. If we'd started showing the cricket, I could have understood it, but a crowd shot that anyone with a camera phone could upload in minutes was hardly cause for a slow sensual whisper in my ear. Cricket Australia, however, did care about it, and even asked to approve any photo used for an Ashes book. Stalin would have been proud.

When Sam came in we had a quick crisis meeting. We decided to stop the crowd shots. *Two Pricks* had just found an audience, this wasn't the time to end it because we broke the rules, even if the rules were stupid and pointless. The fans that we weren't allowed to film looked quite excited after the previous day, their summer of suck replaced by "Magic" (now you see him, now you don't) Johnson's spell. There was more strut in the waddle of the fans as they came in. Australia were back; Mitchell was back; the world was right again.

It was a flight of fancy. At the press conference Mitchell had admitted that he hadn't worked on swing, or really tried that hard to get swing, or even known how he had got swing. You could explain his spell by him essentially shrugging his shoulders and saying, "Jolly Gosh, I don't know how it happened, but I am happy it did, gee willikers." Whilst his honesty was refreshing, it was also kind of sad. This man had so much pressure on him, and even in a moment like this he had to know that the chances of him getting it right again were about 50-1.

England started the day's play with three men out on the boundary for Watson. Modern captains might spend too much time looking at analyses of where bad balls are hit. It was the start of the day, Watson restarted his innings like a kid entering a house of horrors, we know he barely converts fifties into hundreds, so how about a touch of pressure? Get in his face; make him think of something other than not mis-hitting a rubbish ball to a sweeper. It's not just Strauss: modern captains are all about keeping the runs down by putting sweepers out. Tremlett looked their best bowler in this game, and doesn't bowl a lot of four balls, so why start him with a scattered field to a bad starter?

It was clear that England had been studying fielding positions all night when Anderson bowled to Watson with a 7-2 field, mid-on and deep midwicket the only two fielders on the leg-side. How much say Anderson had in this was unknown, but he continually targeted the pads and Watson cashed in. If Anderson also thought this was a bad idea, bowling on the pads was a quick way to end it.

Watson was looking good, and over the last couple of years when he had turned from someone who thought he deserved to be worshipped to someone who demanded to be worshipped, his body language had changed. For years if Watson hit a big shot he immediately posed for every camera in the ground. Sometimes the ball would have landed, been passed to a fielder by someone in the crowd and slowly walked back in to the bowler, and Watson would still be in pose.

Now, he had grown. There was still the occasion where he posed. But he'd also got the macho Matthew Hayden walk.

It was the big swinging dick walk that has been used in Hollywood and playgrounds for years. He knew he was the shit. "That's right, I smacked that, and if you're not careful, I'll smack the shit out of you too." It was all part of the reinvention of Shane Watson from being everyone's target for abuse, to Australia's best player. His promotion to opening the batting still didn't quite work or make sense in Test cricket, but since he had come back, he had been Australia's marquee player. Before, he was the player who was repeatedly picked when he never performed, seemed to be on the verge of crying at all times, and when he did something right he'd pose for an hour, but most of the time he'd just be injured.

There were also the press conferences outlining exactly where he was in his rehab, what changes he'd made to his action, how he'd taken up Pilates, or what his latest approach to batting would be. It was endless. The thing is, the first time I'd really had any contact with Watson was in a press conference, and he'd seemed like a nice guy. Sure, I'd heard all the stories from other players and press who thought he was a wanker. And I'd read and written the bad press about him for years. But in person, he just seemed like a largely unaffected, if vain, man.

I'm sure he still took longer to put his hair into a gentle manly bouffant, and he even waxed his chest and used moisturiser, but for all his faults, he was now liked by the Australian public. The Australian public will mainly overlook every flaw if someone is really damn good. His broad shoulders, surfer hair, and chiselled physique barely ever won anyone over, but start pulling the ball off the front foot, taking the odd big haul of wickets and making regular runs, and suddenly you're the man.

I think he might also have something that people like: no bullshit. Built like he is, with the power he has, and the pace he once had, he could have pretended to be a badass. He didn't. In fact, like it or not, Watson is always Watson. Watching him in a press conference you got more real reactions than you got from the entire English team. Watson was just Watson. In the past I'd seen this as a bad thing. But being in press conferences day after day, I'd fallen for him. Watson just seemed honest. Sometimes that made him an asshole, sometimes a douchejuice and sometimes an easy target. But after weeks of seeing him up close, I realised I preferred an honest bloke who occasionally was an asshole, to someone who just repeats the word "execute" or talks only about plans and units.

That didn't mean that Watson would stop pissing me off now I'd learned to live with him. Because of him I would owe Sarge 100 bucks from the bet before the series, and I knew he wouldn't make his hundred today. I could just smell it. You know you've watched too much cricket when you can accurately predict when someone will get out based on their body language, but the minute he took his helmet off while the sightscreen, flapping around like a hose, was fixed, I feared he wasn't going to get his century. It could have been my imagination, but his neck looked like it was twitching and he seemed to be thinking the malfunction was a conspiracy to defraud him of the landmark. He was on 93, and as good as he had looked, this couldn't have happened at a worse time for him. He was not a man that played well after stoppages or in his 90s – combine the two and you've got his worst nightmare.

Watson had faced four balls after the sightscreen stuff-up when Tremlett hit him in front, and the finger went up, Watson on 95. He reviewed it. Perhaps out of hope. Or because he loves a review: this is his second in this Test. It was definitely out. He then spent 28 minutes walking off the ground. Nothing annoys me more than a batsman walking off the ground slowly. You're out: fuck off. Don't trudge, even in your 90s. I know it hurts, in fact I can see it hurts by your face, but the trudge off the ground by Watson is the one thing I will never be able to get past.

It's hypocritical of me to like him for being honest and then slam him for walking off in a disappointed fashion, but like most humans and several animals, I am a hypocrite. When he does it I secretly want the zombie apocalypse to start right then, with one of the undead slowly walking up behind him and biting his flesh and feasting on his organs. Sadly, I know that a slow-moving – traditional – zombie would never get past the security guards.

There was no zombie, but instead an excitable young vampire in Steve Smith came to the crease. Tremlett tried to stab him in the heart first ball; Smith didn't seem to see it. From there on, Smith top-edged, missed, periscoped and reviewed his way along. The longer the innings went, the more he proved that he and number six may not be the perfect match. Smith and Hussey got to lunch, Hussey with ease, Smith with luck.

Graeme Swann hadn't bowled an over yet today.

After lunch Smith started to play some more assured shots, and two hours and 20 minutes into the day Swann came on. It looked like Swann had been hidden from Hussey. Obviously the pitch was an issue as well, but I felt it was more than that. There seemed to be some odd tension between Swann and Strauss. You kept hearing rumours about Swann becoming the new Flintoff in the changing room.

You often hear rumours about players' sexuality, how they met their wife in a threesome, or how a player was stopped from sledging by an opposition player threatening to out their infidelity via the stump mic. Who knows what to believe, but there did seem to be some less-than-loving body language from Swann to his captain. It could just have been the 30 overs he hadn't bowled, or maybe Strauss used his box.

John Stern, the kind and soft-spoken editor of *The Wisden Cricketer*, who would be acting as Jonathan Agnew's autograph mule when the Test finished, thought it had something to do with Strauss not stopping a single at short cover. Stern was clearly only giving me this information because he hadn't seen how I'd taken the piss out of him on the latest *Two Pricks*.

England had decided to bowl short to Smith. You'd think bowling outside off stump to someone as eager to hit the ball as Smith would be the way, but the WACA does weird things to bowlers. That bounce is Viagra, and suddenly every batsman has a weakness with the short ball. Tremlett came round the wicket to him and tried to do what my old man would call armpit bowling. Tremlett round the wicket to Smith didn't last that long as he gloved one behind and left us with a bizarre 36 to dissect. Was he lucky to get to 36, or unlucky to fall for 36? Was he lucky to be in the team, or unlucky that he'd played as a batsman and bowler in different Tests and looked like neither?

There was talk that Tremlett had bowled a back-foot

no-ball, the rarest of no-balls, far rarer than even the three-men-behind-square-on-the-leg-side no-ball. It happened so infrequently that I doubt umpires even looked for it. No fuss was made by Channel 9, so it probably meant that it wasn't one.

With Smith gone, Australia had a lead of over 330. Because of a Test at the WACA against South Africa two years ago when Australia let the Saffas yawn their way to 400, people were bringing up the subject of large chases. No one really believed it though – this wasn't the same pitch – even if that was when the Saffas were opened up with Mitchell Johnson's other kick-ass spell.

Haddin started with a slogged six off Swann, but was out to Tremlett one run later. The six from Haddin, though, was enough for Strauss to dump Swann again and go for Collingwood. It seemed like another bizarre move. Not because Collingwood shouldn't be bowling – the new ball was less than ten overs away – but if you were to bowl him and Swann in tandem, they'd get through the ten overs quicker together, ready for another assault with the new ball.

Mitch came out with four men on the boundary. For Tremlett to Hussey, there were five men out. That Mitch got caught at cover off Collingwood made the field placing seem all the more redonkulous. But it was the kind of wicket that captains love because it looked like it was a brilliantly-conceived decision. It also meant Australia's tail would have to face the new ball.

None of this stopped Hussey, who kept chugging along milking England to bring up his hundred. Hussey hardly even noticed when Ryan Harris got out to the most obvious plan in world history: short balls at the WACA with men in the deep.

Then Swann, still looking a bit sulky, dropped Siddle at short cover. Not one English player went up to him. In a team that would pat your bum when you threw the ball to the bowler at a good height, it was a big change. Perhaps Swann was annoying them all. Perhaps their rule book said no ass patting for dropped catches. Or they might just have already checked out of this match and wanted to save all their ass patting for Melbourne.

Siddle eventually went to Anderson, for his 200th Test

wicket, and Hussey finally fell for that short-ball trap for 116, giving Tremlett a five-wicket haul. Not a bad comeback for the big man, who could expect some more comments about how huge he is from Andrew Miller in the future (Miller flirts with Tremlett at the pressers). Swann did the sprinkler dance after catching Hussey, and I ask you, was it bad form to do the sprinkler when your team needed 391 to retain the Ashes? It may not be too much by modern standards, but it seemed too much at this ground.

The sprinkler, for anyone who hasn't seen it, is a dance ripped off from *A night at the Roxbury*, one of Will Ferrell's early films. It involves you putting your left arm on your head, and moving your right arm around like a sprinkler moving around a lawn. It has so far become far more of an internet sensation this Ashes than *Two Pricks* has.

Australia didn't start with Mitch. To those who hadn't spent years watching him play, it seemed odd. To those who had, it seemed normal. Mitch and the new ball have rarely got along. It's generally felt that he wastes it. It's better in the hands of the men who will try to get the most out of it, rather than the guy who won't know what he is doing with it. It's like he acts differently when he has it, and it seems easier just not to give it to him and risk him losing the plot again.

Some were saying that because Mitch failed with the bat, his bowling would suffer. If only Mitch were that simple to work out. Andrew Miller stopped thinking about Tremlett's impressive physique for a second to look into this theory: when Mitch took his last ten-wicket match haul, he made a pair. I looked into it more closely and discovered that his other ten-wicket match haul was at the WACA when he made only 18 and 21. If anything, the analysis proved conclusively that Mitch loves the WACA and in every other way is impossible to try and work out.

With no wickets and only gentle swing on offer, though, he came on for the sixth over. Straight away he was in the action, almost running out Cook with a kick at the stumps. His first over was quick, but mostly mental. He put it on the pads of Cook, was short and wide to Strauss and let through nine runs.

The good news for Australia was that unlike most bowlers, Mitch was used to the odd nine-run over and he still looked confident.

Cook did not last much longer, out to Harris from the first ball of the next over. Harris moved a fast one back into him and struck him fairly plumb in front. Unlike the review of Watson early in the day, Cook walked up to Strauss, they calmly chatted about the delivery, and then Cook walked off. Australia had removed one of their roadblocks. They had executed their skillsets all over him.

After seeing so much of Cook, in real life and via dreams, it was weird to see him fail. If I'd been a drug-taker, I probably wouldn't have accepted that this was going on in front of me. Cook was a sweatless, indestructible reptilian alien – he shouldn't have been getting out so easily. If he kept going like this, people would think he was human. Although that was probably what he was counting on. He knew England couldn't win here, so why pretend? The cunning bastard.

Or, maybe there was just something about Perth that was taking England down. For the first time since the first day at the Gabba, they looked like the side without a clear idea what to do. Perhaps Andy Flower was not here. There was no doubt that Flower was the ultimate puppet master. He was cricket's Jim Henson. Everything that had happened in this series so far was because of him. Any other England side would have lost at the Gabba, drawn at Adelaide Oval and gone down at the WACA.

Even if England were to lose here, Australia still wouldn't win two Tests (or draw one and win one). That was because of Andy Flower. He had turned a flakey outfit into a military unit. If there is a stone left unturned I'm sure he goes and turns it himself. If he is still in charge in three years England will be close to unbeatable in a series, even without any star players. It would take something special like a Sehwag innings or a Steyn bowling spell to beat them, because no other team in world cricket is going to be this prepared.

If I were the ECB, I'd have given Flower five million quid a year for five years, just to ensure that by the time he leaves,

England are so ahead of the opposition that it would take ten years for anyone to catch up. In this series he'd hardly said a word to the press, but you could see his stamp on the way England batted, fielded, talked, and played. If you watched when England clapped someone for reaching a milestone, he clapped with them, but he didn't go overboard like KP or look like a proud father the way Strauss did. Instead, he gave the cold, calculated clap of a man happy that someone had done well, but who didn't want to get ahead of himself.

If Flower won the lottery, he'd be back at work the next day, and he'd be early.

Then Strauss was dismissed by Mitch. The ball before the wicket was quick, short and wide, and Strauss got an easy four, but the next ball was quick, full and swung away and Strauss barely played a shot, but the ball ended up in the slips. The England batsmen just didn't seem to handle the extra pace of the WACA that well. It wasn't the bounce that undid them, like it did for many touring teams; it was more that England just didn't seem to play their shots on time.

Just after the Strauss wicket I ventured out of the press tent and into the stands to catch up with my friend Sarah who had flown over for this Test. Sarah is the photographer for Kent County Cricket Club and the eye behind sarahcanterbury.com. She was staying in Mandurah, which sounded like a long way away, so it was easier for us to meet at the cricket. I got there just in time for this serial photographer to put her camera down as a man streaked across the ground, undressing as he went.

It was poor form from him. Had he stripped beforehand, he could have made a real impact; instead, he fell over from trying to strip whilst running. I apologised to Sarah for ballsing up her shot of a pasty white man's ass, and Astrid's friend Ruth tweeted me to inform me that she had seen a touch of balls in the whole exchange. I'm not sure she could have seen his balls from her view. However, I'm sure she knows what balls look like, so it would be rude to doubt her.

The semi-streaker was punished by the security guards. They have nets up at the WACA to stop people from the hills streaking. The hills on either side of the WACA are where the drunks gather, and then occasionally streak. This man was obviously not on the hill. The WACA was on the ICC shit-list for pitch invaders already, after a Pakistani player was tackled there, so this wouldn't help them. Although, even those at the ICC could laugh at this. Maybe.

It didn't lighten the tension out on the ground. From the second KP walked out it seemed that almost every Australian player took the chance to abuse him. The WACA crowd was even into him. As England's most recognisable player and the easiest target as a pantomime villain, he was the one that people were hating on.

It's often said that sledging a player like KP can come back to bite you, because when they make a run-a-ball hundred your bowlers are left looking for the razor blades. But KP barely had time to abuse anyone back or make any bowler feel silly as he edged to slip to give Hilfenhaus his first wicket since the first over of the Ashes at the Gabba.

Collingwood came in, which really made the score 55 for four not three. It was a shame, because in the past Collingwood would have been the backbone of a chase like this. Now he would be nothing more than roadkill. At the start of his innings Collingwood hardly played a shot, but whenever he did, he almost played on or was caught. He soon got back to his nudging self, but you knew it wouldn't last.

Which was why Trott's wicket, leaving his bat dangling at a wide one, was actually a bit of a shock. Trott was not known to dangle. The WACA was doing strange things to England. Mitch just bowled a typical wide-of-off-stump ball, and Trott found Ponting's hands at second slip. However, Trott is a fighter, and although he'd left England at 81 for four with Collingwood at the crease, he'd also taken out Ponting.

Ponting's catching hadn't fallen away in the same way as his batting, but he wasn't as good as he used to be. Some blame could be attached to his crazy attempts to get below any catch so he could take it with his hands pointing up. Or it could have just been age. For this one he did drop low to take it with his hands pointing up, but not as far as he had for others. The ball smashed into his hand and rebounded to Haddin to take the catch.

It's almost impossible ever to know if Ponting is really hurt. You could shoot him and he'd just look down to see where the bullet hit him and then handle the pain. When he was hit in the face at the Oval in 2009, he spat the blood about and abused those who asked if he was OK. This was the same. You could see him trying to work out how to fix his finger, working out that he may not be the best person to do so, and leaving the field. When he is hurt enough that he leaves the field, you wonder how many pieces his finger is in.

The wicket brought Jimmy Anderson to the crease as nightwatchman. In my last book I wrote a huge hate chapter about nightwatchmen. I'll paraphrase it: I hate nightwatchmen. And the way Anderson does it is even more infuriating, because as stupid as the job is, it is pretty easy: face the last few balls of the day, and make sure no real batsmen get out. Anderson is generally good at not getting out before stumps, but the part about no more batsmen getting out he doesn't get.

Collingwood had faced the first four balls of the final over of the day and did so without incident. The fifth ball Collingwood was never quite in control of but somehow he managed to squeeze it out on the leg-side, and wanted a run. The problem was that Anderson did not want a run. Now I'm not saying this was the world's easiest single. It was tight. Not suicide tight, not Ponting-at-the-Oval tight, but it was the sort of single you really had to want. Anderson did not want it.

It could have been that Anderson had mentally switched off. It could have been that Anderson just didn't think a tight single was the right thing to do at that time in the evening. It could just have been that the last thing that Anderson wanted to do in the whole world was face the last ball of the day.

It was clear that Collingwood wanted this single. Not just because he set off for it, but because in his mind it was there. The single meant he had done his job and got through the day. England were probably not going to win either way, but Collingwood still had his own battles. Had this been Brisbane or Adelaide, Collingwood would have firmly defended the last ball, or even left it. This, however, was the WACA.

Ryan Harris' ball was not some unplayable monster. It didn't fly up at Collingwood's throat or move away in a deadly way. It was a length, corridor ball that barely moved. It could have been left. It should have been easily defended. Instead, Collingwood played a shot that didn't look horrible until you looked at it four or five times. Collingwood's first step was no smaller than his normal first step; he put his foot in the general direction of the ball so his weight was on his front foot without him being fully committed. He'd done this movement a million times in his life. It was the safe, calculated Collingwood shuffle. One built for someone who is trying to choke the best out of himself, and preparing for the worst to be thrown at him. If the ball keeps low or rears up, he'd still be able to cope with it somehow.

The way he moved, it looked like he was in the perfect position for the Collingwood dead bat. It wasn't a forceful forward defensive stroke like you'd get from Ponting, or a solid, confident one like Strauss'. It was a cold cup of coffee to the ball, bunting it to the ground, letting all the pace from the ball evaporate in one hit. Collingwood was not trying to make a statement; he was just trying to survive. It was his backyard bomb shelter shot.

Then, something changed. You could blame the Anderson single, his age, the situation or just Australia's aggression, but Collingwood forgot to dead-bat, and pushed at the ball. His bottom hand was choking the bat even more than usual and his top hand was almost a foot away from it. All he needed to do was dead-bat it. Every replay I saw, that is what I wanted him to do. It never happened.

Instead, he pushed through at the ball in a half-hearted, limp-wristed way. It was the defeated man's push. He was searching for the ball, groping and hoping that somewhere in his loser-push he would find the ball and get back to the changing room unharmed. The ball took the edge and flew off it.

Almost immediately Collingwood tried to correct himself. It could not make a difference, the ball was already flying towards slip, but Collingwood's hands tried to find where they should have been. They headed left, like they were suddenly trying to leave the ball. Some of the movement was because of the edge, and some of it must have been from the realisation that something had gone wrong. Collingwood's head, out of pure reflex, spun around, and watched the ball go straight into Smith's hands. That was stumps: England were 81 for five.

"Mummy, is that capped?" said Sam.

He had clearly lost it. He now thought I was his mother, and I draw the line at spanking. It turned out he was asking a grammatical question to me, which was almost as weird. We'd now become so close that I can guilt him for not inviting me to *The Wisden Cricketer* special dinner. But not so close that he could call me Mummy.

Sam tries to stick around for as long as possible after the day's play. He does it because he feels guilty at all the editing I have to do. Sam is one of those people. He truly cares what other people think, for someone who is putting so much of himself up on the net, and not just any part of the net. YouTube is like the WACA of old – you could put up a clip of yourself kissing two chicks at once, and someone would post a comment calling you a faggot.

Every single bad comment Sam took to heart. I'd spent many a late night on the phone because we'd had one bad comment on a YouTube clip. Whilst I felt bad for him, it also meant that when the bluebloods of *The Wisden Cricketer* had dinner and I wasn't invited, I could show how much this hurt me just to upset Sam. To be honest, as good as a night with John Stern, Peter English, Gideon Haigh and Steve Lynch would have been, I really just wanted to finish the editing and then have a beer and a steak.

I was generally one of the last to leave the press box, althoughf for whatever reason, this night everyone seemed to stay as late as me, which meant that I had to tell them how to get out of the ground. While I worked late, I could also hear the races over at nearby Gloucester Park. At any stage I could have got up, strolled over, and enjoyed a meal and beer there while watching people ride around in sporty little carts behind horses. I never did. The thought only really occurred to me just as I was uploading *Two Pricks*, and by then it was too late. I'd spent my life hearing about this racetrack that was about 200 metres from the WACA. I could even clearly hear the bloody announcer calling the horses.

Once I'd finished, Astrid asked if I needed to be picked up. I said yes, and then finished about 40 minutes before they arrived. I was waiting outside the ground as punters left the racing. And with my wife stuck on the tarmac at Heathrow Airport, snowed in. My last conversation with her seemed positive; the wings were being de-iced, the snow seemed to be clearing and in about 33 hours I would be seeing her in Melbourne. When Astrid and Ruth turned up and asked me what I wanted to do, I said I wanted a beer and meal. I was told there were only two nice places to go. According to Ruth, one was good, and one full of emos. It seemed weird that on a Saturday night there were only two places open and one was for kids who were wearing tight black jeans and listing to My Chemical Romance, but I trusted them. So we drove to the first place, and there were no parking spots. We drove to the second place and there were no parking spots. We went around the block at the second place and there were still no parking spots, so we went back to the first place, and there were still no parking spots. We ended up getting McDonald's.

It was at around this time that I became truly convinced that Perth was not the city for me. I'm not really into beaches; I just want to be able to eat and drink after 8pm and have a cricket ground that has been updated to the standards of the decade I'm living in. Perhaps that makes me an asshole, but drinking beer with a McDonald's burger is never that pleasant.

A few months earlier, in August, I'd been to Sri Lanka, and, predictably, had got sick. My stomach is so weak that water can upset it. During that time, I must have lost about 10kg. Then I came back home and put it all back on and then some. As for how: as I eventually admitted to my wife, I was a McDonald's addict.

She laughed at first, because it is ridiculous, but once I took her through what had been happening without her knowing, she no longer found it funny that I was a quarter pounder junkie. After commentating on cricket for Test Match Sofa, or on any night that she wasn't around, I was having two quarter pounders, two large fries and all the Coke I needed to get me through the night. Sometimes I'd eat McDonald's twice in one day, meaning four quarter pounders.

Just saying it out loud, for the first time in years, was therapeutic. Now I feel sick eating McDonald's. In Brisbane I'd done it once, because it was the only food source between Sarge's flat and the Gabba, and now Perth and its early closing hours meant that I'd had another. I didn't feel good about it, but on tour you had to improvise, throw out the playbook, and eat shitty food.

I was taking it one bad burger at a time.

DAY 4 – THE WACA

When I woke up in Perth the next morning, I had somehow forgotten where I was, what I was doing where I was, and how I'd got there. I started having a massive panic attack. Now, I don't generally panic attack, so I didn't know how to stop it. And I'd never ever had a panic attack on a blow-up bed, which turned out not to be the ideal place. I couldn't even tell if I was awake or asleep, having a nightmare, or stuck. I was just sort of flopping around trying not to fall off the air mattress, like it was 70-foot high. I was freaking out, sweating, having trouble breathing and was convinced that I was in the wrong place.

I hadn't even dreamed of Alastair Cook in Perth; there was no need.

Then the panic stopped, I remembered I was in Perth, at Astrid's, and that everything was all right with the world, although I still checked the room for signs of Cook. Perhaps I had been dreaming of him after all. A few years ago I had a recurring dream that Adolf Hitler was in my room. I would wake up 100 per cent convinced he was there. One time, when I was living with an ex, I woke up convinced I'd seen Hitler walk past the door to my room. I went out to the lounge stark naked, utterly convinced that Hitler was watching the TV. It was actually my ex. For two years after that, I slept with a Samurai sword under my bed, which, thinking back on it, would have not helped much against a dream Hitler.

The reason for my bad dream and panic attack must have been the combination of travel and lack of booze. Or Alastair Cook. When I settled back down I checked my phone for the date and cricket scores, just to make sure I was in Perth and that Australia were winning. When you think about that, as sensible and level headed as it is, it is also the sort of thing you'd do if you were dreaming about waking up from a dream. Until I was at the ground I couldn't be sure that this was really happening.

Checking the phone, I learnt that while I was in Perth, and Australia were on the verge of victory, my wife's flight had never left London. For five hours her plane sat on the tarmac before they told her to piss off. So any hopes of seeing her when I got to Melbourne were gone, and any hopes of seeing her before Christmas were fading.

It also seemed that other partnerships were in trouble. The newly-formed Liz Hurley and Shane Warne super-relationship was, apparently, off, after Warne was caught sending frankly shit sexts to an uninterested married woman in Melbourne. Everyone has an opinion on Warne, but you've got to admire him; if we know only 20 per cent of what goes on in his life, and we know about this many scandals, think of the shit he could really be getting involved in. You could make an awesome ageing lothario play about him. Have a well-lived man, perhaps less artificially enhanced than Warne, in the lead, and show him chasing women his whole life and how it affects him as he gets older. Actually, come to think of it, throw in a mincing brother and a fat nephew and you've got *Two and a Half Men*.

The morning's play went as you'd expect, only quicker. Anderson barely stuck around, Bell was hit in front and referred the decision just for kicks, and Prior was undone by pure bounce. The pitch was too quick and bouncy for Swann who tried to hit out, and Finn went quickly. England made it to only 123 and lost by 267 runs. It was no innings defeat, but it still stung.

Ryan Harris ended with six wickets in the innings and nine for the match, the same as Mitch. Someone asked me if I knew anything about him touching the ball close to his heart where he has a tattoo for his dearly departed mother. I didn't, but I told them to run with it anyway, as it sounded great. Tattoo or not, I was very excited for the big man. If I ever own a large dog, I will call it Harris in honour of this guy.

That he ever made it to Test cricket, let alone to take a six-for in the Ashes, was a hell of an achievement for a man who pushed his broken body barefoot up lanes of broken glass. He was my kind of fast bowler: quicker than he looks, smarter than you think, and willing to break down for a wicket.

In his press conference, Strauss sounded like a man who wasn't too worried about the loss, who knew that he had a plan, and who wasn't winning Tests just because one bowler came up with the odd magic trick. Sam asked him a question. I hadn't asked a question all series, and Sam hadn't either. His question was about whether Swann was disappointed that he hadn't bowled before lunch the day before. It was a good question considering Swann had looked pissed off in the field and no one cared about him dropping a catch. From behind us, you could hear the sniggering of some hardened old men who only asked important questions like, "How did you feel taking that wicket, no really, tell us exactly what was going through your mind, no, what I mean is, name every emotion and thought you had in great detail for me." Strauss took it seriously enough, although his answer was less than convincing. "No, I think he understood the situation, and that's the way it goes sometimes," he replied. "Sometimes he's going to be less effective. The great thing about him as a bowler is, you know he's proved over the last two years or so that he's going to be a threat more times than not."

Ponting and Mitch then replaced Strauss. Ponting, like every Australian player in this Ashes, used 45 clichés when only one would do. I'd have loved to have known just how many words per answer the two teams gave. Of all the stats in this series, I'd find that the most interesting. You got the feeling that the Australian players were so coached in stock phrases that it actually took them an extra minute to answer every question. The English players used the clichés too, but fewer, and usually answered the questions more concisely.

Ponting was not as coached as the other players, but still

fucken wordy. You wouldn't think he would be – from afar you'd expect him to just sit there and grunt. But he doesn't; he gives a lot of detail, often even looks like he is thinking it through, and is fairly honest. I don't mean honest, honest. I mean he says what those in the Cricket Australia bubble think.

While he was answering all his questions, Mitch looked bored.

Gormless is not a sufficient description of Johnson when he is bored. He is gormlessness personified. He's like a religious fanatic who believes his spirutal being has left his body and he is now watching himself. All his body did while Ponting was yapping away was perform rudimentary functions like breathing and scratching. Even when Ponting was asked a direct question about Mitch, Mitch didn't react. He just sat there, looking into another dimension. It's his Keanu Reeves face, from *Bill & Ted* or *The Matrix*. The completely-drained-of-awareness face.

Sam and I were sitting about a metre from him, and I started by filming Ricky. But I couldn't look away from Mitch's face. Just as I started to film him, Sam told me the same thing. For us, there was only Mitch in the room.

For a while, it was more of the same. Mitch would pick up his drink bottle, often without looking at it, drink it, put it back, scratch his leg, and then continue to just stare into the abyss. Then Mitch and the microphone took over. For six minutes Mitch was focused on one of the microphones in front of Ricky that kept toppling over. He caught it, moved it, tried to find things to hold it up before ultimately being told by Ponting, "Do you want to just hold it, mate?"

Mitch still continued to play with it though. Pushing it, pulling it, twisting it, he was as determined with this microphone as he is with a ball in his hand before he comes in to bowl. Then, he just smiled, a simple smile, but the smile of a man who had achieved something even though Ricky doubted him. It was the saddest fucken thing I'd ever seen.

Finally, 16 minutes into the press conference, Mitch was asked his first question. He was like a kid getting a present, he was so excited. He was honest and talked about being dropped in Adelaide.

Dropped. Not rested. Greg Chappell was not there to correct him.

I don't mind bullshit sports crap. I live it. I know that no matter what someone says in public, they're probably meaning something else. Fine, that's the game. There is a limit, though, to bullshit. That limit is claiming that you will be resting a player unless he plays well in his next game. You can't corporate speak around that – it's pure bullshit. What you are in fact saying is that you will drop a player unless he plays well in his next game. As fans – forget the hungry media for a minute – we deserve a bit of truth in your nonsense. Not much, but without fans, sport does not exist.

You can go on about how important the stars are, but without fans, sport stars are just fitter, better-looking people than the rest of us. Sure, say your clichés, invent new phrases that are completely useless, and even make sure you never answer a question directly, but don't expect us to believe any of it.

Australian cricket is struggling. And it's been struggling for ten years. Forget on the field, I'm talking in the schoolyards and on TV. People weren't watching it as much as they used to. James Sutherland, Cricket Australia's CEO, has had about ten years to do something, but he and his cronies have not got it right. Now England were out-professionalising them. Something was terribly wrong. Perhaps Australian cricket should take the power back. Instead of spending all their time making sure their players and officials used just the right corporate bullshit speak, they should be encouraged to be honest.

"Mitch, tell me how it felt, really felt, deep down inside, to be dropped?"

"Aw look, I felt like strangling Greg, chopping him up, and feeding him to my dogs. That bastard better watch his back around me, because I want nothing more than to play for my country and he took it away."

"Greg, why was Mitch dropped?"

"He bowled a complete truck load of garden fertiliser at the Gabba."

It'd be risky. But honest. This cliché-driven corporate

wankfest is a complete waste of everyone's time. The only reason I took the piss out of the press conferences on *Two Pricks* was that the press conferences were good for nothing else. For the reporters, it is a cut-and-paste exercise. For the cricketers, it's about getting away with saying nothing.

Two Pricks took me hours, and by 6pm I was finally finished. It was amazing that England lasted for only a few minutes yet I was left with a day's work. To celebrate surviving another Test, Sam, Oli and I met up at Claremont for food and drinks. Sam assured me Claremont was a cool little party district of Perth. That seemed to mean that it had one bar and one nightclub. It started badly when we struggled to find anywhere to eat and then found out that many Perth restaurants were bring-your-own booze only, and ended worse when two of the poshest people I've ever met were not allowed into a nightclub because they were wearing flip-flops, probably Ralph Lauren ones.

The good news was that I got to hear a story about a guy claiming he once put his dick on Kate Middleton's shoulder, and finally got to hear the end of Oli's train story involving Dutch lesbians. We also talked about the cricket.

The WACA was a bit of a Headingley 2009 remake. They kept several of the same cast, but also brought in new, younger faces and changed the script a little. The coming back from the dead arc of Chris Tremlett was good, Ryan Harris' "this time it's personal" hitman was awesome and Hussey's starring role was a nice touch, but all anyone really saw was Mitchell Johnson.

His performance at Headingley was patchy. Sure, it ended with a five-wicket haul, but no one thought he was the star. This time, though, it was all about Mitch. His performance was so totally badass that you knew his character would be spun off in a bunch of films that got progressively worse. But that would cheapen what he achieved here. This should have been his last performance. He should say, "Thanks, but I'm out, I want to try other genres, do some Shakespeare, and maybe even direct." Sure, he'd stuff all that up too, but after a performance like this one, Mitch deserved to do whatever he wanted.

It also set up the series quite well. A win here for England would have made the last two instalments rather pointless. This way, though, England had the chance to win while everyone was watching. Because this wasn't some return to form for Australia, and this wasn't them getting things right – their script was shit, most of the actors phoned it in, Ricky was hurt in a stunt, and the directors and producers were all clearly licking angel dust out of each other's assholes. The film only worked because three or four of the performances were amazing.

For some Australians, this was the light at the end of the tunnel – "look, our boys aren't that shit". For me it was the scene in a horror film where it looks like the hostages are going to get away, but instead they're caught and they really piss off the serial killer. If it happens this early in the film, it's never going to end well.

It was now obvious that my wife would not make it out for her first Australian Christmas. Snow sucks. Of course Australians still have fake snow on their stupid Christmas light-covered front yards. It's as if they've never noticed that it's summer in Australia for Christmas.

It's not just my wife I'd missed this Ashes: I'd also missed meeting up with most of my Australian friends. For some reason I thought the Ashes would be like a rap video with pasty writers instead of girls in bikinis. Just parties, good times and the odd bit of cricket. Because of *Two Pricks*, though, that hadn't happened. Maybe it wouldn't have happened anyway. When you do the tour on the cheap, you stay nowhere near the hotels that the other writers are in. But that didn't really explain why I hadn't met my old friends that live in the towns I'd been in. The real reason was that I spent most of my time handcuffed to my computer-editing.

At Brisbane I missed a guy I worked with for years. Apples, as we called him, was a good guy when I worked with him – well until he was my boss – but he'd always followed my career since then. He was in Brisbane for a bunch of days, and I just never had a chance to catch up with him. Also in Brisbane was the most perverted man I've ever met, Schembri. He was working for Channel 9 as a cameraman, but I only got as far as getting his phone number off him in a five-minute chat. In that five minutes he hardly had a chance to be perverted; I felt ripped off. In Adelaide there was Matt, a long-term fan of cricketwithballs.com. In Perth there was Sally, the illustrator of the cover of this book. Not only did I not get a chance to catch up with her, but my head was so fucked up by living the Ashes life that I didn't even remember she was in Perth.

I hadn't even caught up with other friends who were on the tour. Lawrence Booth and I tried to catch up for a beer in Brisbane, which very nearly happened except that I got there late and he was on his way to somewhere else. Gideon Haigh and I had three or four conversations in a few different cities about the potential for catching up. The closest we came was when I saw him between speaking engagements.

It's not that I hadn't had a good time – I had. I'm just naturally allergic to work, so once I do some, I can't then push myself to meet up with people. And I like to chat to friends and speculate wildly in bars. Perhaps I was a representation of the new cricket media. Unable to just file off some quotes pieces and talk about the day's play, this new breed had to find fantastic stories, record podcasts, and film, edit, and upload internet TV shows. Or, I was lazy and like to whine about not relaxing enough whilst on a paid holiday to cover the Ashes.

MELBOURNE (AGAIN)

Christmas was then taken up by family. Not in a bad way – I enjoy Christmas with my family, mostly. My parents still make sure they eat roast turkey, and I make sure there is good fresh Australian summer seafood available. There is plenty of drinking. This year, we started at our place with about 17 people, with Sarah the photographer, who was now staying with us, as the only Pom. She got plenty of flak, but enjoyed the seafood. My mum walked through a screen door and my dad set fire to the BBQ, which everyone enjoyed.

The news from the Australian squad was that Ponting had got through his Christmas lunch OK, and his broken finger was never sat on by Peter Siddle. This meant Ponting would play on Boxing Day at the MCG, ending very little speculation that he wouldn't. If his hand had been stuck in a machine, I think he would have dragged the machine out to the middle and played anyway.

There was another Christmas party on at the same time. The cricket writers' Christmas dinner. Sam and I had been invited to the dinner, but I was with my family and he was staying with other people. There was no reason that I should know any details about this dinner, except that Sam and I had become table conversation. In fact, according to some of our sources, it wasnt just there, but we'd been a discussion point more than a few times.

On tour, the majority of cricket writers talked about three things. Sex and cricket were the main two. I get that they talk about sex – most of them are away from their ladies for a long time. Sam and I managed not to turn every conversation with each other into one about sex, although we did mention *Two Pricks* in public so often that I could understand why people might think otherwise. As yet, we have still to consummate our relationship.

After talking about sex, cricket writers talk about cricket, or sometimes sport in general. It's the one thing that binds them. I'm sure that if a bunch of art critics get together they talk about art a lot. That doesn't mean that it doesn't get tiring after a while. It's also true that if you don't know people that well, you talk to them about the one thing you know about. It even got to the point that I would start the cricket chat even though one more conversation about Steven Smith's bowling was going to send me postal.

The third thing that cricket writers talk about is other cricket writers. And when they do it in private, it's rarely in a positive way. The intellectual writers are often called boring; writers who believed in themselves were called arrogant; writers who didn't believe in themselves were called bumbling idiots. The non-professional cricket writers' lack of cricket knowledge is mocked. The newspaper writers are called dinosaurs. The online cricket writers don't deserve to be there. The young writers ask stupid questions. The old writers are past it. Everyone is a cunt or a bore.

It appeared that at this Christmas cricket media dinner, Sam and I were accused of being arrogant assholes who didn't deserve to be in the press box and who asked stupid questions. It got back to us that our big crime was that we didn't go and introduce ourselves to people. At the Gabba there must have been about 100 people in two press boxes. Were Sam and I supposed to go from person to person introducing ourselves?

Generally, in a press box I'll introduce myself to the person next to me if they look approachable. On some occasions I don't, because if someone is not talking to me at all, or is busy working, I'm not just going to introduce myself to them. It's not a hard and fast rule, but if I chat with someone next to me, I'll often say, "I'm Jarrod from wherever," just so we don't spend the whole day next to each other not knowing who we're talking to. On those occasions when I have sat next to someone and not talked to them, these people, mega famous cricket writers that they might be (or just someone who works at the ground who has taken a spare seat) also haven't introduced themselves to me. It doesn't bother me. I didn't become a cricket writer to join a fraternity or get new friends. I became a cricket writer largely by accident. I don't want to lunch with Michael Vaughan or golf with Richie Benaud.

A further complaint appeared to centre on whether Sam and I deserved to be in the press box. It seemed that by not introducing ourselves and saying who we worked for, people had assumed we were only there to produce *Two Pricks*. As if we could contact Cricket Australia, about as conservative as a Southern Baptist church, and ask for accreditation for our show, "Two Pricks at the Ashes". It doesn't work that way. We were in the press box because *The Wisden Cricketer* and *Cricket Victoria* asked for accreditation on our behalf.

Not that I don't believe cricketwithballs.com shouldn't get accreditation. In the UK I'm often left out of press boxes that include organisations with far fewer readers than cricketwithballs. Between cricketwithballs.com, *The Wisden Cricketer* and Cricinfo, more than a million people read what I do. Most of these people are deranged, but that's why I like them. Sure, it's not for everyone; some don't like swearing, sex, unrestricted content, fantasy, jokes and bullshit. That doesn't, though, stop cricketwithballs.com from being a massive website that gets more readers a year than the three English and one Australian cricket magazines combined. But every time accreditation came around, the ECB denied me. Last season they told me it was because I swore on my site. I pointed out that *The Guardian* swears. They then told me that it was because I wasn't a member of the cricket writers' club. I called the cricket writers' club, and they said that access to the cricket writers' club had nothing to do with accreditation. Then the ECB told me that I wasn't going to be accredited because they didn't want to let bloggers in, as if by letting one blog in they'd have to let them all in, just like they let in every newspaper that ever writes about cricket. Eventually I got accreditation for the Australia–Pakistan series in England. Not as cricketwithballs. com, but for work with Crikey, an Australian website that is just a glorified blog. I'm convinced that I got more readers on cricketwithballs.com.

My accreditation this time was from the organisation, Cricket Victoria, who hosted the Boxing Day Test. The Test that helped pay for this whole series. With them behind me, I felt pretty damn sure that I deserved to be there. And as I didn't have an assigned seat, and was just finding one that wasn't taken, I was pretty damn sure that I wasn't keeping any really deserving person out of the press box. Sam was there on behalf of England's biggest cricket magazine. There were far more people in that press box that by that standard were less deserving than us of being there. In a strange way, producing our videos was having an impact that our writing couldn't.

However, there was an upside. If they didn't know who you were, they couldn't get angry with you. It was Sam who pointed this out to me. There were far more people in that press box that by their standards deserved to be there less; they just didn't know who they were. We were now known. This meant we could be slagged off with the rest – we'd made it. Press box fame.

There is no doubt that part of the reason we did *Two Pricks* was to enhance our profiles. Not in a "hey, look at me" way. We just wanted to get more work, and things like *Two Pricks* stood out (sorry). We also thought that we were lucky as hell to get people to pay us to go to the other side of the world to write about cricket, and that it might not happen again, so we tried to do what any underdog boxer in a film would do: give it everything we had. We could have just written, or done podcasts (as I did in 2009); instead, we tried video because no one seemed to be doing anything like it. And it was about the only thing in the world in which I had formal training.

It had more of an impact than anything we could have written. It was harder to ignore video than words, and it attracted far more attention. That brought suspicion and the odd criticism. I'm sure there were other young people writing good stuff on this series, but there are so many words on cricket that it's hard to find a new insight. A daily light-hearted video was a whole different medium. It was something that the cricket media hadn't done. So we did it. And some people liked it.

It also wasn't only Sam whose questions were being picked on; we heard it happen to other young writers too. The experienced guys forget that when you haven't asked an international cricketer a question too many times before, it's not that easy. Sometimes you have quite a good question in your head, but when the smooth, good-looking James Avery, an ECB media manager, nods in your direction and everyone is waiting for you to talk, you don't get the question out exactly as you want to.

I don't blame the older reporters for this; it's hard to miss some of the worst questions. They hear them every tour from some new guy, and it must get frustrating. To them it becomes a sport in itself – reliving the worst moments of the tour in the bar afterwards and all joining in on a laugh. It was just that Sam and I had this special bond now, and so any attack on him really pissed me off. Unless it was done by me, in which case it was totally acceptable.

If Sam's questions were being dissected for stupidity, it meant people knew who Sam was. If we were seen as assholes who made stupid little videos which took the piss out of other journalists, then it meant they'd seen or heard about them. And if they were saying we didn't deserve to be there, they probably knew of cricketwithballs.com.

Unlike most people, I get a certain satisfaction from someone not liking me. I don't trust it when everyone likes me; I'll think I'm doing something wrong. There are valid reasons that some of these guys don't like me. Imagine having been a newspaper guy your whole life, writing to word limits, making sure not to offend and often having your opinions stripped from the copy or added to by editors. Then some young Aussie guy pops into the box and writes any old shit, takes the piss, doesn't live by the rules of journalism, and runs around with a camera having fun.

If I was some guy who worked for some dying form of communication knowing that there was a chance that my whole industry would be different in a couple of years I'd probably be pissed off at me too. But I wasn't. I was the bloke who couldn't get into the press box 80 per cent of the time because I was part of the new media. It's why I had no problem with Brett from The Roar getting into the box despite him not being a lifelong cricket writer from a major website. He had an audience he was writing for, and there were spare seats in the press box.

The really bad thing about all this is not knowing who to trust. You get told so much shit that you have no idea who is being honest and who isn't. One person tells you they like what you're doing, but then others tell you that the same person is saying you don't deserve to be there. It does feel at times that if you aren't filing daily reports for a paper or agency you don't get looked at as a deserving member of the press core.

Then there is the almost one-man war that Andrew Miller of Cricinfo seems to be fighting against the dinosaur core. Trying to get in on interviews that are deliberately being hidden from him because with Cricinfo, and its massive audience, he has the chance to scoop them all. I find that harder to understand, because I don't care what sort of newspaper you write for – we're all online writers now. Whether you're from a newspaper or a website, everyone has the ability to post something online straightaway and few wait for the print edition to come out to find out what the score is.

And how anyone could try and keep Andrew Miller out of a press conference is beyond me. I'd invite him just for that moment after he asks a question, when he softly strokes his chin and looks deep into the eyes of the cricketer in a flirtatious way.

DAY 1 – MCG

I'm one of a few people who loves the G when it's empty. Sitting in this big bastard with only about 12 others makes it feel more personal and spiritual. It's probably the same feeling that others get when they walk into a delightful meadow and no one else is around. Having been to many Shield games, I was just used to having the ground to myself. So when it was a big game, it was like my ground was throwing a party and everyone was invited. Boxing Day actually tramples on the G a little. It's not the cricket crowd that will turn up for days two to five; it's an event crowd.

Somehow Melbourne turned itself from a sport city into an event city. The Melbourne Cup carnival, Melbourne GP, and Australian Open were not really for fans of horse-racing, motor-racing or tennis; they were just days when everyone turned up. Formula One was not a big sport in Melbourne. No one cared about the rules or knew much about the competitors. They just liked to turn up with thousands of others and get drunk. The Boxing Day Test was much the same. A lot of devoted cricket fans avoided Boxing Day because they knew the G was going to be packed with the idiots who liked ODIs and footy.

Whilst it could be annoying as a cricket fan to be trying to see how Shane Warne was setting up Brian Lara while piss was getting thrown up in the air around you, it was also worth doing just once. The Melbourne crowd has always been slightly more animal than the rest of the country. Part of the reason is the numbers. No other ground can get in even half the number that Melbourne can. In one stand alone, Melbourne accommodates more than the WACA.

Now add booze and the G itself. Because there was no doubt that of all the world cricket stages, few seemed more like a coliseum. Eden Gardens in Calcutta was probably the only one that comes close. I've never been to Eden Gardens, but on the TV it seemed more like a wave of noise that comes at you. The G was different – it came at you in pieces. Bay 13 was where the majority of the abuse came from, but there wasn't a pocket of the ground, the members' included, that didn't volley something at you. There were days when you could close your eyes and just listen to the whole ground saying "faggot", "fucker", "shit", "cunt", "poofter", and "soft-cock", all at once. It was almost like a symphony of swearing. All out of tune and vile. It was disgusting and wrong, beautifully so.

The G might be a place for sick people to say sick shit, but it was my place to hear people be sick. It was Melbourne's mouthpiece for all the idiots, racists, homophobes and general fuckwits. Actually it was Melbourne's asshole – where the best and worst of the city came out in one place. If anyone from the MCG or the Victoria Tourist Board likes that phrase, they are welcome to it, free of charge.

Getting to the ground early and stealing myself an overflow press box seat in the Great Southern Stand, I then just went out and watched this magnificent asshole slowly fill up. While I was out there Jay Masters from the *Daily Star* came over. We had a quick chat, he tried to get a gig on *Two Pricks*, and then we just sort of looked around the ground. You could tell this wasn't just another Test match. The G was giving me chills, and only some of those were from how cold it was. Jay and I did that sort of bullshit banter you do when you both just want to soak up the atmosphere.

Fuck I love this place.

Eventually it started to really fill, as did our tiny overflow room. Instantly I felt more comfortable in this room than I had in any of the others. It felt like a dungeon (which is quite an effort with a wall of windows) but in a good way. It was one of those rooms I had passed a million times at the G and always wanted to be in. The main press box was something I'd never seen before I was in it. Every time I'd been to the G I'd seen the press boxes, and I'd wanted to get into them right from when I was a small boy. There were only about 12 of us in the overflow box. I knew most of them – Chris Ryan and Gnasher McGlashan of Cricinfo, Chris Stocks of the *Metro*, Gemma Ward of *Spin* magazine, Jon Norman, and of course Sampson – and for the first time it seemed like a place in which you could be comfortable saying out loud what you thought.

Today was going to be much tougher for me than usual. Instead of just writing for my site and making *Two Pricks*, I was given real work to do. When we were in Perth, Cricinfo's Peter English had asked me if I wanted to be a stringer for AP (Associated Press) at the Boxing Day Test. I said "sure". He then asked me if I could write straight. I assured him I could. Then he walked away, and I googled the term "stringer". It meant freelance hack. Today I had to write at the toss, then at lunch and at tea, and put real live quotes in at the close of play.

England won the toss and decided to bowl.

I then went about writing what everyone had told me had to be the most lifeless copy ever written by a human being. I was so afraid I'd say something that I took out all sentences that meant anything and started writing like I'd been coached by Cricket Australia. I got Sam to check it all, as he'd been a stringer before. He found it very amusing that I was trying really hard to write how the normal people write. I just didn't want to fuck up.

On the first morning of most Shield games here, Victoria try to bat. They believe that no matter how bad the pitch is, they can get enough runs to put pressure on the opposition. Usually they do this in a far-from-pretty way for a few hours, then David Hussey and Brad Hodge are released and the runs come flooding in. I've seen it many a time.

As had Dean Jones. For about 15 years, maybe even longer, he'd been making the same point about the G. It wasn't a good point, or even that funny, but you just got the feeling that the first time he said it, someone had laughed, so he had been saying it ever since. "The only time you drive on the first day at the G is on the bus to the ground." There were other slight variations, but that was the gist. When I was told about his article in *The Age* I just scanned down looking for it. I knew it would be in there.

"Now, you must watch your driving in the first session," he'd said. "Every ball that is pitched up has to be treated carefully. It might look like a Christmas present, but treat it as if it has a bomb in it. DO NOT DRIVE IT, no matter how good it looks. These deliveries tend to stop, and easy catches can be offered to loose driving. The only drive you should attempt on the first morning is the one to the ground in the bus!" The exclamation mark was the best part. Kept it fresh. Jones' Test record at the G was six tests with an average of 25(!).

England obviously thought that the best way not to drive on this wicket was to bowl first. This was where David Saker's local knowledge came in handy. As a man who'd spent years bowling on this ground, he knew that this pitch might have something a little more fresh to it. Not that you should expect anything special from a G pitch. You should expect it to suck the life out of the fans in minutes. Most G pitches were, by definition, shithouse. It was consistently one of the worst pitches in world cricket. It offered no pace for batsmen to play their shots or for bowlers to get zip off the pitch. The ball bounces like a tennis ball. It spins after a few days, slow spin that really doesn't mean much. Most first-class or Test matches here involved dreadfully slow cricket, followed by tragic collapses when the batting side fell asleep waiting for the ball to come off the pitch.

Just to take the piss out of me, the game started with Watson being dropped off the fifth ball and Tremlett getting hit for ten runs by Hughes in the second over. On the 13th ball Watson was dropped again. The ball was swinging, there was some seam movement and you could already see the tennis ball bounce that once inspired Dean Jones' bus joke. It *was* bloody hard to drive on the first day at the G because of this bounce; the ball bounces straight up, rather than on a normal trajectory. From side on you could see this clearly, and you could imagine that facing someone on it is more difficult than you'd want. On the 20th ball of the day, this tennis ball bounce was exploited to perfection by Tremlett, who took the shoulder of Watson's bat, the ball floating slowly to gully. This time, unlike the second drop, KP took it easily. Watson had been dropped twice on the way to five. There's no better way to say that.

Ponting came out, and you wouldn't hear many bigger receptions on this ground for anyone, not even a Victorian. The G loved Ricky. He wasn't hated at any other ground, far from it. But at the G, he was God. That was when the bogans and footy fans showed themselves, reacting like they wanted nothing more than to be him. He was everything they wanted to be. The working-class kid who made it big but still feels like one of them.

There weren't many places on earth that elevated legends like the G did. Whether it was cricket or footy, it took someone it loved and canonised them right in front of you. There had been no runs for Ponting this summer, his team had been lucky to win a Test, and there had never been more pressure on him. But there was no way you could tell any of this from the adoration he got here, especially on Boxing Day.

Ricky reacted to this adulation by trying to run out Phil Hughes. He needn't have bothered; Hughes survived a referral down the leg-side, but then broke Dean Jones' rule and heart by slashing at a wide one like a maniac. KP took another catch and Tim Bresnan – England's only change from Perth, replacing Finn – took his first wicket in the Ashes.

Finn was the leading wicket-taker, and if stats were the only thing that mattered, he would have stayed in. The official story was that he was being rested. There were two other stories going around. Quite a few of the English press believed he was injured; Jay Masters was convinced that this was the case. It didn't really make sense to me. That was the easy story, but my theory was that like Australia, the England hierarchy had used "rested" to mean "dropped".

They couldn't come out and say, "We've lost the last Test and we are panicking so we've dropped the leading wicket-taker for the Ashes." So they'd basically said, "Poor Finny is a bit tired, we're going to give him a rest." This made me really angry, because they'd just gone and copied Australia, and yet again they'd done it better. I didn't mind being beaten by a better side. It was the fact that England were better at being Australia that really pained me.

And so Bresnan came in for his first Ashes Test, and sixth in all – and in his second over took a wicket. Andy Flower could do no wrong. If he picked a backpacker who he spotted sunning himself on the beach at St Kilda, the guy would make an important 60 to further England's cause. Bresnan was a bit better than that.

I liked Bresnan. I wasn't convinced he was a long-term Test cricketer, but he made the most of himself. When Samit Patel was offed for being fat, Bresnan wasn't. He just did what the team asked and got himself fit. He was far from an Adonis, yet more than fit enough to bowl long spells without getting tired. To me he came across as a simple character, a wicket-to-wicket type who was clever with the ball rather than brilliant. And a solid batsman who could chip in with runs.

He was actually the sort of quintessential Victorian all-rounder. A more masculine, chunkier version of Tony Dodemaide. Victorian all-rounders were always more deadly at the G. There was something about the G that helped the slightly slower bowlers who relied on gentle swing. In my lifetime I'd seen Dodemaide, Ian Harvey, Jon Moss and Andrew McDonald all just put it on a length and move it a little each way and be insanely successful here. In Test cricket it was much the same. Steve Waugh was unplayable at the G at times, Ricky Ponting has swung a wicket here, and Andrew Symonds has taken a few wickets as well. Bresnan was actually slightly quicker than the others I've mentioned, but he's much the same sort of bowler.

The Hughes wicket had little to do with swing; it was just wide, and shouldn't have been driven. Gully was deeper, which was perhaps a far better idea to Hughes than trying to bounce him. Michael Clarke's reception was about a tenth as loud as Ponting's. Ponting was still out there, barely. He was mostly defending and leaving. Everything he did looked gentle and unPonting (as UnAustralian as you could get). He was revealing his leg stump a lot, and you could see why he'd been caught down the leg-side a bit. Tremlett smashed the ball into his pads a few times and the Australian captain just didn't look right. Then he punished Anderson with two pull shots. It was classic Ponting (very Australian) and maybe I'd been looking for the bad signs too eagerly. His broken fingers seemed to be gripping the bat OK, and if he could pull like that off Anderson, he couldn't be too bad.

I'd barely finished writing that line when Tremlett found his edge and Ponting was out. It was a good ball, and the kind of ball that Ponting had had trouble with throughout his career. Tall bowlers made it harder for him to get forward, and he pushed at them hard, so if they got seam movement he'd nick them to the slips.

Shortly after, Hussey showed he'd never read or listened to a word from Dean Jones, nicking Anderson while driving. The only thing that saved Australia from further embarrassment was the combination of lunch and rain, who put together a small partnership before the Australian players were thrust back into the middle. They were 58 for four.

Steve Smith, Australia's extremely temporary number six, pushed very hard at a ball he didn't need to play, to give Anderson and Prior another. Clarke had been Australia's best batsman to this point, but he played an awkward pushing drive to a ball he should have left. There was absolutely nothing he could do with that shot other than edge it. He ended up on the move with one hand on the bat as Prior completed the catch for another Anderson wicket. Clarke was the top scorer at this stage. He had 20.

Haddin then played a shot that was not only representative of how shit Australia were now, but how shit they had been for the entire summer. It was as if Haddin thought Australians needed to see the entire summer reflected in one ball. So he put a summer of shitness into his on-the-up drive off Bresnan that landed in the hands of Strauss. It was almost impossible to believe that he would play a shot this stupid. And I don't say that lightly of Haddin.

Just look at the facts. People had been saying for years, and not just dearest Deano, not to drive on the first day. Three of his team-mates had already got out this way. He was the last recognised batsman. And you could see that the ball was moving around a little. So what would possess you to then play a wild drive, your feet nowhere near the ball? It was the shot of a losing team. More than that, it was the shot of a team that still believed it could hit its way out of this. It couldn't. Not like this. England were too organised and Australia too ordinary for a Haddin cameo to change this match

Johnson got out pushing, Siddle got out driving. Hilfenhaus was just not good enough for Tremlett. It was only the first and last wickets that seemed to come from genuinely good bowling. Australia had made 98.

The whole event happened in slow motion for me. Years ago I saw Big Daddy get run over by a car. I turned just as the car hit him, saw his knees take out the headlights, his ass make a dent in the bonnet, the exact part of his shoulder that hit the windscreen, the glass cracking and then breaking, and then him hitting the ground. It wasn't until he hit the ground that life sped up again. When Ryan Harris walked off he reminded me of Big Daddy going off to pick up his shoe after the accident.

There could be no coming back from this. Australia didn't have the talent, strength, planning, or commitment. They had almost done it against Pakistan at Headingley, but this wasn't Pakistan – the English team hadn't hopped on a flight with the hope of playing some good cricket. They knew what they were doing.

Every dismissal had been caught behind the wicket; just like Australia's best cricket, it was behind them.

I didn't write anything as deep or meaningful for Associated Press. I just kept with the platitudes and nonsense. Every sentence I wrote I tried to keep as boring and factually accurate as possible. Anything that looked like I had an opinion was taken out. Then Sam would sub it and make it even less opinionated. It was like my writing style had been gelded. And I took far more time over these few words than I did for anything for the rest of the tour.

Interest was added to the England innings by the question of whether Australia would sledge them, as they had at Perth.

That – and the lack of it beforehand – had been put forward as one reason for Australia's performances. Paul Marsh, the chief executive of the Cricketers' Association of Australia, had said, "I think there is no doubt the team's performance has been affected. Hard, aggressive cricket is in the Australian team's DNA and unfortunately the players started second-guessing their natural instincts in the heat of battle for fear of reprisal from Cricket Australia or a public backlash from the vocal minority. I know for a fact that many of the opposition teams were seeking to exploit what they now saw as a weakness in the Australian team."

It was amazing that you could take one win – a lucky win – and spin it however you wanted. Australia didn't win in Perth because they were sledging; they sledged in Perth because they were winning. It was plain as day. Australia would always sledge, because that is who we are as people. But the over-the-top, in-your-face sledging of Perth would only happen when Australia thought they had the opposition down. Xavier Doherty wasn't in the face of the Poms in Adelaide, but that wasn't because of some Cricket Australia directive – it was because he was getting a cricket beating. Marsh's comments were as mental as the Indian fans who thought that everything that has happened to Australian cricket was directly related to what happened in Sydney in January 2008, when the Test between the two nations had been soured by allegations of racial abuse, dodgy low catches and a series of umpiring blunders, most of which went against India. Some sort of a cricket karmic payback. I thought they were mental, but they make Paul Marsh look properly insane.

The start of England's innings was what you would have expected – far calmer than anything Australia had done. It seemed like there had been a solemn pledge not to lose a wicket. Mostly, they left the ball, something Australia didn't do. England had the patience to let the bowlers wear themselves out and wait for the ball in their area. When England did go after one, it was because the ball was so terrible that they couldn't help trying to cash in. Strauss got one past gully in the air, then, when he did get an edge, soft hands made sure that it didn't get to the slips.

Johnson also gave England another gift, a wide ball down the leg-side that went for four byes. It's more than they could have ever wished for. Ponting had brought him on for the sixth over, but his first three went for 17. England were 42 without loss off ten overs. England hadn't just beaten the Australians, they'd beaten the G crowd. This was by far the tamest crowd I'd ever seen for a Boxing Day Test. I was once at a fifth day for a Test in which Australia expected to bowl out South Africa and win. Kallis kept them out almost on his own. There were only about 10,000 people in the ground to watch what should have been an easy victory for Australia. Instead they saw Kallis block, but they never shut up until the end when Lance Klusener and Shaun Pollock ensured the draw.

It hadn't even been this quiet at the G for games that Australia had lost.

The attendance wasn't even the amazing figure the authorities had expected. Sometimes I wondered if the G didn't do itself a disservice by constantly telling everyone it was going to break records, that no seats were left, and that you'd be lucky to get in. Because not for the first time the crowd was well below the 90,800 record for a cricket match that they had forecast. It was still over 84,000, though, so wasn't bad.

The record at the ground was 121,696 for an Aussie rules match and 130,000 for an evangelical revival service. Which ended talk once and for all that Aussie rules was like religion in Melbourne; clearly it was about 8,000 short of a religion. That said, when Billy Graham did preach his nonsense, I suppose it was like Oprah coming to Australia, and I reckon she could pull about 130,000 on a round stage with Travolta beside her.

Strauss and Cook continued to bat with the sort of religious fervour that Billy Graham would appreciate. It was not a fun, happy-clappy religion when Strauss and Cook were involved. It was a sombre, thoughtful affair with lots of incense and serious faces. Cook and Strauss seemed to have found the one true faith. Australia, though, were clearly dabbling in some sort of cult, like Scientology. Sure, all religions at the base of them are kind of nuts. The thing with Scientology is that even on the face of it, it's nuts. They electrocute you softly while taping your confessions. That is early on in the process. If that doesn't get you running for the doors, what will?

Australian cricket was sort of the same. Since 2005 they'd been making odd decisions regarding selection and playing style. In that time nothing had really improved. For a while Australia still had the team to be able to paper over the cracks, but now they were too wide.

That they'd made mistakes seemed not to affect them at all. They'd invented the exact same sort of bubble that Scientology built, that all cults build. The outside world didn't know the real ins and outs – only they did – so any decisions they made couldn't be wrong. It was the dumping of Andrew McDonald after South Africa, the non-use of Nathan Hauritz at the Oval, the batting first on every wicket because of Edgbaston, the not enforcing the follow-on without considering VVS Laxman and the keeping Mike Hussey through a dip in his form and the team's form when the best thing to bring him back to form was the fear of being dropped or actually being dropped.

In the past six months, I'd twice seen Australia fail to make 100. In the past 18 months, they'd not made 150 on five occasions. In the 18 months before that, it had never happened. This wasn't some Warne and McGrath hangover; this was an experienced and settled batting order. Yet, nothing changed. That was the Church of Cricket Australia, where Phil Hughes could be the saviour for three Tests, and the devil for the next two.

This was by far the worst day of cricket from Australia that I had seen in my lifetime. It could be the worst day of cricket they'd ever had. It was hard to see a day worse than this unless their plane ended up in the mountains and they were forced to eat each other. A day like this should make Australian fans happy, though. They should look at it as an all-time low and know that those in charge would face up to their errors and get better.

But I didn't think that would happen. Instead they'd continue to pretend to fix problems while continuing to hire people like Tim Nielsen, who everyone had great respect for without him actually improving the team.

Today this gross incompetence from Australia and quality cricket from England meant that after 72.2 overs of play,

England were in front. There must have been a time before when a team was in front in a Test match at an earlier stage, but I doubt they would have done it without losing a wicket. It was a phenomenal effort. Even at Australia's best, you couldn't see them doing that.

England powered to stumps and ended the day at 157 for no wicket. Someone told me it was only the second time in history a team had been in front without losing a wicket after one day's play. Australia had helped England make history. Wasn't that sweet?

It seemed wrong that at the end of this day's cricket we still had to play out the rest of the Test. England should have just been given the keys to Melbourne and told to have their way with it while the Australian team were made to write on the blackboard, "we will not disrespect the G". England started the day with two dropped catches, and ended up with Andrew Strauss and Alastair Cook doing a slow romantic waltz around the urn.

For the first time in the series, Michael Clarke did a press conference. His career was at an all-time low, and considering he'd been dropped before, that was pretty low. All over the country I'd heard fans tearing into him, so much so that I had to really look again into how I felt about him.

Michael Clarke should not be the next captain of Australia. I'd said this for longer than it's been fashionable. And it is fashionable. Other than Justin Bieber, no person in the world seemed to be an easier target than Michael Clarke. Like a manufactured pop star, Clarke's public persona had been planned, polished, and tweaked to be just right. That didn't give much room for the real Clarke to come out, should there be one.

He was the perfect modern sportsman in many ways. He helped charities; never said anything controversial; didn't get involved with politics; stayed clear of sex scandals; looked good in front of a camera and had the clean-cut appearance advertisers liked. He did his job well most of the time (this summer not included), yet the majority of the Australian public didn't like him, and even some who did like him didn't want him to captain Australia.

Sort of like a young politician, everything seemed to have been carefully mapped out for him so that no mud could stick. His relationship with the famous model Lara Bingle might have been the only time he really made a PR mistake, and I thought that relationship matured him very well. Then he broke up with her in such a calculated way that people stopped holding it against him almost minutes after it ended. Even the "I love you poopkins" type of tweets he sent to her were ignored. He just had a way of never being the one who had done wrong.

He reminded me very much of General Casey in that seminal 1950s sci-fi parody *Mars Attacks!* Upon learning that he was in line for a very special and prestigious honour, he rang his wife.

"Yes, I get to greet the Martian ambassador. Isn't that great?"

"Oh, it's a hell of an honour."

"Didn't I always tell you if I stayed in place and never spoke up that good things were bound to happen?"

Clarke stood still, and never spoke up, but then they turned. The public did it first. It was hard to have a cricket conversation between three people without one of them being violently opposed to Michael Clarke on every level. When he made runs, he did it only when Australia had already put on hundreds (which was true), he refused to go into another gear in one-dayers (which was also true), he didn't bowl enough (back problems), he was a wanker (beaches, tattoos, pretty girls, expensive haircuts, photo shoots and fast cars) and he should never captain Australia.

My dad's reasoning for why he didn't want Clarke to captain was that he whistled when in charge of the team. Not wolf-whistling, but whistling for attention like a farmer to his sheepdog. My dad thought that was about the single most disgusting thing he had ever seen an Australian captain do – although he never saw Warwick Armstrong in the bath. It would be funny if that were the most outlandish reason to hate Clarke, but many had other reasons.

Most of them seemed to be class related. He didn't feel working-class anymore. Perhaps he didn't mention the words "working-class" anymore. To me, a fellow child of the working-class, he felt painfully working-class. He liked fast cars, faster blondes, fancy tattoos, and looking good. I grew up with about 50 blokes who were the same as Clarke. Many of them never made much money, but they still tried to hang out in cool places, spend all their money on their cars and chase women who would look good next to them. They all dressed in designer clothes and attended the clubs where the local celebrities turned up. It's working-class; it's just a different breed.

It was not even a new breed. Australian cricket fans had been exposed to it already. The name would be Shane Warne.

Warne was working-class. He also liked blonde women (and movie stars), fast cars and now spent his time travelling in first class to poker tournaments. He's also done some work to make his appearance better. The thing about Warne was that we knew so much more about him too. We knew he had trouble keeping a woman, what underwear he liked, that he smoked, that his mum gave him tablets, and we knew that he was the best of the best.

Clarke may have been the same sort of flashy working-class boy as Warne, but his personality had been wrapped up in so much secrecy that even a former team-mate told me he only talked to managers, his bat sponsor and a few players. All we saw of Clarke was superficial; Warne (accidentally or not) gave us everything, meaning he came across as human whereas Clarke was like a cardboard cut-out. I'm not saying Clarke should get involved in a sex scandal, although it couldn't hurt. I'm saying he needs to show the world that he is human. Plus, and this is more important in Australia than anywhere else, he hasn't quite fulfilled his potential yet.

There is no doubt that Clarke is an above-averagely talented cricketer. He is no Warne, but he was lauded as the once-in-a-generation teddy bear that cricket experts told us was going to take over cricket – the new Ricky Ponting. But he isn't. He came into cricket after almost all the great bowlers had retired and the pitches had all gone chief-executive-officer-brown.

Clarke is a long way behind Ponting, and in terms of pure cricketing effect, they aren't on the same planet. Perhaps that is unfair, but he isn't auditioning to be a jizz-mopper at his local nudie venue; he's trying to get a job that is the second most commented-on position in the country.

There was always going to be more scrutiny for Clarke than for, say, Marcus North, who most people didn't even notice when he was in the team. That is why his image, more than anyone else's, needed an overhaul. If he doesn't have a personality, they should fake one. Cricket Australia could even fake it if they liked. Especially if they wanted to get rid of Andrew Hilditch. They could send Clarke out there to say something really controversial about Hilditch, like he didn't have facial recognition so he got Shaun Tait confused with David Warner. Then have him publicly reprimanded by Cricket Australia. The public would turn on Hilditch, making it even easier to give him the golden handshake. Or they could just have Clarke skip a team meeting to see *Machete*, get drunk, and get thrown out of a proper outer suburban pub.

Because as it stood, I knew more about Douggie Bollinger, even though he only turned up on the international scene eight minutes ago.

Douggie proved that you didn't have to do much to be liked by the Australian public. Douggie was Douggie. No amount of media training could stop him from saying something stupid. His wife was perhaps the most normal cricket wife in a decade. He was just a knock around Aussie bloke who had a weird head and a big smile. *GQ* wasn't about to offer him a cover photo. Yet, when the endorsement cash was allocated this year, Douggie got a huge proportion of it because advertisers wanted him.

My favourite endorsement was of Douggie dancing and holding his man boobs for some mobile phone company while the rest of the players sang a song. Clearly Douggie didn't know the lyrics, or didn't want to sing, but his performance as the moob-grabbing dancer was the highlight for me. The reason he was in all these ads was that focus groups and market testing had told ad firms that Douggie was loved.

There was no magic formula to Douggie; he's a big loveable doofus who on his debut said that he wanted to play at 150 per cent. He was easy to bag, loyal as hell, more like the family pet than potential leader. The story about him getting hair plugs as a wedding present for his wife was priceless.

The irony is that Clarke is exactly what sports boards, advertisers, agents, PR firms and marketing companies had been trying to grow. You can't grow or control a Douggie, but the super slick star players are supposed to be exactly like Clarke. Sports stars aren't told to say stupid things, get embarrassing hair plugs and do comedy dancing. Clarke has done everything right, yet he is the least popular member of the team. Even when he is in form. Clarke has been so polished, tweaked and coached that he is barely the same person who came screaming into Australian cricket. I've watched him for years and I have no idea who he is or what he stands for.

I think it's that, and far less of the working-class snobbery, that sets Clarke apart. Mark Taylor was hardly the knockabout larrikin working-class type, and people liked him. He had opinions, handled himself with the press in an honest, funny way, and most were happy that he was captain. He was taking over from Allan Border, the man who rebuilt Australia with grumpiness and cold steel. A far blokier, swearier, more working-class hero than Taylor could ever be. Taylor was also keeping Steve Waugh, the battler's hero, from the job. Clarke's only main rivals are players from outside the team.

There are those who keep telling me via blog and tweet that they don't care about whether he has a personality, they just want him to make runs. Of course when he did that, he wasn't that popular either. From 2006 to 2009 he averaged 71, 80, 50, and 54 in Test cricket. In 06 and 07 he did tend to score mostly when Australia had already beaten the opposition up, but he still made an assful of runs, and people didn't rate him.

My problems with his captaincy had almost nothing to do with the reasons he seemed to be hated. If he wore a pirate earring, read Sylvia Plath on the balcony and only talked to people who watched modern day French films, I wouldn't hate him more, or think he would be less of a captain. All I can go on is his past actions.

He had publicly stated that he would never captain Ricky Ponting. This made him sound like he was scared of leading him. I want a captain who would say he would captain a sabretooth tiger if he was picked.

He had at times said he didn't always feel comfortable going to Ponting with suggestions. He was the vice-captain of Australia; this wasn't some title you got when you'd sold 100 Whoppers. It meant something, and he should have been chipping in, especially when he saw Ricky losing it.

He wouldn't change his game for T20 cricket. In real terms I care almost nothing about the fact that he plays T20 cricket badly, but in the larger world view, if he couldn't change his game for his team when it was needed, that was a problem.

His apology for not walking. I appreciate a man who apologises. Too many people never do. But don't apologise for not walking. You're Australian, that is fine, don't apologise for that.

His lack of visibility off the field during the Ashes. Clarke did not appear at a close-of-play press conference until the fourth Test. Watson, Haddin and Hussey all came out on days when Australia were pummelled. Where was he?

The speed with which he left the ground after play. To me Clarke just saw cricket as a really cool job. I'm not sure the captain of the side can afford to do that. Simon Katich may agree with me.

The complaints in front of younger players. When you lead the side you don't need to be telling your players that you think the pitch is hard to bat on. It's not what leaders do. Or, they use it to motivate, and don't have a hissy fit.

Watching him delegate autograph duties. At a Victoria v New South Wales one-dayer, Clarke was rested and sitting in the dugout watching the play. Some kids saw him, and asked for his autograph. Clarke said yes, but sent another player over to collect the items and take them back to him. Way to keep your distance from the fans.

It all came down to the fact that I didn't feel like I really knew him. I followed him on Twitter. Read all the cricket press.

Watched his interviews. Had been to his press conferences. So how could this be?

Who is Michael Clarke? What does he believe in? Who does he vote for? What pisses him off? Does anything piss him off? Is he embarrassed by his public acts of affection for Lara? Why did he wait until Lara was in a bind before leaving her? Does he like leg slips? How does he believe Mitchell Johnson should be handled? Why so many bowling changes in Sydney? How will he fix slow over rates? Would he be a better captain than Cameron White? Has he read Mike Brearley's captaincy book? Does he believe in human cloning? Will his back ever be truly healed? Is he nervous or energetic? Why should he be the next captain of Australia?

The most I knew about Clarke was that he had said he never wanted to be dropped. It was the most human I'd ever seen him. And although it was a bit depressing at the time, it showed that he had a fire inside him. I wanted more of that and less of his corporate image.

At times I had even wondered whether I was giving Clarke a fair go. People got so angry about him that it made me doubt my position. The Australian public had turned on him in a vicious way. So I asked a few players about him, and most of them had no real opinion of him. My favourite was a player who played juniors with him, played seniors with him, went on tours and to away matches with him, and who had generally spent a great deal of time with him, and he said, "I have absolutely no idea what he stands for or what his opinion is on anything at all."

Through all this almost no one talked about how he had reshaped his game, made himself a better player and made a huge personal decision midway through a Test series. Clarke was a shit wanker to his detractors, or an injured champion to his fans. Neither was true. But with Clarke, truth never seemed to matter.

After all that, I had to put quotes into my AP piece. I froze. Whilst I had recorded the entire interview, I hadn't actually listened to much of it. After 30 seconds of staring at my screen I emailed Andrew Miller to ask if I could have his transcript of the interview, as I knew he had the fastest hands in the press box. He sent it straight over and I put in a couple of quotes that looked like they would fit into such an AP-style piece. Then I spent ages doing *Two Pricks* and wore a watermelon on my head.

Finally, I left the overflow room and headed to Jolimont station. I made the idiotic mistake of missing my train, and then laughed at the thought that right at that moment it was still statistically possible for Australia to win the Ashes. And then stopped laughing knowing that I had to wait 40 minutes for the next train due to it being a public holiday. It was now after 9pm and it was getting dark, I was the only person at Jolimont station, it was fucking freezing and all I had on was a shirt and T-shirt and jeans. It had been a cold summer in Australia, but this was real Melbourne wind cold, which felt right for Australian fans.

I looked into one of those seated areas that always smelled like piss, just to get away from the cold. The smell of piss was there and so were about ten rats. Now, I'm not afraid of rats, I had no strong feelings about them either way, but I had columns due and I didn't want to be looking out for Willard's mates while I tried to work. The rats won, because even out on the platform they started scattering everywhere, eating the crumbs of the pies that the G punters had carried across with them. Now I was cold, kicking away at rats and trying to finish my column about how bad Australia were. Sam was out with friends. My wife was stuck in London. And I bet I was going to dream about Alastair Cook and rats.

My mind also went back to Australia's 88 against Pakistan at Headingley, and I wondered which day I hated more. It was not even a fair contest. Everything about this day was horrible. The batting, the bowling, the defecation on and desecration of my spiritual home, and now the rats. To make myself feel better I checked out the final version of my AP copy. They had rewritten almost every word. Not to make it more dull, but to make it more exciting. I was now too dull for AP. This had been the worst day of Australian cricket ever, and my writing was too boring for agencies.

Then I jumped on the same train as Sarah and my mum, as

they were heading back from the city. Sarah was over the moon, and I was reminded how little I cared that other people were happy. That night I had a Burger King. I needed a fix of burgers and bourbon to get me through the next few days.

DAY 2 – MCG

Two Pricks was now a global conglomerate. We had two sponsors: David Hopps had given us a fair payment (I think that is the term we decided on) from his travel company reddottours.com for a small ad at the front of each video. And we'd convinced Craig Nott of cricketbetlive.com to cough up some money. Neither payment was enough to secure our future, but we knew that we had something that people liked watching and that companies were willing to give us money to do.

It was also cool because Craig gave us cash in an envelope – and who doesn't like getting an envelope of cash from a bookie. It was delivered to us by our mule Gideon Haigh. And I'd convinced Hoppsy to give Sam a dollar less than me, just so that it would fuck with Sam's mind. Which it did.

Before day two, Australia had a team hug in the changing room. It was nice to see, team bonding and doing it for each other. They were showing the whole country that this meant something to them, that going out there as brothers in arms they would do whatever they could to win this Test. No mountain was too high, no valley too low, and no river, etc. They were Australian men, built of Australian flesh and bone, with Australian hearts and lungs and the most important thing in the world: Australian spirit.

The boys looked so determined it would have been wrong of any of us to tell them that this series had gone.

When the cricket started, I started to doze off. Not because it was particularly more boring than any other England innings; it was just that I expected England to continue to grind the Australian carcass. I was woken by "It's a wicket for Australia" from Jim Maxwell on the radio. He said it like he was commentating on aliens arriving at Epping Plaza. Maxwell had never made anything sound more like a momentous and surprising occasion in Australian sporting history, and he was half right. Siddle had taken the edge of Cook and Australia now had a wicket.

Australia did have an excuse yesterday: the sun came out. Cricket can so often be changed by clouds disappearing. This morning the clouds were in, and Siddle had a wicket. The weather didn't explain away everything, though. Johnson's poor bowling and the eight bad shots were not weather-related. This morning Siddle just looked better, and with the ball moving a little bit, he got Cook.

Last night I did dream of Cook; he was hosting a meeting and I was regularly told off for not listening. Then Siddle got Strauss, and now I was watching. It was a top delivery that bounced more than Strauss expected. It squared him up as well and he tossed his head back like a damsel in distress. The crowd noticed as well. They didn't often miss a Victorian do well and they started to get mildly excited in general, but very excited for Siddle. After 16 overs, he had two for 18. Last night and today he had just bowled. There had been no wacky round-the-wicket plans, he wasn't bowling three feet outside off stump and at no stage was he told to bounce anyone out.

I think Siddle could be a very fine long-term bowler for Australia. He's quick, strong and dedicated. When he gets it right he can take down a whole bunch of batsmen at once and he's only 26. What he doesn't need to be is Australia's plan bowler. Not every time. Not when Mitch and Hilfy almost never do it. The stupid plans should be shared by all the bowlers to ensure the success of Australian cricket. Or, the wacky plans could be thrown out. England don't seem to need them.

That second wicket didn't, however, come at the best time. Siddle had worked hard to get Australia anything, and a few overs later he was looking tired when KP took him for a couple of fours. At drinks it was obvious that Siddle would have to have a break and that somehow they had to break this partnership before the new ball was taken in 20 overs' time.

In 20 overs KP could be on 60, Trott could be on 40, and Australia could be fucked.

They were already, but in the greater scheme of things keeping Siddle on would keep the game open and mildly exciting. Without swing or luck, Australia seemed to have no chance of getting Trott out; their best chance with him was to bowl each ball on his hip and give him a single. KP had to be their man.

Australia seemed to come up with two approaches. Hilfenhaus was going to probe with gentle away swing outside off stump in order to play on his patience and get a wafty drive to be edged behind; Mitch was just going to yell at him. But Hilfenhaus looked like a man out of answers. Coming into this summer I thought he was going to be the key bowler, but now I couldn't see how he could play in the next Test. His swing was still there, but it wasn't going as far and he seemed to have slowed down. Perhaps he had lost pace, but he had really been doing the job that Andrew McDonald could have done this summer: keeping the runs down and getting gentle swing.

Hilfenhaus bowled through to lunch and hardly a harsh shot was attempted off him. In 19 overs he'd gone for 40 runs. The important thing was that he still hadn't got wickets. My bet with Sarge about who would have the better series, Hilfy or Watson, had been lost long ago, and I didn't mind that; I just liked Hilfy and wanted him to be the player he could be. He was never going to be a huge wicket-taker at Test level, but taking just one wicket at the WACA was just not good enough for a swing bowler.

During the press conference after Perth, Ponting had defended him, saying his maidens built up tension so the bowlers at the other end could take wickets. But that job could be done by an all-rounder like McDonald.

At the other end Mitch yelled a bit, bowled fast, bowled wide and went for 57 runs in his 12 overs. He had wasted cloudy conditions, and as Melbourne's weather can change in an instant and looked like it was clearing, he was of no use to this team. He was replaced by Smith who bowled tidy leg-spin without much bite. He didn't look any worse than Doherty, but he didn't look any better.

Lunch came and Australia's chances of staying in this match – already slimmer than Lara Flynn Boyle – had gone. They'd bowled as tight as they could, Mitch excluded. KP was scoring slowly, Trott was doing the same, but at 226 for two, they were already too far in front. They wouldn't be bowled out for less than 300, and in all truth, I would have been surprised if they hadn't made 400.

England could have panicked when Siddle was bowling. They could have chased Hilfenhaus, tried to embarrass Mitch or got sloppy against Smith. They didn't, because they were quality. It took more than bowling line and length at them for a session to get them out. They could have attacked, but they sensed what Australia were doing and played cricket accordingly. If it all sounds so simple, that's because it was.

For lunch we ate pies. On the first day we'd all headed down to the old Melbourne Football Club changing rooms for lunch. Now I liked the idea of eating where thousands of men had been rubbed down in an underground bunker as much as anyone; it's just that I don't like the idea of eating salad wraps in a place that has the best pies on earth. So for day two I went out and pied up everyone who wanted them. The secret was not to look for a shop selling pies, but to find a pie boy who came to you. There are a lot of things I like about English cricket and yet there is one thing they really miss: a person walking around the outer carrying a big plastic container full of pies.

Australia resumed after lunch looking to get to the new ball. Watson and Smith got rid of the four overs as quick as they could. Hilfenhaus then bowled one more ball with the old ball, which KP hit for four, and the new ball was taken. Hilfy couldn't get it to swing. He tried full and straight, full and wide, but it just wouldn't go for him. At the other end Harris was getting it to talk off the seam. The difference between them in menace was massive.

KP moved to 49 and then got a ripper from Harris. It hit the pitch and jagged back in past the bat. Haddin didn't appeal – he did verbal handstands. No one else moved much or made a noise. Watson at slip put his hands on his head as if to say, "How close was that?". Ponting never moved at mid-off. When they discussed a referral, Harris seemed to walk away. Haddin, doing his best Prior impression, convinced Ponting that it was out. The T-sign was made.

The hotspot did show something; at the bottom of KP's bat there was definitely a hot spot. The problem was that the ball was at least two inches higher than the hot spot when it went through. Plus it was a massive hot spot mark on the underside of the bat, meaning that the ball probably would have gone down had it been hit, which it didn't, so it was given not out. Case closed.

Or at least it should have been closed. Instead, Ponting went on one of the most ill-advised rants to umpire Aleem Dar that you could ever hope to see. From the replay that Ponting had seen on a good quality (but not perfect) screen 140 metres away from him, he could apparently tell 100 per cent that it was an edge – way more than a third umpire could tell from looking at a high quality screen inches from his face. Ponting should have just walked away; instead he took up minutes complaining about something that he couldn't change and that he was wrong about anyway.

I'd seen him do some idiotic things in his time. A Pura milk advert where a girl spills milk on her breasts; that goatee he had in the 90s; getting Mike Hussey to bowl in India; bowling first after McGrath did his ankle at Edgbaston; those damn vitamin commercials. This seemed to be the most honest, though. He was chasing again. There was now no difference between him and a guy playing the pokies at 3am and hitting the machine because he believed it had cheated him. If Dar had been a slot machine, Ponting would have been slamming him around, kicking him, and claiming that the whole thing was fixed.

I loved, though, that at his age he still had the passion. I'd prefer he used that passion on Cricket Australia to see why Australia were underperforming in Tests rather than complaining to an umpire that had got a decision right. Even if it was an edge, his behaviour was over the top. If England had been unsure as to whether Ponting was broken, they needed little further evidence. The man had had a mental breakdown right in front of 67,000 people.

KP brought up his fifty a few balls later. Ponting wasn't thrilled for him.

With the new ball doing less than nothing for Hilfenhaus, Siddle was brought back on. Legitimately he got one to keep low and jag back, hitting KP plumb in front. After a quick chat, Trott and KP decided not to review. It was a shame, because if that decision had been reversed, especially in error (whether real or Rickyed) we could have seen a Test captain's head explode.

The Barmy Army were in front of us and while they were loud yesterday, today they were louder. They got stuck into Brad Haddin, giving him the referral signal. To his credit he didn't take off his glove and give them the finger; he just had a bit of referral fun with them. If Ponting's finger were not broken, he'd be in the slips, and I doubt Haddin would have acted the same way with them.

Collingwood was now facing Johnson. He might be the only English batsman to fear Mitch. Collingwood had got off the mark with an inside edge, had been lucky to survive an lbw appeal and had managed a more than decent cover drive for three. Then he decided to hook Mitch. It was a terrible mistake. I couldn't figure out why he could think it would ever end well. He wasn't beaten for pace as much as the ball just bounced a bit more than he anticipated. With the ball in the air I sort of hoped that it went wide of Siddle. If England were going to win the Ashes, and they were, I wanted Collingwood to be there in Sydney when they did. I also wanted him to go out with one last innings.

Not a hundred – his career was not one that needed to finish with a hundred – just a gritty 65 as England built on their impenetrable lead. For him and no one else. He'd been there through the highs and lows without making a big deal of himself. I thought he deserved just one more innings, if only to ensure that he finished Test cricket with an average of over 40.

It was a small thing, but I thought he'd earned it.

A few overs later, Ian Bell did his bit to honour Paul Collingwood, playing the exact same shot off pretty much the same ball from Mitch, who had now been gifted two wickets that he did not deserve. Australia had England at 286 for five. The crowd made it feel like 46 for five. Siddle had been involved in all five dismissals and the crowd absolutely got behind him. If Australia were to take the next five wickets for only a few runs, they'd be in a position to get some respect.

I sort of hoped that it wouldn't happen. I actually hoped that Australia would lose this Test badly and then get massacred in Sydney. Now that England had deservedly retained the Ashes, I hoped that they would win the series 3-1. If somehow Australia won at Sydney (by winning the toss on a green top and multiple kidnappings) they might look at this series and think they were close to England and on the path to success. But 3-1 would be a suitable drubbing that would make you realise there was something wrong with the system and that it needed rebuilding.

So this was what I thought they should do.

Tap Ricky on the shoulder. If Australian cricket was to rebuild, they needed someone other than a 36-year-old in a form slump who has refused to drop down the order. Ponting might be a champion batsman but he wasn't such a special captain that he should stay on. I could see no reason other than pride for him to remain in this role. If (when) Australia lost this series 3-1, that would be the perfect time for a change in leadership. The next captain should start now, at the bottom, and see if he can improve the performances of this side. The next leader needed immediately to distance himself from Ponting and lead this team his way. If they decided that Michael Clarke was the man, then he needed to take over as soon as possible to turn public opinion and learn how to lead.

Retire Hussey and Katich. For 20 Test matches, Hussey was a batting behemoth, averaging 84. His next 38 Tests he averaged 38, including this series where he has been as good as he was at any time during his first 20. The problem was that at 35 all he was doing was keeping Callum Ferguson, George Bailey and Cameron White from getting any Tests, and preventing potential young guns like Chris Lynn and Mitch Marsh from coming in. Simon Katich had done the opposite of Hussey, in that his best form was in the last two years since he'd come back to Test cricket. He'd been Australia's most reliable player in that time, but at 35 and injured, he was not the future. Australia could keep picking the same players out of emotion, or take a cold-hearted look at what is happening and drop them. Sport isn't sentimental; it's sport.

Sack Andrew Hilditch. It was now quite clear to most fans that Andrew Hilditch was no longer in charge of the side. Some might argue that he hadn't been in charge for a while and was just giving Ricky the side he wanted. Now Greg Chappell was the spokesman for the selection committee and had taken over the naming of the side unofficially. When Hilditch didn't even know where Michael Beer was from, that should have been enough to give him the axe on the spot. Unlike his hooking, Hilditch's selections had been safe and conservative, and that was part of the reason why Australia came into this series with an old, malfunctioning batting line-up. His decisions to pick seasoned veterans to paper over the cracks never quite worked, and now it is Chappell's turn.

Fix the coaching situation. There was no doubt that the Australians had been outcoached by England. I thought David Saker was the best bowling coach in the world before he was selected by England. At any stage Cricket Australia could have popped down to the Victorian nets and offered him a contract, especially knowing that Cooley was thinking of leaving the job. They didn't, and hadn't Tremlett, Finn and Bresnan picked up some wickets? Mike Young was a part-time fielding coach who wasn't required for all the Tests even though Australia's catching was terrible in the first seven days of the series. Australia also needed to work out if Young was helping their slip catching, which was at a low point. Tim Nielsen's friendly style didn't seem to be getting through to the players. The top order had been collapsing for two years and I'd yet to see any radical plans from him to fix it. I'd yet to see him say or do anything. The players might love him, but perhaps that was the problem. And for Cricket Australia to have extended his reign by three years before the Ashes proves that no one was really looking at the results. The man was a perfect assistant coach for the players to lean on when the main coach was chewing them out. But as the main coach his record spoke for itself. Australia had not improved under him and that was more than enough to get him fired.

Pick solid youngsters. Australia picked two young players this summer who were out of form and had dodgy techniques. From my time watching domestic cricket this season, they had plenty of young talent lying around. Smith and Hughes were positive, talented young men, but they had flaws. Smith wasn't good enough as a batsman or bowler, and Hughes didn't believe in himself anymore. Compare them to Finn, who had a decent action, was well coached, and believed in himself. So when Australia pick from the young players, find the ones that have form, confidence, and belief in their techniques. Chris Lynn, Usman Khawaja, Nic Maddinson, Mitchell Starc, James Pattinson, and James Faulkner all looked like legitimate players with solid repeatable skillsets that were made for executing. Let them execute.

Cricket Australia had to be changed. I wasn't an expert on how Cricket Australia was structured, but from what I knew, it seemed to be an archaic system that meant some state teams got fewer votes from the board. All I really knew was results. Australia's marketing and performances were bad. James Sutherland had been there for almost ten years. At some point, he had to be made accountable. Something had to change, and if the team was struggling, the coaching poor, the selection nonsensical and the marketing absurd, then you probably needed to move on.

And I hated the whole "sack them all" routine. It was a reflex of all sports fans when their team lost. The thing was, Nielsen should have been sacked long before, based on Australia's results. Ponting should have told Australia exactly how long he was going to stay. Sutherland had had more chances than either of them.

It is no crime to rebuild your cricket team when it is

struggling. The Australian team could, though, still be more professional. They could plan a team for two years' time, instead of two Tests. They could employ full-time selectors. They could pay for spotters at their opposition's matches. They could employ full-time wicketkeeping and spin-bowling coaches. They could test all their players' eyesight and reflexes. They could hire professionals from well-run American sports to come in and step up their game. They could even question whether a marketing-driven Test-squad announcement is the best way forward. They could.

Instead they watched as Prior edged behind from Mitch. It was a regulation sling across the batsman with no real movement, which Prior was just a bit late on. Except that Aleem Dar was not sure. I liked Aleem Dar, because he was cautious, didn't want to make himself the centre of the story, and was generally a good umpire. He had seen something he didn't like and, from recent history, this probably meant a no-ball. The replays showed it straight away: Mitch had overstepped. On the face of it you could say two things for sure: technology was not Australia's friend and Dar had made a clever decision to refer a wicket that he was unsure about.

There was, though, more to it, in my mind. Imagine that Mitch had not just bowled one no-ball, but that he had bowled several, all of them very close to the line, so close that Dar was not sure about them. Then he took a wicket and Dar referred it. Now, if a no-ball had been called earlier, Mitch could have adjusted his run-up and stopped bowling them. Also, since this had now happened on at least three or so occasions in Test cricket, how many no-balls were just not being called? You could have been losing vital runs or a wicket based on the fact that the umpires only correctly called one no-ball.

In this case, though, it was probably only the difference between a defeat and an innings defeat. Had Australia got Prior out early, all it would have meant was that England might have led by less than 250. Prior's form had been shaky all series, mostly because his ass had gone numb waiting for Cook or Trott to get out. But sometimes all you needed was an overly cautious umpire who was unsure about a no-ball call, and luck.

Prior was a hard worker. Somehow he managed to be largely invisible and yet beset by controversies involving sledging young Indian batsmen for being poor, jelly beans on the pitch and his wife sitting on the lap of L Ron Stanford. Prior claimed that most of these things weren't true – except the lap thing, we all saw that. He's got a head like an Essex lad – it looks like it's made for headbutts.

Not that long ago, his wicketkeeping was a joke, and his batting was grand. Now he had found a happy medium. In this series, he had been outbatted by Haddin, but there was now a huge gulf in class between them as wicketkeepers. Prior had worked hard at his 'keeping, and slowly he had become the best 'keeper he could be. Not England's best 'keeper, in my opinion – James Foster is like wicketkeeping heroin – but Prior had the complete game to keep Foster out.

Without his wicket, however well Siddle continued to bowl, England just piled on the runs. Prior took his second chance, scoring freely. The innings was completely pressure-free and England were looking at another scary total.

Jonathan Trott, meanwhile, continued to be the best invisible batsman of all time. Trott's innings, like many of his innings, never quite seemed to be *the* story, but without them Australia would be in one hell of a position. When Trott's no longer in the team, you can bet there will be some intellectual chin-stroking articles about how good and important Trott was.

Once the Prior and Trott partnership pushed England past a 300-run lead, the Barmy Army got into full voice. I don't have a big problem with the Barmy Army. On some days, like the last day at Brisbane, they were the only thing in the ground giving it atmosphere. Their Mitchell Johnson song, "He bowls to the left, he bowls to the right, that Mitchell Johnson, his bowling is shite" was funny.

The problem was, if they found something funny, they'd do it over and over and over again. I can watch an Adam Sandler film and find it funny, but if I was trapped in a space where that is all I was allowed to watch, I think I'd go crazy. That is what the Barmy Army does: they come up with a good joke, and then they spend all day spamming your ears with it. If they are far enough away it is all just atmosphere, but if you were, like I was now, trapped right behind them, it wasn't atmosphere – it was noise pollution. They liked cricket enough to travel around the world supporting it, so I admired them, but if someone in a bar kept repeating the same joke I'd walk away. In the crowd or press box, I didn't have that luxury.

They seemed louder since Prior survived, because England had been in such control that the Australian fans had just switched off. Or gone home. No supporters like to see their team getting bashed, and Australian fans always seemed to leave before the close of play anyway. This time it just made more sense. By the end of play, it seemed like only the Barmy Army were in the ground. England were 444 for five, Trott on a century and Prior a fifty.

The Australian press conference after play started with Lachy Patterson stating that they couldn't say anything about Ricky's umpire meltdown. Then Peter Siddle, who had been put before the media, was asked about the incident. He said "no comment" with a natural smile on his face. Then he was asked about the incident again, and again he said "no comment" with a forced smile on his face. Then he was asked about the incident one more time and this time his face went into some sort of weird shape and he shook his head like an actor in *Law & Order* telling the cops he didn't commit no rape.

It was ugly and pointless. Siddle was involved in the incident as much as anyone other than Ponting, right in the face of the umpires. The whole thing was a farce and, just to relieve the tension, I wanted to ask him if he'd ever struck a woman.

A few hours later Ponting got a fine of 40 per cent of his match fee. It was like slapping his wrist with week-old celery. I don't actually eat celery, so it might take two weeks, but I know that really limp celery wouldn't hurt when it slapped you. No suspension or suspended sentence, just a small fine for a man who has been playing Test cricket for over a decade and should know better. Considering he went up and complained to both umpires separately, it was really only a 20 per cent fine per incident. Bargain.

Ranjan Madugalle, the match referee, was the person who

slapped Ricky with the celery. When you do something that piss-weak you might as well go the whole hog. Why fine him – why not just apologise to him for the whole situation? Make the umpires come in and grovel before him; go out in the bay, catch him some fish, scale them, cook them in a garlic and lemon sauce, put them on a naked woman and have them delivered to his room. It's the sort of punishment a parent afraid of pissing off their kid would give.

Luckily, on this trip I'd been well behaved, and my parents had had no need to punish me. But it wasn't like I hadn't had my fair share of mummying on this tour. My mother had treated my return like a grand event. She had arranged a whole social calendar for my wife, and had planned visits, parties, and nights out for me. Family members had all been allocated a day. Mum also had many day trips at the ready that my wife and I would enjoy, and she seemed to change the sheets of the bed twice a day. She was loving being a mother again. But it wasn't just me. It seemed to be the natural instinct of mothers, that I'd forgotten about in my now largely motherless world.

While in Adelaide, Sam's friend Mimi had tried to empty our plates as we were eating, because she said she could make a better meal than the fish and chips we'd brought home. I had no doubt that she could have – in fact she did on another night. The thing was, at 9pm at night, having not eaten since 1, this meal was the single best thing ever, because it was on a plate in front of me and filling my belly. Meems' meal would have been better from a taste and health perspective, but it would have taken at least 30 minutes to prepare, and who has that kind of time at nine at night when a piece of battered flake is in front of them?

Astrid's mum June was also a complete doting mother to me, Astrid's friend Ruth, her own kids, and probably everyone who wasn't a complete stranger. You could actually see the pain on her face when I walked in with a Hungry Jacks burger. I felt guilty eating the deliciously fatty, greasy burger in front of her, although that didn't mean I didn't eat it. When I tried to take her out for dinner to repay her for letting me stay at her place I practically had to drag her out. And even then she wouldn't let me get her an ice cream.

When I was at Gideon Haigh's book launch, Mike Atherton had talked about seeing the look on the face of Ponting during the bad times and seeing himself in him; the way the job became who you were, ground you down, changed who you were, and how you became a captain ahead of everything else. I thought this mothering thing was similar. Your life became about mothering, and your first instinct was to try to look after those you loved – or those who happened to end up in your house.

It also explained away some of the mistakes. I thought that for anyone who was that devoted to any one thing, however brilliant as they might be at it, it would chip away at their sanity. I'm not just talking mothers. It could happen to fathers, politicians, lawyers or used car salesmen. You started doing the job and then you become the job.

Ponting wasn't born a Test captain; he became one over time. He tried to become what he thought he wanted to be, what he thought the job was, and what others expected him to become. I could now barely remember what he was like as a person before he was captain. I think he was cheeky, although it doesn't feel right to call him that. He was just totally Ponting the captain to me now. And on days like today when he was having a complete mental breakdown, when he couldn't see what seemed to be right in front of his face, you could tell that the job had become too much for him.

It happened to everyone. Mail workers shot people, lawyers went on gardening leave, politicians started working with charities and sportsmen tried to become business people.

When I think of the women I'd been around, you could see it in them. They saw a scruffy bastard like me and went straight into maternal mode. My mum could run the country if she was given a chance, and Meems and June were obviously smart as hell as well, but that mother thing was still there. While I was with these three amazing women I saw one print out the entire internet to give to someone else, another try to turn on a TV by putting the remote in the hands of someone else and pushing the same buttons with the other person's fingers that they had already tried with their own, and one have a conversation on speaker phone about bowel movements while I tried to convey that speaker phone might not be the best way to have that talk.

Ricky's moment wasn't any more mental than these; it was just angrier and more public.

DAY 3 – MCG

Over the last few days the whispers had started: Australia had lost the Ashes, so it was time to assign blame. It seemed that Michael Clarke was to blame. You could have blamed his poor form, the shocking dismissal to KP at Adelaide, or playing through an injury for the majority of the series. Instead, it was breakfast that was to blame. A charity breakfast at that.

Players are asked to do a lot of things during a series. It wasn't a new thing, but now they tried to pack all the nonsense stuff into the shorter tour times to the point that some of the players don't even get time to improve their best scores on *Call of Duty*. Or golf. So when Shane Warne's charity asked Phil Hughes and Michael Clarke to attend a charity breakfast on the morning of Boxing Day, the players probably thought that they didn't have any *Call of Duty* to play, it was too early for golf, and that they had to eat breakfast anyway.

I didn't think that breakfasting with a few hundred people before a Test match was an ideal warm-up, but I hardly thought it was that big a deal. Hussey did it in Perth, and he did well. From what I heard, the players took about five minutes to get to this breakfast, which was less walking than you'd have to do to get from a cheap room at Circus Circus in Vegas to get breakfast. If Brad Haddin had been in Clarke's place, I doubt anyone would have cared about this event at all. Not that I'm saying bacon and eggs aren't important; they're just less important than random selections, confused tactics, poor coaching, confused running between wickets, and shoddy fielding.

In the press box I was shown the back of *The Age*'s sports section, which called KP a wanker. The English media couldn't get over it; I couldn't see what the big deal was. I call my dad a wanker. Plus, it is pretty much a universal truth that we are all wankers, literally and figuratively.

People on Twitter and in the press box started to talk about a possible guard of honour for Ponting as he came out. Chris Stocks from the *Metro* said he saw something, but we have a sightscreen-impaired view of the players' gate. Some told me it was definitely a guard of honour, others claimed people were just letting Ponting go down first. A fan on Twitter at the ground showed me a video that they had made of the incident. It was similar to a UFO video – there were various things in shot, and the camera swerved around violently without any chance of you working out what was happening.

Siddle shook free of his press conference form and his bowling was very good again. Early on he got Prior nicking short of slip and then the same batsman spooned one to mid-on. Ponting took it without anger and without his broken finger causing more damage.

But there was some damage out on the field. Ryan Harris pulled up halfway through an over, and it didn't look good. Automatically, with Harris, you think "knee". He tried to work through it, but there was nothing to work through and Michael Clarke finished the over for him. With someone of Harris' size and history of injuries, you feared the worst.

It hurt me to see him pull up like that. The man was a quality bowler that Australia could use; the problem was that a 31-year-old infrequent player might not really be in their future plans. With a knee that could have used an artificial joint, any prolonged absence could end his career five Tests in and after his breakthrough match at Perth.

That was just harsh. I know cricket can be a prick, but it was still unfair.

Siddle took the edge of Bresnan's bat to register a hand

in the first seven dismissals, and his fifth wicket. The crowd started the "Siddle, Siddle" chant, as they realised that this Victorian was about the only bowler out there with any chance of finishing the innings.

The goods news for Australia was that they had never lost a Test in which Siddle has taken a five-wicket haul. So even though it looked like there was no hope left for Australia, clearly they were about to stage a remarkable comeback and win or draw this match. Because, as we all know, stats don't lie.

Even with all this statistical hope, the Australian fans had given up, the most visual representation of this being a blown-up condom that floated above the Barmy Army that said, "Fuck you England." It was a beautiful effort in summing up the Ashes, but it may have also done even more by accident. The missing comma between "Fuck you" and "England" is telling. This was not a very well thought out prank. Had the English fans done it they would have got the grammar right, put more effort into the writing, brought in more condoms, put on a variety of slogans and just done a better effort all around.

Swann came out and played a few shots, and the Aussies tried to bounce him. He got a quick 22 and then played a hook shot that made it look like he'd never played the shot before, giving Hilfenhaus his first wicket. Just like Mitch, he needed a batsman playing a terrible hook shot to get into the game. Hilfenhaus then bowled Tremlett and for a minute or two it looked like Siddle's effort would only result in a five-for until he cleaned up Anderson.

Siddle ended with six for 75 from 33 overs. It was the sort of performance that would have Victorians on his side for years to come. The ones that weren't already.

Australians now had the four best bowling performances in this series. Four tasty six-wicket hauls, and in a way it was like a reverse of their previous Ashes in 2009. There, the batsmen all made hundreds, but then went missing when they were really needed. This time the bowlers had popped in with big hauls, but gone missing for days on end.

Siddle might have had two six-wicket hauls, but had had three dry Tests in the middle. Hilfenhaus looked slower and his swing earlier than any-time in his career. He would only play at Sydney because Harris was injured. Then there was Mitch, about whom it was impossible to talk without swearing and making weird nonsensical noises.

This was the same attack from the last Ashes. And Australia were going to lose again. Sometimes the proof is actually in the pudding, whatever that means.

England's attack hadn't been God's gift to bowling. It had just been really good. What they had done was sustained the pressure on Australia. Australia hadn't put together partnerships. Even when things went well for them in Perth, they only had one really big stand in the game. England got regular wickets from clever, sustained, tactically sound, efficient, bowling. Purely on a skill level, they weren't dramatically better than Australia; England just looked like they knew what they were doing. England's attack was quite different from the last Ashes. This time there was no Graham Onions, Monty Panesar, Steve Harmison or Freddie Flintoff. Those four bowlers could all be better than Bresnan or Finn, yet Bresnan and Finn had come and fitted into the unit quite well.

At the break, I got a phone call from Big Daddy, who told me to look left, where he was leaning over the fence and waving like a madman. It was great to see that two kids, a fiancée, a mortgage and a job with the council had not yet made him grow up. I left the press box to have a chat with him and he informed me that he had come to see Ricky Ponting's last Test innings. He did say "in case". Big Daddy and our other mate Sime went to Sydney for Warne, McGrath and Langer's last Test. Big Daddy really liked to see the end of things. If they did executions at the G, I think he'd come.

We bullshitted for a minute, but after he mentioned the end of Ponting there was a certain awkwardness to our conversation. For two men who can bullshit for hours on end about everything, and who have done since we were both able to talk, it was quite weird. Eventually he went off to sit with Sarah, who refused to give up her good seats to sit with him so she smuggled him into the upper tier with her wits. Or they were dazzled by her hair.

Australia opened up like they had many times in this series, with runs. Hughes smashed anything wide, Watson was like a salivating dog waiting for any length that was full or short, and after two overs, they had 18 on the board. They hadn't looked like getting out; it just made me nervous, all this shot-making. Sure, Australian batsmen were usually rubbish when they played defensively, but the Cook and Strauss partnership showed that defensive play could work.

Hughes and Watson were never going to be that kind of opening partnership. Hughes was impulsive and careless. When he is seeing the ball well and believes in himself this means he can score very fast and take the game away from the opposition. Watson is bullish and a natural run scorer, Australia's most consistent batsman and the one most likely to change the game.

Hughes just needs form and confidence. His technique might never work in Test cricket. Bringing him back during a form slump was not really the way to tell if that was the case or not. The selectors created this indecision. Their move to drop him two Tests after his successful tour of South Africa broke him. Young men don't always handle rejection that well; usually it results in stalking, love letters or threatening suicide to the one who didn't want them. Hughes it seemed to rock to the core.

It could have been handled so much better. Hughes could have been given one or two more Tests to prove that he could handle the short ball; Hussey could have been dropped after 18 months of poor form; Watson could have taken his position. Then when Hussey rediscovered his spark he could have been brought back for North. This would have put a confident Hughes and Katich together, the cocky young shot-maker and the stout old man. Katich still would have been injured in this fantasy, but Ed Cowan, Michael Klinger, Ryan Broad or Liam Davis could have come in to play the anchor role.

I was dead against Shane Watson opening the batting for Australia, and I wasn't exactly happy for him to come into the middle order. Now I was desperate for him to bat in the middle order. Every time I saw Watson leave the ball, I wished they'd re-jigged the batting order into what Ponting asked for.

When Watson drove or played the pull shot, a collection

of masculine images flew through your head: Lee Marvin in *The Dirty Dozen*, Muhammad Ali on the ropes, Henry Rollins performing on stage. When Watson left the ball you saw perhaps the most effeminate shot in world cricket. Watson put all that weight on the front foot and then violently whipped his hands behind his back and almost pirouetted 180 degrees. It was far more dramatic when the ball was close to him; when it was wide of the stumps it almost looked OK.

But none of it is natural. Good leavers of the ball do it so naturally that you hardly notice them leaving the ball. When Andrew Strauss left there was no fuss at all. Ponting or KP did it in an aggressive "I could have hit that if I wanted to" way. They wanted the whole world to know that the ball was theirs. They were not natural leavers. Still, compared to Watson, they seemed to make it work. He didn't.

Watson's leaving of the ball seemed to be to prove to himself that he was an opener. The more balls he left, the longer he would be out there. The longer he was out there, the greater chance he would make a big score. Big scores would make him an opener. The problem is, he didn't make big scores. I thought that letting him loose in the middle order would bring run-a-ball hundreds, but as an opener in this series he was scoring slower than Cook, Trott or Hussey.

That I was writing this the one time these two looked really good didn't make it any less true. Watson hadn't got into his leave-and-defend mode yet, and Hughes looked more confident than in his previous three innings. They brought up the 50 partnership in ten overs, forcing Strauss to bring Swann on earlier than he probably planned to. Bresnan was brought into the attack as well.

Watson didn't need Swann or Bresnan, because he got rid of Hughes on his own. A simple push to Trott at cover was all that was needed, but Hughes couldn't make the run. Trott and Prior did nothing more than execute their skillsets. Run around the ball so you can throw it with your right hand, throw the ball next to the stumps, take the ball in front of the stumps, remove the bails, and Hughes was about a foot short.

It wasn't Hughes' fault, but there were two things Hughes

could have done that I would have expected an English batsman to do. Saying no could have worked, even though Watson's turning circle wasn't great. If Hughes had said no early enough he could have prevented a run-out, or at least *his* run-out. Then if he did trust his senior partner, when he saw it getting tight, he could have dived.

England had not had a batsman run out in this series. This was partly because they hadn't run badly, and partly because Australia had not capitalised on several mix-ups and stutters. This was Australia's third run-out. Twice with Watson. There was a time when the one per centers like this always went Australia's way. Perhaps after a good call the Australian batsmen should go down and pat the ass of their partner to let him know he'd done a good job.

England bowled only one bouncer to Hughes the whole time he was out there. Eight overs earlier. In every innings, England had bowled progressively fewer and fewer short balls at him. It actually said a lot about England. While everyone in the world was going with the short ball theory, they'd seen other flaws that they thought made him easier to get out. Compare this with the way Australia had bowled to Alastair Cook (in my latest dream he was a maths teacher with chalk dust all over his Cosby sweater). He had flaws in his game, but Australia had not changed their tactics for him, or even got close to working him out. If Hughes and Cook swapped teams, Hughes would have made some runs in this series and Cook a lot fewer. And not just because Watson would have run him out.

Now Ponting was in, and didn't look right. For 14 balls, he left the ball or defended. Ponting was not always a quick starter, but this didn't feel right. England were pinning him to the crease and he wasn't doing anything to counter it. It was the first time in my life that Australia had a weaker number three than England.

That sounds weird, knowing that England's number three was a gritty, late-blooming grafter, and Australia's was one of the best batsmen in the history of the game. History was an important word there. But you'd have to be a drug addict who shot speed into your eyeballs to pick Ponting over Trott at the moment.

At the other end, Watson had shut up shop. With Hughes

there, Watson was scoring at will, but once he ran Hughes out you could see him blame himself. As Hughes went off Watson looked like he felt responsible for the possible end of Hughes' Test career. There were some batsmen who, on running someone out, found that it helped them focus and score; there were others, though, where it messed with their heads, and Watson was one of these.

It was hard to know what Australia's plan was, or if they had a plan at all. They were strolling at five an over when Hughes was there, but since his dismissal they had scored only ten off ten overs. Given that the wicket was a run-out, and not caused by brilliant bowling or something strange from the pitch, why had they locked up?

It seemed that some tight bowling from England, together with the finger of Ponting and the conscience of Watson, had just stopped play. Ponting looked actually unable to score; Watson looked unwilling to score. All it did was help England build the pressure, and if they were to get a wicket, the next batsman would come in with England completely on top.

Hughes and Watson had moved slips away, punished bad balls, and got Australia rolling, but Watson and Ponting had done the opposite. This was Australia's most reliable batsman and their captain, and they were just handing the advantage and an innings win over. Not that it was Ponting's intention to do so – he was fighting like a dog to stay in – but it wouldn't last. You didn't have to have a degree in medicine to know his finger was stuffing him up. And even though he was batting about as badly as it was possible for him to do, and showing that on batting alone he shouldn't have been out there, I still thought he had to play in this Test. Australia's only chance of winning this Test was with Ponting there. He knew that, and that was why he was now holding onto the crease as tightly as he could.

Watson was nicking short or wide of slips and playing and missing. Somehow he got to his fifty, and Ponting, at one point on five from 39 balls, made it to tea at 19 off 54. It was ugly. At 95 for one Australia had done well to get to tea. It just didn't feel safe or permanent.

The break didn't come at a good time for Watson; he was in his 50s, not looking good at the crease, would see Hughes' sad puppy face in the changing rooms and doesn't usually bat well after a break. All these things combined to make him play perhaps the worst shot of his career. It was as if his hands were playing the stroke and his bat wasn't. What started as a ball he wanted to leave ended with him wafting his hands at the ball as Bresnan smashed it into his pad. A disgusting non-shot shot. Like Paris Hilton making a concept album of gangster country songs about paedophile priests.

Ponting walked over to straight in front of the stumps to check the line, which made little sense since you couldn't argue that Watson played any kind of actual cricket shot, so it didn't matter if it hit him outside off stump. Only the height was of any importance. But they reviewed it. The ball clipped the digital bails so it stayed out. And even if it wasn't, it should have been given out on aesthetics alone. Hopefully any news coverage of this dismissal would contain the warning: "This almost cricket shot may distress some viewers."

Prior finally gave Australia some respite by missing a stumping as Clarke danced down the wicket to Swann. It didn't last long.

Ponting got a length ball from Bresnan that kept a little low, and he dragged it back on to the stumps. My stomach felt like shit, my head hurt and I wished I was anywhere else. It hit me really hard. I tried to write down notes on how the ball might have kept low and moved back in, but replays showed neither really happened. Ponting was just old and slow, and as he walked away he let out a bellowing "fuck".

I might have just seen Ricky's last Test innings, and if not the last, then the last at the place I'd spent my life watching him. Back from when I was 15, two people had been paramount in my life: Ricky Ponting and the actress Natalie Portman.

Ponting started his Test career when I was 16. He was the young pup way before there even was a pup. I followed his career through dodgy lbws at the WACA, scratchy knocks at number three, not wearing a helmet to face Curtly, a fight with a fence at Sydney, a fight with someone else at Sydney, a dropping from the team, that terrible goatee, getting wickets with gentle outswing, the face of milk in Tasmania, the centuries rolling in, runs, World Cup finals, grumpiness, backing his team, captaincy, backing Roy, bad captaincy, over rate problems, losing an Ashes, winning more World Cups, more runs, more bad captaincy, losing faith in spin, losing another Ashes, losing the number one spot, winning a pointless trophy, losing cricket matches to everyone, and losing the Ashes again. I hadn't been there for every moment, but I'd lived it all.

I doubted we'd get on that well if we met, even though Ponting and I had a few similarities. Both of us left school early and flirted with the idea of becoming groundsmen. I can't say why it was attractive to Ponting, but for me it was a way of really learning the game and was a far better job than the collecting of shopping trolleys that I had been doing. Both of us were quick to anger, and hugely defensive when criticised. Over the years it had got both of us in trouble and I could see, when Ponting wanted to fly off the handle, how he reined himself back in. There was also the painfully working-class upbringing we both had. The footy and cricket, and the belief that we had one skill each and the hope we could eventually live off it.

Whether at the ground, on the TV, in press conferences or in the field, there were few sportsmen I watched as closely. I'd even once tried to review his book, but *The Wisden Cricketer* binned the review, probably because I made it all too complicated in my mind. I wasn't just trying to review his book, I was thinking of every instance of him I could remember, and that is hard to sum up in 400 words.

As a batsman, he was one of the best I had ever seen or would ever see. When he was in control of his game, he was in control of the Test match. It felt like Ponting wasn't batting for any reason other than to put his side into the best possible position, and most champion batsmen aren't like that. It was something that I loved, and tried to emulate when I played. His shots were great to watch, but it wasn't about that for me – it was how he tried to get on top that I loved. Strategic singles when a bowler had the better of him; forcing the fielding side to change away from positions that might have got him out; attacking the weak bowling link to finish him before the next batsman came in; and the way he would change his game for each innings depending on what was needed.

As a captain, he got better as his team got worse. When he started, he was a confused man, and needed a lot of help from others. There were times when Warne or Darren Lehmann seemed to be setting the fields instead. Ponting had the heart of a captain, but never the brain. Not that he didn't try to get better; his use of catchers on slower pitches and the way he used Andrew McDonald in South Africa showed that he was getting better. It was just that his faith in his players, as inspiring and wholehearted as it was, couldn't put life into a team that was poorly coached, badly selected and rarely prepared. Some of this was his fault, some of it was not. By the end of his captaincy he was no better or worse than almost all Test captains in the world.

As a competitor he always stood out for me. The more he fought, the more I admired him. Even when he was wrong, I loved that he would fight for what he was wrong about. Winning mattered to him; being liked didn't seem to matter as much. The more that modern sportsmen wanted to be liked, the less it seemed to bother Ponting, and the more it bothered him to lose. He could play for ten more years with a team that never won a Test series and I don't think he'd ever get used to losing.

Ponting would always have something that neither Michael Clarke nor any of the next generation of captains would have: Aussie cricket fans felt like he was one of them. Even if they didn't like what he said or did, they had that same bond with Ponting that I felt. They felt like they knew him. It didn't always mean that they liked him, but they could predict that he would get angry, have trouble with things going against him, and would do anything he could to win. Even if you didn't like Ponting, you could feel comfortable and happy knowing how he would react to situations.

For years I'd abused him for his captaincy, his misuse of bowlers, and the bubble he lived in. I'd called him the hairy-armed troll, once doubted that he wanted to win as much as he said he did, and got angry with so much of what he had to say. I'd jumped on his mistakes, pointed out when I thought he was wrong, and told anyone I could that he was not doing the best job he could for Australia. I'm not talking about as a cricket writer; I'm talking about before that as well. I'm not sorry, because I think if the tables were turned Ponting would do the same as me. I wouldn't miss his captaincy any more than he would miss my criticism of him.

The reason I felt sick was that I'd miss watching him bat. From the first ball I saw him face, I'd always treasured watching him bat. His batting *was* Australia to me. Not the cricket culture, but all of Australia. You couldn't see Ponting bat and think he was from anywhere else. His batting said more about Australia than the national anthem, Australia Day or the Australian flag. There will be those who would pick Trumper, Ponsford, Harvey, Bradman, Border or Waugh, but for better or worse, Ponting was mine. We picked each other. He was my Australia, the best and worst of it. The Australia I loved and despised.

At about the same time Ponting dragged onto his stumps, Natalie Portman's pregnancy was tweeted around the globe. Portman and Ponting really came into my life at about the same time. In many ways I wanted to be with one and wanted to be the other. Now I was old enough not to want either. Not that I ever had any sort of shot with Natalie Portman, realistic or otherwise, but five years ago, news of her being pregnant would have stopped me for a moment and made me think.

Ponting's bad shot and exit from the G hurt me. This was my ground, and I felt like a part of me was leaving it, never to return.

Ponting might yet be back in Test cricket; he could even play again at the G a few more times. He was someone that I'd never write off, but the best of him had gone. I felt older when he went out than I ever had in my life. The Ponting I grew up with didn't exist anymore. And maybe that's what hurt me.

Clarke and Hussey went way too easily. Clarke had had the worst series of his life. KP had hardly done much more for

England, but would come out of the series with a 227 that guaranteed victory at Adelaide and the wicket of Clarke which double guaranteed the victory at Adelaide. I remembered when Clarke would take the odd important wicket for Australia.

Hussey may have been the only Australian to outplay his direct opposite. It was partly because his counterpart was Paul Collingwood, and partly because Hussey had had a career-saving summer. Yet as great as it was, he needed to go. I felt bad, because it really meant everything for him to play for Australia, but I just couldn't see how someone his age was helping Australian cricket if he only played a series like this every three years.

Smith and Haddin put together a bit of a fightback, although maybe that is expressing it too strongly. It would be better for everyone involved if the game finished that evening, but Australia couldn't even seem to get that right. Smith even looked OK for a while, then pulled a short one from Anderson straight back onto his stumps. There was a cold, dead look on Anderson's face when Smith did it, like he was trying to audition for a role in Sly Stallone's *Expendables 2*. He needn't have bothered – even if he'd giggled like a schoolgirl it wouldn't have mattered anymore.

Ian Bell bats at six for England, and it took him fifty Tests to become any good. I doubt Smith will get to fifty Tests, and unless he finds a way to stop pushing at the ball and tightens his technique, he might not play 20 Tests.

Australia ended the day 169 for six. Our little overflow press box had by now bonded as one, the outsiders all together, when one other person joined us. That person was Scyld Berry, the editor of the *Wisden Cricketers' Almanack*. He sat in the front row in his regal, otherworldly way. When I found myself meeting Scyld for the first time, it was clear to me that my life had changed. I could have lived in Melbourne my whole life without ever meeting anyone like Scyld. If I ever had to show an actor how to perform the role of a dignified alien, I'd introduce them to Scyld. He's not actually an alien, he's just alien to a boy from the northern suburbs of Melbourne. Today, sitting in the front row of the G's most public press spot, he was in my home, and a drunk fan ran up to the window and screamed the Barmy Army Mitchell Johnson song at him.

At the press conference that night you could tell that there was a big difference between Australia and England. Peter Lalor, from *The Australian,* asked Watson if he'd accepted that he'd lost the Ashes, Watson "Ummed", then paused, and breathed out, "Just about." Later on Bresnan was asked how it felt with only four wickets left to get. Bresnan paused, "Ummed" for a moment and then said: "Yeah, we've still got the three [sic] wickets to get so I'll describe that tomorrow – or if we do that; we've still got a lot of hard work to do."

Australian cricket didn't just wake up one morning and lose the plot; this had been a slow painstaking process. Up until a few months before the Ashes, Merv Hughes was a selector. He was a selector without a subscription to a pay TV channel. This meant he could watch international cricket on Channel 9, the home summer matches, and that was it. He couldn't watch Pakistan take on England before the Ashes, or the West Indies take on England before the last Ashes. He justified this in a few ways; one was that watching cricket on TV was not that important anyway and the second was that he couldn't afford it.

I have no idea how much money Merv Hughes has, or even how much a Foxtel subscription costs, but if he couldn't afford it then Cricket Australia should have been paying for it. Foxtel shows overseas tours that Hughes could only see if his tour company sent him over or when he was the selector on tour. He should have been watching all of this, because TV has taken us deep into the bowels of cricket. You can now learn far more watching at the ground with a TV above you than you ever could in cricket before.

High Definition had given us seam position, wrist position and super slow motion shots of where the batsman's feet and hands were at the point of impact with the ball. Pitch maps, beehives and wagon wheels told you where the ball was landing, where it went past the batsman, and where he hit it. You could get a close-up of the batsman or bowler's face to see how he was handling the pressure. Stump cam told you which batsman made the call in a run-out. Watching at the ground was still the best way to watch cricket because you could see everything that the production crew missed, but the TV took you up close and showed you the sort of subtlety that you really needed if you were selecting the best 11 players for a Test match.

Merv's actions and comments showed that somewhere along the line, Australia's professionalism had gone awry. They were so far ahead of the rest of the world with their professionalism and their great team that no one had noticed the others closing in. England were now as professional in every single facet of cricket off the field – and on the field, they were ahead.

I'd always assumed that the reason that Australia was so good at sport was not so much to do with Australians living in a sunny country, being more naturally athletic, and wanting it more, but more to do with the fact that they were the most disciplined planners and trainers in the world. Australian cricket benefited from this as much as anyone. That they had a great team was beyond doubt; that it happened at the exact moment they were twice as professional as all other cricket sides was also beyond doubt.

Now that had gone, and Merv couldn't even watch repeats of *Gilligan's Island* or the stupid 45-over List A tournament Cricket Australia has sticky-taped together.

That night, I went out to Lygon Street to eat with my parents and Sarah. My dad was angry at Ponting, and Smith, plus Clarke, and Watson, but like most Australian fans the real rage had left on Boxing Day. Now it was time for our favourite Kimber family game: let's fix the whole thing over a beer and a meal.

I loved Lygon Street, and after taking a while to find a place to eat, I ordered a big kick-ass steak, the biggest they had, and I wanted a bowl of fries on the side. I usually wouldn't order a bowl of fries on the side because I was an adult now. When I was a kid I'd order a bowl of fries on the side even if my meal had fries. Now I've grown up, I make healthier choices, think about what I'm eating, and usually find I just don't need the fries.

Tonight I wanted fries, but my waiter never brought them.

I asked him a second time, and he nodded, but no fries ever made it to my table. On any other day I think I'd get fries. Today was not a good day for feeling like a kid again.

DAY 4 – MCG

The G had practically no staff on duty for the last day, and spectators found it hard to get in because of the small number of gates that were open. I thought that all the English should be let in for free, just for coming all the way out. And if they'd come out for previous series they should have been given a private box as well.

It started badly for Australia when Mitch was bowled by Tremlett. It didn't really start badly – it just continued to be shithouse. England managed to drop two catches, completely missed another, and stuffed up a simple piece of fielding. Perhaps they'd been told the crowd was stuck outside the ground.

At this point I decided to go for a walk around the ground. I kept my eye on the game, but the whole Ashes kept coming back to me. It started off with a non-stop flash of images of Australian mistakes on the field, in the changing rooms, from the selectors, from the marketing department, everywhere. Then I came to England.

England were better fielders.

Graeme Swann was a better tweeter than all Australian cricketers combined.

England's bowlers were better.

The whole Ashes preparation by England was better.

The English coaches were far better than the Australian coaches.

The selection of England's team was better.

The Barmy Army were better organised, executed their skillsets and banded together far more than Australian fans.

The English batsmen handle almost all kinds of pitches – green tops or brown tops – better than the Australian batsmen.

The Lord's press box had better food than the MCG changing rooms.

The white whites of England looked better out on the ground than Australia's creams.

England were better at handling the pressure.

Yes, the word "better" appeared almost as much as the word "obviously" in a Peter Siddle press conference. It appeared so much that this wasn't an accident. The only thing that springs to mind when thinking of something Australia did better was collapsing.

Even when England shat themselves on the WACA pitch, they looked like a composed side that would bounce back. On the other hand, Australia's win looked like it was based on a freak occurrence that couldn't be replicated, and it wasn't. Nothing from England looked accidental, not the bum patting, the sprinkler, the testing of Clarke's back, the way they kept Hilfy out, or the way they thought through the referrals.

And that is how you win a five-Test series.

Australia weren't just beaten; they were outplayed, outthought, and outmastered in every aspect of cricket, both on and off the ground. This wasn't a knockout, but a slow strangulation. England didn't do it with a brilliant cricket team; they have more support staff than Mariah Carey for a reason and that was to build a professional, well-drilled and organised cricket team that was better than its opposition.

One of the few places where England weren't better was in the captaincy, but Andy Flower was a giant puppeteer who worked Strauss to perfection. Strauss captained by defensive numbers; Ponting let his emotions get to him and then captained like a pissy child. During this series Ponting had often used the word "betterment" when talking about improving the Australian cricket side.

Betterment is a rubbish word.

At the end of the day (which is when the press conferences were) Andrew Strauss used far better words.

Standing in the G watching this, it was clear to me that cricket isn't a funny game: it's a sadistic torture that we enjoy because each and every one of us is sick and wrong. I'd been out here for weeks, and the feeling I had was more like being a prison bitch than a sport fan. Kept away from my wife, sharing a room with various men, hardly drinking or sleeping, watching my back so I didn't get shivved, and knowing that even when I got out, I was always going to be affected. I could imagine my grandkids being apprehensive in years to come. "Should we ask," they'd say, "I mean, he still has nightmares about Alastair Cook."

It wasn't the losing that I minded; it was how long it all took. But that's what makes cricket such a great game. In other sports, the band aid gets ripped off. In cricket, they keep you alive for as long as they can, cut your toes off, slice your calf off, put your genitals in a blender, get flesh-eating ants inside your thigh, show you your intestines, put your arms in a wood chopper, cut out your tongue and stick it up your ass then back to your mouth, draw and quarter you, dip random bits of your body in acid, make you listen to Christmas carols, and keep you conscious during all of it. Cricket never cuts your eyes out, though. It keeps them in, so that you have to watch all of this, for weeks on end – your body just being abused and damaged for the pleasure of others. It was, to use a Siddleism, "obviously" why we loved it. It was why I was still in the ground, seeing England run around for the fans. Seeing Cook one last damn time. So much Cook. Every day. Cook was the blender.

England weren't a brilliant team yet: they were just really good at what they did. What made them good was not necessarily what got you excited about cricket. If they were your team, you didn't care how they won, but for the rest of us, Australians and everyone else, this was a long series, filled with well-drilled quick singles and bowling units.

Australia were the entertainment in this series; their comedy ineptitude on and off the field had kept us all wanting more. They didn't trust technology or each other. They just kept building brick walls and running into them.

England won. Quite fucken rightly.

I can't remember the ball they did it with, or even who it was that got the wicket or who got out. It was just over. I was standing with Christian Ryan, there we were, just two Cricinfo freelancers standing together. We didn't know each other that well, but well enough. We stood in silence as we looked around the ground. Taking it in, seeing what it meant to the fans of England. Having travelled around the world following sports teams, I knew how much the fans deserved this. Not just the ones here, but all of the fans who had followed England on a tour. They could have chosen another sport, found another hobby, spent time with their loved ones. They didn't. They chose to follow their country around the world.

At the press conference, Strauss said all the right things, while Trott still seemed to be in his batting zone. Then Ponting was probed, gently, by the press. They all asked their questions and he did his best to give them what he thought.

Then the last question was by Brett from The Roar. When they said it was Brett's question, everyone turned to him. He looked pale, and he struggled to get his question out cohesively. "Do you see an immediate thing that you can change to lift the team in a couple of days?" It was a good question, and Ponting answered it as well as he had the others. It couldn't have been scripted better: if this *was* Ponting's last Test, as a player or captain, Brett was the best person in the room to ask him the final question. It was as if the last question was saved for a fan, rather than for another journalist. It was probably my favourite moment of the whole series.

Later that night we went out drinking; I'd bloody deserved it. Somehow I'd been sober for almost the whole two months, and this wasn't the time to be sober. I hit Fitzroy, the birthplace of Neil Harvey, and caught up with David Hopps, Simon Briggs, Richard Hobson and Nick Hoult. Hoppsy even tried to cheer me up about my accent by saying that I didn't have an Australian or an English accent but that I just sounded like me. Of course, Sam was there. The night wouldn't have been complete without Sam.

We drank, changed bars, spoke as eloquently as possible

to various radio and TV stations back in the UK (strangely I was all over the BBC), perved, talked shit, lost the older guys, were joined by Jon Norman. Sam, Jon and I ended up at some too-trendy-for-its-own-good Fitzroy bar, shoved in a nook with funky seating, drinking Coopers. We sat there till the place shut, just talking nonsense, planning to take over the cricket world, talking about the future, taking the piss out of each other, discussing the various hostels/pissy motels/friends' accommodation we'd used, and enjoying the night. Right then, it didn't matter that the Ashes were staying in England. I had drink and good friends at 4am in Melbourne. With Jon there, it also meant that Sam and I wouldn't get together, and our love would remain unrequited.

Sam and I had accomplished something this Ashes; it's just that we weren't even sure what that was.

There were two things I kept thinking of all night through the drinking and frivolity and bar-hopping and press interviews. When I'd gone on that walk around the G when Australia were seven wickets down, I'd bought a pie. I kept the pie with me the whole time I stood with Christian Ryan, and then I took it into the press box with me. It was a beautiful pie, cooked to perfection. The pastry snapped in your mouth, the meat was perfectly heated, and the gravy was beautiful. It was the best pie I'd ever eaten. I'm sure of it. Even if I wasn't sure at the time.

The other thing I remember was that earlier that day, I'd been standing with Jon and Sam, and we saw Ponting walk off the ground to the sound of Dave Grohl singing "There goes my hero". The song wasn't for him – it was for England's win – and Ponting wasn't my hero. But it just seemed right, wrong, fucked up and perfect all at the same time.

SYDNEY (AGAIN)

Blood was spread all over the SCG. Bits of bone fragments were in the grass. Toenails were found in the pies, bits of skin and hair in the beer and if Australian cricket had a consciousness, it had been raped. And I'm talking rape rape, not just rape. After all the chest-stabbing at Sydney, I finished the last *Two Pricks at the Ashes* and jumped in a cab to see my wife for the first time in seven weeks.

The final Test was still playing through my mind. The temporary Australian captain was booed on his home ground, another spinner was chucked into the woodchipper, Lawrence Booth had been named as editor of *Wisden Cricketers' Almanack*, batsmen stared at each other from the same end, people stopped mentioning my accent, England won the series and not just the Ashes – the third innings win in the series – I think I was hit on, a 37 (Usman Khawaja on debut) was talked up like it was a double hundred, Paul Collingwood retired with class, and Australia were broken. It was the first time in my life that with every ounce of me, the Australian and UnAustralian parts, I wanted Australia to lose a Test match. Sometimes you have to reach the bottom to know why you want to get back to the top.

On the way out of Sydney the taxi driver (yup, Ricky had been in his cab, it was freaky) had one of those popular crap radio stations on. The DJ said, "Up next is Ant and Dec." That was it; Australia was now completely conquered by benign presenters from England. I didn't know why Ant and Dec were on Australian radio, but I just knew that their safe, family-friendly comedy routine would be a hit, because I'd now seen what well-trained English people could do in Australia. There was no stopping them. They would take over. One meticulously-researched well-planned excellently-implemented procedure at a time. Even I was about to see my English wife (who had finally flown in) as if I needed more proof they were taking over. You didn't need to be UnAustralian to see that.

That night, my wife went to bed early because of jet lag. I stayed up for a while. I was very tired and I needed a week of sleep to get back to normal. The problem with sleeping, though, was that I knew what I'd dream of.

Above me was a smooth-looking surgeon. It was hot as hell in the operating room, which was actually my family's kitchen. He wasn't sweating. Not even a drop. He was focused, calm and knew what he was doing. I tried to tell him I was awake, that this was all a mistake and that I could see what he was doing, but I couldn't move or make a sound. His impressive chin and nose were hidden from sight by his surgeon's mask and all I had was those eyes. Those deep, dark, smoky eyes, piercing straight through me. He raised his steady hands, and in them was his tool. Then he gently and easily cut me. Some would argue that it wasn't technically perfect, and that he could have cut into me with his scalpel in a better position, or with his feet closer to the table.

You couldn't argue with his results, though. I was sliced open on my family's kitchen table.